THE WORLD
SKI
ATLAS

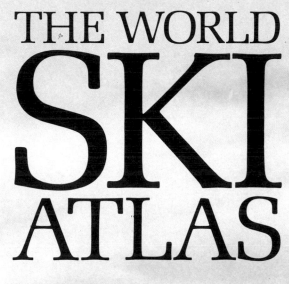

THE WORLD
SKI
ATLAS

by Mark Heller

A & W Publishers, Inc.
New York

Introduction

At least thirty million people throughout the world ski every year. So potent is the enthusiasm for this recreation and sport that it drives men and women to climb mountains and glaciers for endless hours, to trudge from the Bay of Whales to the South Pole, to cross Greenland from Umanak to Scoresby Sound, even to find satisfaction in a joyful slide across half an inch of slush on the South Downs of England.

The first formal winter-sports holiday ever to be held took place in 1865 at the Kulm Hotel, St Moritz. It was primarily devoted to skating, tobogganing and sleigh-riding. In the years since, the world has come to think of 'winter sports' as a fancy way of saying skiing.

Around this superficially simple activity – sliding along on a pair of expensive planks – has grown a leisure industry which earns the equivalent of a small country's fiscal budget. The sport and recreation of skiing has grown at a phenomenal rate in the last two decades. It has changed the face of mountain country in Europe, the Americas, Japan and Australasia. With it have come tens of thousands of hotels and apartment complexes, hundreds of thousands of ski lifts, chairlifts, gondolas and cableways.

This book ranges the whole world of skiing. It shows 50 super-centres and 150 major and popular mountains and very many smaller resorts. It shows you what they look like, exactly where they are, and what they may be like to ski. If you should discover that your own favourite ski paradise is not mentioned and if this should make you unhappy, then you need look no further for the culprit. The choice was mine.

Let Ull, the ski deity, decide who is right or wrong.

Contents

A Quarto Book
First published 1978
© 1978 Quarto Limited
© Text Mark Heller

This book was designed and produced by Quarto Publishing Limited,
13 Burlington Street, London W1.

Phototypeset in Britain by Filmtype Services Limited, Scarborough,
Yorkshire
Printed and bound in Hong Kong

First published in the United States of America in 1978 by
A & W Publishers, Inc.
95 Madison Avenue
New York, New York 10016

Library of Congress Catalog Card Number: 78-58333

ISBN 0-89479-027-7

12,000 Years of Skiing

1882 Nansen crossed
Greenland on skis.

1868 Sondre
Ouersen Norheim
redesigned skis and
bindings.

1936 first chairlift
designed by
Jim Curran for
Sun Valley.

1070 Bishop Adam
of Bremen describes
skiers in Scandinavia.

1867 first American
Ski Club at
La Porte, California.

Jon Torsteinson Rue
known as Snowshoe
Thomson carried US
mail across the Sierras
from 1856 to 1876.

Earliest recorded
skiing in Switzer-
land, Mitlödi,
1868 by Wild.

Mid-19th century
Scandinavian miners
and loggers emigrated
to California.

1921, First downhill
World Champion-
ship race, Scheidegg.

1924 First Winter
Olympics,
Chamonix.

1911 first Downhill
race from Plaine
Morte to Montana.

Where and when skis were first invented is a mystery for the few known facts are inconclusive. Surprisingly sophisticated, recognizable skis, at least 4,500 years old, have been found in Norway, Sweden, Finland and northern Siberia and, more recently, in southern Kazakhstan in the Altai mountains. They are all either both short, such as the Hoting ski from central Sweden dated about 2,500 BC or both long such as the Kalvträsk ski from Finland dated at about 2,000 BC. Rock carvings in Rödöy in northern Norway showing a skier with very long skis wearing an animal mask have been dated as the same period as the Swedish skis. Other rock carvings found near Soroki by the White Sea show a band of hunters wearing short skis and carrying a single pole. These have been dated at about 1,000 BC.

The discovery of the Altai skis and the known migration of the Steppe or Reindeer people from the area of the Altai to the north and west in the period after the ending of the last, Würm, ice age between 15,000 and 10,000 BC, suggests that these hunter-gatherers took with them the knowledge of skis in the migration into northern Europe.

The curious coincidence of the similar dates for all the known finds of prehistoric skis can now be explained by a radical change in climate, commencing about 3,000 BC, known as the great thermic maximum which resulted in a long period of snow-less winters making the possession of skis unnecessary.

The earliest written account of skis is in the official history of the T'ang Dynasty (AD 618–907) which describes a 'Turkish' (Kir-

1520 Gustav Vasa raced from Sälen to Mora to liberate Sweden.

c2500 BC Hoting ski found in Sweden.

13th & 14th century earliest ski literature, Rune 7 Old Kalevala.

Rock carvings in Rödöy and Soroki (White Sea) dated c1500 BC.

15-10,000 BC migration of Steppe or Reindeer people.

Skis dated 2500 BC found in Altai Mountains, Khazakstan.

(7th century) Earliest account (Chinese) written of skiing by Kirgiz tribe.

1934 First commercial skilift Davos designed by Konstam.

1896 Matthias Zdarsky started the Lilienfeld ski school.

19th-century migration of Scandinavian miners to Australia.

1861 first ski club in the world founded in Kiandra, Australia.

giz) tribe who 'skim over the ice on wooden horses (MuMa) which they bind to their feet'. A later work, the Kuang Chi (the Sung Dynasty encyclopedia 960–1127), describes skis in very great detail as well as giving instructions for their use.

Europeans of the Middle Ages first read of skis in Bishop Adam's account of his ministry in Scandinavia where he describes the wild hunters of the north as 'borne on bent boards'.

The earliest literature involving skis other than descriptions is in the nineteenth-century transcription of the Old Kalevala, a Finnish collection of sagas dating from the 13th and 14th centuries. Rune 7 is a dramatic account of the feats of Lylikki, a Hanseatic merchant now identified as Wilhelm Lüdecke.

Two events of this period of history describe the use of skis as the central ingredient of the events. In 1206 the infant King

Haakon Haakonson was rescued from a successional murder by his bodyguards, the 'Birchlegs' who carried him from the Guldbradstal just outside Lillehammer to Østerdal on skis in mid-winter. In 1520 during the complicated wars involving Denmark, Sweden and Norway, Gustav Vasa returned on skis from Sälen to Mora to lead the popular movement to oust the Danes from Sweden – a distance of 85 kilometres. This is now celebrated annually by the Vasa cross-country marathon.

During the early 18th century ski troops were used by both Norway and Sweden. The first of these, the 'official' Norwegian ski infantry, were called up in 1716. In 1733 Captain Jens Emmahusen wrote the first instruction manual for skiers ever to be published.

Apart from the everyday use of skis in Scandinavia, notably in south-west Norway, which had continued since prehistoric times, skis were unknown and unused in the rest of Europe. The people had no interest in winter sports for they lived in a continent which was almost continuously at war in one form or another. Winter was a time for surviving misery and snow before yet another trial.

A disastrous economic depression which coincided with the westward expansion in the New World and the emergence of Australia as a country in its own right promoted a massive emigration of Scandinavians, mostly from Norway. They were employed as loggers, miners and general heavy-work handymen in their new countries. Those who found themselves in mountainous, snowy environments instinctively turned to skis both for transport and recreation.

Ski clubs were founded in La Porte, California in 1867 and in Kiandra, Australia in 1861. Kiandra was the first ski club in the world and is still in existence. C. C. T. Bjerkenes was the first skier in Australia in 1853.

In the Californian Sierras, 8,000 miles from Kiandra, a former Norwegian, Jon Torsteinson Rue, had been employed to carry the U.S. mail across the Sierras to the outlying mining and farming settlements. From 1865 until 1885 he carried out this task on skis which he had made himself. Just where he acquired this ski mastery is a mystery for he came to America when he was two years old. He adopted his stepfather's name of Thompson and has gone into skiing history as 'Snowshoe Thompson'.

Alpine skiing had a delayed start. Gut

The Rödöy skier (right) dated c 2,500 BC has always puzzled ski archaeologists. It is a man wearing an animal mask for reasons that are not apparent. The Italian drawing of Swedish skiers (below) is dated about 1550. At that time both Norway and Sweden employed ski-shod troops.

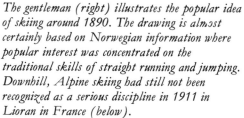

The gentleman (right) illustrates the popular idea of skiing around 1890. The drawing is almost certainly based on Norwegian information where popular interest was concentrated on the traditional skills of straight running and jumping. Downhill, Alpine skiing had still not been recognized as a serious discipline in 1911 in Lioran in France (below).

Legend has it that children used beer-barrel staves for sliding on snow long before skiing was introduced to Switzerland. These boys in Grindelwald were photographed in 1900; note the bindings. The early 1930s were a golden age for British lady skiers (below). Members of the Lady's Ski Club competed in every international race with very great success.

Modern ski dress has nothing like the elegance of the lady from Chamonix c 1905 (left). The earliest moguls appeared in the late 1940s and caused great consternation. Speed on trails was much higher before 1940 than they are today.

Muths is said to have been the first skier in Germany in the Thüringer Wald in 1795, but the first authenticated account of a skier in Germany was a Norwegian, Mr. H. Möller, in the 1850s. In 1868, in Mitlödi, Konrad Wild became the first person to ski in Switzerland. All this skiing was on long, crudely shaped and ill-attached Norwegian skis.

In 1868 a virtually illiterate cottager called Sondre Ouersen Norheim journeyed from Morgedal in Telemark to Oslo and demonstrated to an incredulous public 'modern' controlled skiing. He had invented or developed a waisted, arched ski (the dimensions are unchanged to this day) which he attached to his feet by means of twisted osiers which held his toe and heel firmly to the ski. It was the birth of skiing as we know it.

In 1888 Nansen crossed the Greenland ice cap on Telemark skis and his book published three years later brought skiing to the notice of the general public. Among Nansen's readers was an Austrian reserve officer, Matthias Zdarsky, who realized that the broken steep territory of the Alps required a new technique. This he perfected at Lilienfeld near Vienna.

The scene shifted to the British who were busy skiing in Wengen, Mürren and Grindelwald at this time. Through them, during the years 1910 to 1924, Alpine skiing became downhill skiing as they used the Jungfrau railway for uphill transport.

In 1921 the first international downhill championship was held in Sheidegg. In 1924 Arnold Lunn revived the modern slalom and during these golden years of skiing – the 1920s and the early 1930s – recreational downhill skiing became a popular and accepted winter sport.

Davos in Switzerland was the site for the installation of the first commercial ski tow. The incomparable T-bar, the invention of a Swiss skier, Erich Constam of Zurich, revolutionized the sport. Now people could learn to ski without toil, as they no longer had to climb up before slithering down the fields of snow. In the United States, Jim Curran invented the chairlift, and installed the first one at Sun Valley.

These two developments were the main foundations for the great ski-boom. The boom has been aided and advanced by tour operators and modern air travel, which have taken advantage of the social developments of winter holidays and increased foreign travel to the extent that there are now in excess of 30 million skiers.

Ski Disciplines

Skiing is a generic word describing the activities of sliding on snow with the aid of skis. It evolved from a primitive means of transport over snow-covered ground into a varied sport and recreation. This development was the result of changes in the living patterns of people in Europe and North America which, in turn, promoted the application of modern technology to the manufacture of skis.

Nordic or cross-country skiing is the form most closely related to the traditional form of skiing in Scandinavia, where the skier travels over relatively flat ground. There was little need for robust skis nor a technique other than that required for moving smoothly in straight lines. Technology concentrated on perfecting light and durable equipment.

Alpine or downhill skiing demanded a ski and a technique which would move the skier safely over steep and broken ground, enable

him to turn and brake effortlessly and control the high speeds which this kind of skiing involved. Within a very few years of the perfecting of the basic Alpine techniques, the equipment became so specialized that the two forms of skiing, Nordic and Alpine, became incompatible. Even within the Alpine disciplines equipment was developed for specialized use, such as in Alpine touring and ski mountaineering, which, in turn, became unusable for recreational skiing.

In both disciplines, Alpine and Nordic, the competitive elements rapidly separated themselves from the purely recreational. Both developed a technology and language of their own and evolved a series of identifiable competitive disciplines completely divorced from recreational skiing.

Nordic skiing developed distance races, jumping, the compulsory combination of both and the para-military Biathlon which

combines distance racing with target shooting.

The Alpine racing disciplines have divided into the Downhill, the giant Slalom with about 30 gates over a vertical drop of not less than 300 metres and the Special Slalom with about 60 gates over a vertical drop of 150 metres. Men and women race separately over roughly equivalent courses. In addition to the so-called amateur disciplines there is a professional downhill discipline over two parallel slalom courses raced simultaneously by two skiers.

The three disciplines, Aerial, Moguls and Ballet, of freestyle, the latest addition to the family tree of skiing, are still in a state of development. They have been instrumental in popularizing short skis and while they are essentially competitive disciplines they appear to be readily accepted as part of normal recreational skiing.

ALPINE SKIING

Recreational

Ski mountaineering

Competitive Alpine skiing

Downhill

Slalom—Giant, Special, and Head-to-Head

Flying Kilometre

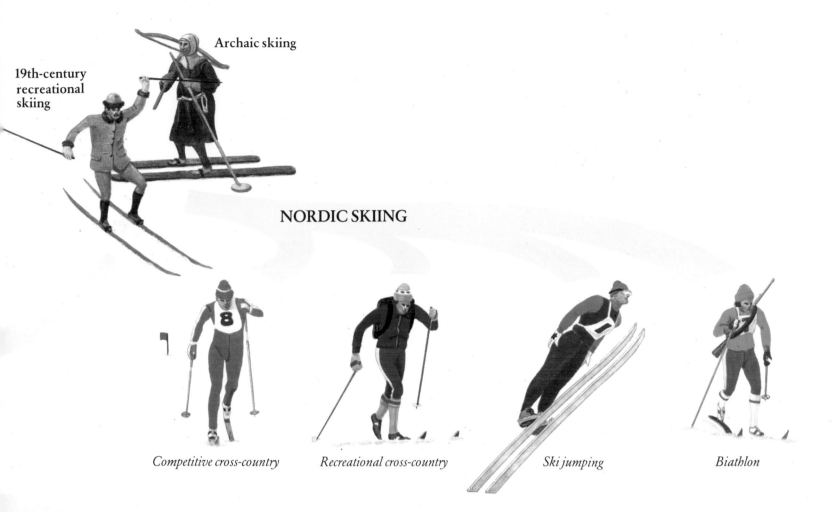

Archaic skiing

19th-century recreational skiing

NORDIC SKIING

Competitive cross-country *Recreational cross-country* *Ski jumping* *Biathlon*

Freestyle

Moguls *Aerial* *Ballet*

Trail Standards

To ski from the top of a trail which starts at the summit of a mountain to the valley floor is a hazardous business. In certain circumstances it can become extremely dangerous. It is too easily forgotten that, having arrived safely inside a building supplied with all modern amenities, from a three-course meal and vintage wine to toilets and souvenir shops, the skier may be at the top of a very high mountain and, once outside, is exposed to all the dangers and vagaries of a high-Alpine environment. No amount of technical expertise can alter the fact that danger from weather, snow and precipices exists. Yet, just as the skill and experience of a deep-sea sailor can reduce the ever-present dangers of the open ocean, so the skill and experience of the downhill skier can exaggerate or diminish the dangers he might face when taking a recognized trail to the valley.

The sign at Corviglia, St Moritz, gives some idea of the many routes that can be taken in this area.

For full enjoyment, a skier must match his skill to the difficulties he is going to face, keeping in mind the variations in snow and weather conditions. What is easy in perfect visibility can become excessively difficult in fog or storms. For one skier deep new snow is a delight; for another it is purgatory. There are excellent skiers who, when faced with a narrow and very steep pitch, suffer complete technical paralysis, and others who are incapable of skiing an ungroomed trail.

To overcome the risk of a skier finding himself on a trail which is beyond his skill,

virtually all resorts make use of signs and warning symbols, both on the trail maps and on the routes themselves. These signs are loosely based on accepted international standards. Those adopted in Europe and North America differ slightly in emphasis and design, and despite many committees and international conferences there has been no agreement on a universal definition of such terms as 'difficult' and 'easy'.

It is now common practice for a trail to be marked at the start, at forks or divisions or at the beginning of alternative routes by a pointer signpost indicating the specific trail in terms of a number or a name or a destination. In every case this should coincide with the information shown on the trail maps available in the resort.

The space between these main signposts should ideally be interrupted by posts with coloured discs at the top. The colours identify the degree of difficulty of the slope and the posts are placed at intervals sufficiently close to one another that they can be seen even in bad weather.

In addition to the trail indicators it has become increasingly common to make use of signs similar to those used on roads to show narrow passages, the meeting of two routes, or a hazard such as one route crossing over a skilift track.

Dangerous edges or closed areas are customarily roped off by bright orange polypropylene cord from which hang pennants made from fluorescent material in orange or green. A sign is planted at the entrance giving the reason for the closure.

The classification of the difficulties that may be encountered on a route is relative to the geography of each particular resort. Moderate trails can vary from being comparatively easy on one mountain with shallow hillsides to being difficult where all trails are steep and frequently narrow when passing through rock barriers or forested areas. The classification of a route will be the average for the entire trail and will never indicate short passages which are either easier or more difficult than the average. In addition, a moderate trail can become excessively difficult purely as the result of snow conditions. In general skiers are advised to stay clear of trails which require skills in excess of their previous achievements unless the conditions are very favourable, or the resort is known for exaggerating the difficulties of its trails for publicity reasons. Speed as such plays no part in the classifications.

North America   **Europe**

Danger from avalanche or other adverse conditions. Route closed. Definitely not safe for skiing.

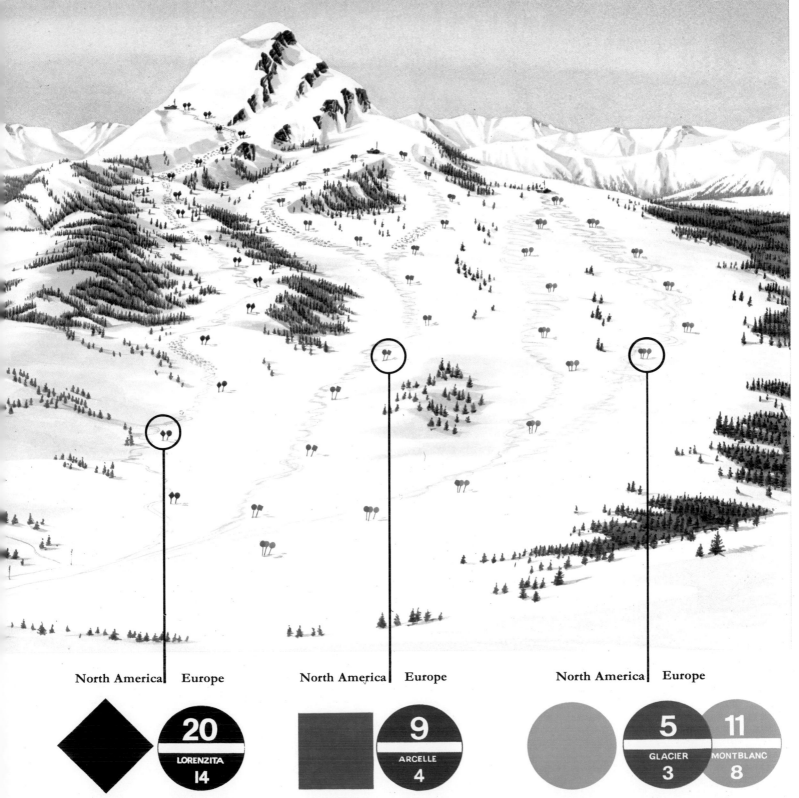

North America   Europe

20
LORENZITA
14

North America   Europe

9
ARCELLE
4

North America   Europe

5
GLACIER
3

11
MONTBLANC
8

The trail is steep and may also be narrow and difficult. Experienced and good skiers enjoy these routes.

A wide and not excessively steep trail with occasional passages of greater difficulty. A route for moderate skiers.

A wide, relatively shallow trail with few, if any, steep sections. These routes are good for inexperienced skiers

Mountain Transport

The comfort, location and safety of the mechanical uphill transport are key factors in the popularity of a resort. The skier needs to be carried, with his equipment, to a point from which he can begin his descent.

The earliest vehicles climbed the hillsides on tracks, by means of a rack-and-pinion system driven by steam or electricity. Many of these are still being used and well-known examples are the Wengen-Scheidegg-Grindelwald-Jungfrau railway in Switzerland and the Mount Washington railway in New England.

The funicular also travels on tracks. The ascending and descending cars are pulled by a continuous cable. As a means of uphill transport, the funicular is regaining popularity, and one was recently installed to travel almost entirely underground half-way to the summit of the Kitzteinhorn from the valley station of Kaprun-Thörl.

The earliest railway in Switzerland was at Rigi.

Draglifts were the earliest forms of transport designed specifically for skiers. The simplest of these consist of a loop of rope driven by a slow petrol engine. Attached to the loop are smaller loops which the skiers hold to be drawn up the snow slopes.

Erich Constam, a Swiss engineer patented the T-bar draglift in 1934. This is an anchor-shaped bar held to a traction cable by means of a clamp. A pair of skiers lean against the bar and are dragged up a snow track. This

invention revolutionized the teaching and practice of skiing, since the time spent travelling up the mountain was considerably reduced, and more frequent journeys could be made. An American variation is the J-bar.

The T-bar is restricted to pulling the skier in a straight line. The Poma 'button' lift was developed by the French engineer Pomagalski, and is capable of negotiating up to three changes in direction. It also has the advantage of being self-service, is used by one skier at a time, and is easily adapted to changing frequency demands. Unlike the T-bar, the Poma is stationary until a skier wants to use it. It is then coupled to the traction cable.

Up to four skiers can be carried at once on a chairlift or in a Gondola, and these or similar mechanisms are now the most common form of skiers' transport. The chair can be a cold and uncomfortable vehicle, and as it moves continuously it can be difficult to mount. The enclosed Gondola solves the problem of exposure and is entered while it is stationary.

The most dramatic, but also the most expensive, mountain vehicle is the cable-car, which is also called a cableway or tramway. A large cabin which holds up to 120 people, is pulled on a suspension cable, often travelling at heights up to 300 or more feet above the ground. It is particularly useful for negotiating vertical cliffs, ravines and glaciers, and is the usual vehicle for ascending high summits. Among the most spectacular of these cable-cars is the Aiguille du Midi – Méré de Glace – Dent de Géant crossing in France, or the dizzying ascent of the Plateau Rosa from Cervinia. The cableway is probably the most ancient of all mountain transport. It existed in some form in China in the 11th century.

Top left: A French engineer, Pomagalski, invented this form of draglift. Centre left: The chairlift is an American invention. The first one was designed by Jim Curran and installed at Sun Valley, California. Left: Tracked vehicles are used mostly for preparing the trails but they do tow people and supplies up the snow. Above: The T-bar is well known to skiers visiting Europe, particularly Switzerland. Above right: The gondola provides frequent, comfortable uphill transport at no cost of effort to the skier. It is the answer to the discomfort of the chairlift in bad weather. An early form of transport was the funicular, and this is still in use. Right: The funicular at St Johann i. Tirol. Far right: The cableway, or cable-car, is used for carrying large numbers of people to high points over cliffs and ravines.

Trail Preparation and Safety

The grooming of trails and the constant watch for possible avalanche danger is not entirely the altruistic activity which many skiers seem to believe. The legal responsibilities of a resort organization extend to the provision of reasonable safety for the visitors whom it transports to the hill-tops. Nor would a poorly maintained trail network in any way contribute to profitability.

In practice, the mountain organization is concerned, in the first instance, with making the trails safe to work on, even in extremely adverse conditions. They must be safe not only for the manual workers but for the costly machinery which is employed and which has now almost completely supplanted the manual labour formerly used.

In addition to safety, the grooming of trails is essential for the conservation of adequate snow-cover. Rolling and compressing the freshly fallen snow has the effect of making it less sensitive to sudden changes in temperature and, in particular, it resists an early thaw in the hot March sun.

Trail maintenance and avalanche safety precautions start in the summer, when the ground can be cleared of obtrusive rocks and tree stumps, narrow passages can be widened, water courses bridged and, in the autumn, further tree-felling is undertaken to widen trails passing through forested land. As the trail machines are limited by the steepness of the ground which they can climb, it is necessary to build access roads for them.

Trail grooming is carried out by specialized snow vehicles which tow behind them ridged rollers. In addition they can be equipped with scrapers to level out moguls, or bumps, caused by the skiers. Three or four parallel journeys by a machine are required to roll the average trail width. They cannot travel at a speed much greater than about ten miles per hour and are limited to a steepness of approximately 35° on hard snow, and rather less over loose snow cover thicker than six inches.

Trails are planned, as far as possible, to avoid known avalanche areas. Avalanche protection has for practical reasons to be restricted to actively dislodging newly created snow layers. This can be carried out in a variety of ways, though all involve the use of explosive charges. These can be introduced into the snow cover either in advance of a snowfall and exploded by remote control or they can be placed into the snow cover by a rocket, recoilless gun or mortar, by dropping special grenades from an aircraft, or by patrols inserting the charges by hand.

Sno-makers (above) cover many trails in resorts in the United States. (Right) a tracked vehicle remaking a trail after a fresh fall of snow. (Below) a snow-blower clearing a lift site.

The black trail (left) has been well skied and is too steep for the trail preparation machines. The skill of the men operating this unpopular form of downhill transport (right) has to be admired.

Clothing and Equipment

Ski clothing and equipment form, together, one of the most sophisticated sports packages ever marketed. A complete set of equipment costs far more than that needed for any other sport. The requirements of the skier are many and often conflicting – the result is an artful compromise between the demands of the sport, technology, fashion and the tourist industry.

The specifications for clothing and equipment required for the two basic branches of the sport – Alpine and Nordic – differ radically and are incompatible. The former requires weatherproof clothing which will keep the skier warm in the face of sub-zero temperatures in a continuous air stream which together produce a very serious chill factor. It has to be robust enough to stand up to the wear and tear of falls and abuse on skilifts. It should not obstruct the very considerable physical activity of the downhill skiing movements. At the same time it must be designed so that the skier will not get too hot while skiing but will not be chilled when standing still, waiting for the next lift.

The Nordic, cross-country skier cannot ski happily with heavy restrictive clothing, and requires light, wind-and-shower-proof outer covering, over light, thermal under-garments. He relies on his physical activity to provide the warmth and on his clothing to prevent heat loss.

The basis for both types of clothing is the theory of trapped air insulation by means of a closely-woven material enclosing a thermal interlayer which will not prove to be a vapour barrier. The wearing of woollen, fluffy outer coverings which collect drift and falling snow is now a thing of the past.

Increasingly for downhill skiing the one-piece or matching two-piece suit consisting of padded trousers or dungarees, and a similarly padded and pocketed jacket is replacing the once familiar, close-fitting trousers and separate anorak or wind-jacket. The material should be a matt-surfaced, closely woven, shower-proof weave which will not slide excessively if the skier falls. Many jackets are provided with a hood fitted into the collar. Sleeves and trouser bottoms should be fitted with inner cuffs, designed to prevent snow from building up inside the suit.

Skiers always seem to have to carry many items such as lift tickets, sun protection creams, sunglasses, goggles and food and the familiar banana bag removes the need for large pockets.

Gloves are made ideally of proofed leather with quilted or padded lining, but more usually they are made of soft synthetic leather. They can be either finger gloves, which makes doing up zips and bindings easier, or mittens, which are warmer. For many years now, skiers have worn some form of knitted cap on their heads, and many children now wear crash helmets. Socks, ever since the warm, foam-lined ski boots were invented, are either knee or ankle length made from loop-knit, wool-and-nylon mixtures, worn for comfort rather than warmth.

Cross-country skiing has developed its own, most attractive fashions, for while it is perfectly feasible to wear downhill ski suits they are clumsy and hot compared with the light-weight clothing most people prefer. Matching knickerbockers and jacket, made of light, wind-proof cotton and polyester mixtures are the universal choice. Both jackets and trousers are cut to permit completely free arm and leg movement. Additional warmth is provided by thermal underwear and light wool sweaters. Long, heavy-rib, woollen stockings in matching or contrasting colours are popular. A tight, knitted woollen bob-cap is the traditional headwear and gloves are usually knitted mittens.

Ski equipment consists of boots, skis, bindings, poles and goggles or sun glasses.

The Alpine Skier

Hats, goggles, glasses and barrier creams protect the skier from strong sunshine as well as freezing fog, wind and driving snow.

The downhill skier's weatherproof clothing provides warmth and protection, will stand up to abuse in lifts or from falls, but will not restrict energetic movements. An inner, elasticated, second lining prevents snow from rising up the skier's arms and legs. Many jackets have a light-weight hood concealed inside the collar for use when the weather changes from sunshine to drifting snow.

High speeds, and occasional, imperfect trails make it essential that skis, boots and bindings are very strong indeed. At the same time they have to assist the skier to perform his sport well.

Alpine equipment is totally incompatible with that for cross-country skiing.

Although the outward appearance of skis has not varied very greatly in the last 30 or 40 years, their detailed design and construction has now become a very sophisticated engineering project. A ski consists of a curved point, called the spatula, a front section between the spatula and the foot, a narrowed and arched section called the waist, and the tail section. The ski is held on to the boot by means of the binding which serves as a firm link between ski and foot through the boot. All downhill skis are fitted with safety bindings designed to open when the pressure from twisting or forward falls becomes dangerous.

There are three basic types of safety bindings. The commonest is known as a toe-and-heel set and consists of a toe-gripping mechanism which permits the boot to swivel sideways in a serious fall. The heel clamp, usually of the automatic, step-in type, opens with an upward and, occasionally, a forward pull. Both are adjustable for the skier's individual weight, ability and boot size.

Increasingly popular are the plate bindings in which the boot is held to the plate permanently while ski-shod and the plate in turn is held to the ski by means of a front and back latch. In the case of a fall the plate can detach itself from either or both latches by a lifting, twisting or combined movement.

In order to prevent loose skis being lost after a fall and possibly disappearing down hill, it is now virtually compulsory to wear some form of safety strap or brake.

The construction of a modern downhill ski, whether full-length competition or compact leisure ski, is a complex sandwich of metal, wood and synthetics. Basically it consists of a top metal surface, a central core made of either a variety of synthetic materials or of specially selected wood blocks or a combination of both. The sandwich is completed by a base plate, again of metal onto which is applied a running surface, the sole, which is made of a special high-density polyethylene. Incorporated into the sandwich, often as part of the base plate, are the bottom outside edges of the ski. These consist of a strip or strips of special steel alloys of great hardness and springiness which are ground to a very sharp right-angle.

The character of a ski is determined by the stiffness of the spatula and the radius of its curve, the longitudinal and torsional stiffness of the front section, the height of the arch and the radius of the waist, and finally by the flexibility and torsional strength of the tail. The central groove in the sole serves to promote directional stability. The edges provide a sharp cutting grip on hard or icy snow surfaces. All these characteristics can be varied while still keeping a strict proportional relationship to each other and so provide a specialist ski for beginners, a perfect ski for powder snow or a downhill racing ski which would be unmanageable on a slalom course.

It is now recognized that the average recreational skier is best served by a ski which is head high or an inch or two more. This length reduces injury potential and makes all ski turns easier to perform. The limitations are restricted to the maximum speed which this type of ski can handle safely. As this top speed is considerably in excess of the fastest even the expert recreational skier requires, the limitation is theoretical rather than practical.

The downhill boot has become a massive, ungainly and often uncomfortable piece of highly specialized footwear. Increasing understanding and development of ski techniques required a boot which would serve as a perfect transmitter of weight and movement from bare foot to ski with a minimum of lost motion. At the same time, the safety binding had to have a rigid sole and one which would stand up to compression forces. The result

The Nordic Skier
The knitted bobble-cap is traditional head-wear for the cross-country skier. It provides protection from all weather.

Clothing must be very light to wear. It is cut to permit free arm and leg movements, and the fabric helps to retain the heat which the skier's activity creates.

Downhill suits would be too cumbersome for such action. The knickerbocker's are the traditional style and are worn with knitted colourful socks.

Cross-country boots are as light as running shoes. The heel is not attached to the long, narrow ski to allow for long strides, but the toe is fixed to push the ski forwards.

was a moulded plastic shell with a narrow, flat, metal reinforced sole and a high shaft from the heel. To make this wearable the plastic shell is padded by means of either a thermoplastic, pre-shaped foam or a semi-plastic, putty-like substance which will, when warm, adapt its shape to the wearer's foot. The boot is closed and tightened by means of adjustable lever clips.

Ski poles are balancing and support aids. They consist of a metal tube with a sharp point which will grip on ice, a small round basket about 3 or 4 inches from the point which prevents the ski pole from sinking into the snow, and a shaped handgrip to which is attached a wrist loop, or a shaped, loopless hilt and guard rather like that of a cavalry sword. The length of the pole should be such that when in the snow, the forearm is parallel to the ground.

Ski goggles or glasses serve to protect the eyes from snow-drift and snowflakes as well as to protect the eyes against excessive reflection of ultra-violet light off snow. They are designed to give full vision and protection as well as having adequate ventilation so that they will not steam up.

Whereas downhill, Alpine clothing and equipment are designed for hard physical wear and as a result can be very heavy, all cross-country equipment is designed for lightness, comfort and flexibility.

Cross-country skis are made in four basic designs: the very narrow, very light racing skis, the so-called training ski or light touring ski, the touring ski which is slightly heavier, wider and often provided with a hard-wood edge, and lastly the *Fjellski* or mountain touring ski which is very similar to the old-fashioned wooden ski used before 1960, but now built by modern methods.

All these skis are worn very long. When stood on end they reach to upstretched hand and arm length. The spatula is very curved to permit a long stride which lifts the tail of the ski, the arch is much greater than is customary on Alpine skis to provide a measure of lift when striding forwards and the waisting is minimal, while the tail is stiff to control straight-line running.

The construction of the racing and training skis is based on a light-weight polymer sandwich with a special micro-pore polyethylene sole. Both the top and bottom layers are of very thin wood veneer – usually birch or ash – sandwiching a polyurethane core.

The traditional sole is usually prepared, by the skier, with a series of special waxes immediately before setting out and it is often renewed during the course of an outing as weather, temperature and snow change. The purpose of these waxes is to prevent the ski from slipping backwards while still allowing it to slide forwards freely. This is achieved by designing waxes which, over a given temperature range, will allow snow crystals to embed themselves partially in the thin wax layer when weight is applied vertically to the ski sole. When the ski is pushed forward, the snow crystals are brushed off the sole leaving a fast sliding surface. The waxes are graded into temperature groups and these are colour-coded.

For recreational use the development of the 'no-wax' sole has done away with the mystique of cross-country waxing. This type of sole, which can be had in three different forms, consists of a moulded polyethylene base which is shaped either into very shallow, backward-pointing steps or as a series of fish-scales. This patterning is used only under the central third of the ski and serves to prevent the ski from slipping backwards on the snow. A third, and less popular system is to embed narrow strips of mohair into the sole with the pile pointing backwards.

Cross-country skis are held to the shoe or boot by means of a simple, light clamp known popularly as a rat-trap, after the patent name of this binding – Rottefella. The clamp presses the welt of the boot between two sidepieces so that the sole engages between three blunt spikes. The size and placing of these spikes and the shape of the side-pieces are standardized and known as the Nordic Norm. For top-class racing, the shoe and binding are made as a single unit, doing away completely with the metal clamp. For rough touring it is customary to use a rather heavier boot with a very simple cable binding.

Cross-country boots and shoes are designed for lightness and comfort. They are rarely above ankle-height and have a specially flexible sole and the upper part is designed not to crease across the toes. For touring and occasional recreational use, a heavier shoe is worn which resembles a light walking boot.

Ski poles used for Nordic skiing are long, light and very carefully balanced. They are made of fibre-glass or split tonkin cane. The tip is a long, curved point, and the baskets are very small and light, although for deep snow larger baskets are used. The handgrip is designed for use with the minimum of effort and the wrist thong is adjustable so that the pole can be pushed backwards without having to grip the pole.

Ski mountaineering and Alpine touring equipment is basically identical with the Alpine downhill equipment which was used 15 or 20 years ago, although every use is made of modern materials. The skis are usually of compact length, and specially designed for deep and variable snow. The boots are a

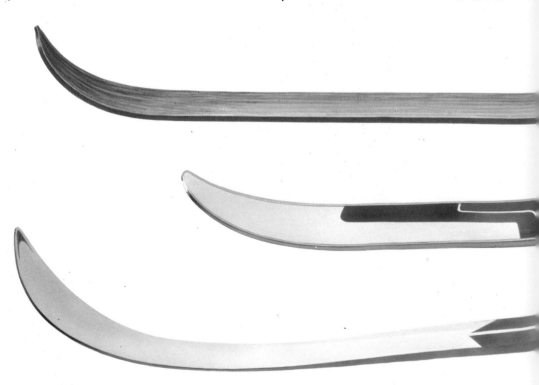

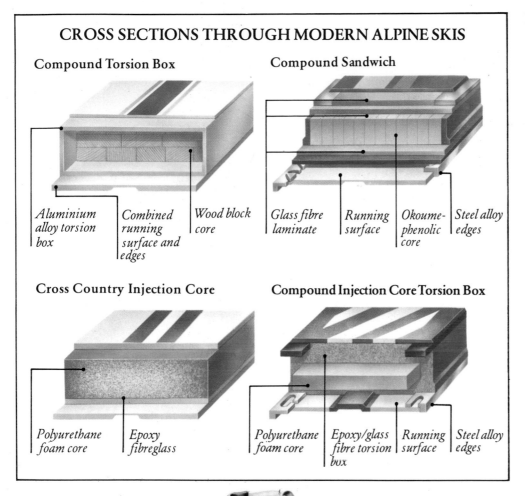

CROSS SECTIONS THROUGH MODERN ALPINE SKIS

Compound Torsion Box

Aluminium alloy torsion box   *Combined running surface and edges*   *Wood block core*

Compound Sandwich

Glass fibre laminate   *Running surface*   *Okoume-phenolic core*   *Steel alloy edges*

Cross Country Injection Core

Polyurethane foam core   *Epoxy fibreglass*

Compound Injection Core Torsion Box

Polyurethane foam core   *Epoxy/glass fibre torsion box*   *Running surface*   *Steel alloy edges*

compromise between a high Alpine climbing boot and a modern ski boot. They must be soft and comfortable for walking and climbing while still be suitable for wearing with compression-type safety bindings and downhill techniques.

The binding has to be of a special design which will permit the heel to lift freely while the skier is climbing but be capable of acting as a normal, fixed-heel binding for downhill running. A number of such bindings are on the market though none is an ideal solution.

In order to climb the often very long and steep distances, use is made of what are called skins. These are now long strips of mohair (formerly they were seal-skin), the width and length of the ski and are attached to the ski by means of special waxes and/or patent clips. They allow a relatively smooth forward glide but resist a backward pull. They are removed for downhill skiing.

Ski mountaineering and touring in the high mountains requires that the skier carries food, spare clothing, and equipment. Although the weight is normally limited to about 15 lbs, considerably heavier weights are carried on major trips involving a number of nights on the mountains in club huts. Use is made of the modern rucksack or back-pack which has no frame which would be an unacceptable obstruction. The width of the back-pack is less than body width and is fitted with an additional waist strap to prevent movement.

Hickory laminated ski *with Alpina binding and soft leather boots. Similar skis to these were in use from c. 1890 to 1930.*

Alpine compact ski. *Sophisticated compound construction. Heel-and-toe safety binding set and thermoplastic, moulded shell boot. 1978*

Cross-country racing ski. *Sophisticated injection core construction. Rottefella type binding with light leather and plastic shoe. 1978*

The Cross-Country Classics

THE HAUTE ROUTE

The classic high level ski mountaineering route from Saas Fee in Switzerland to Chamonix in France, known simply as the Haute Route, means to ski mountaineers what helicopter skiing in the Canadian Rockies means to downhill skiing enthusiasts.

The route is not absolutely fixed and the choice of detailed itinerary depends on skill, endurance, time and conditions. In general, it follows the line of the major glaciers and glacier passes which cut through the most impressive scenery of the highest ranges in the central Alps. The complete route is about 120 kilometres long and, although there is

The afternoons (above) are time for rest or gazing at views like this one from Cabane de Valsorey. The dawn start from the Schönbiel hut (above right). It is a scratchy route down the Zmutt glacier.

Moving from left to right the red line marks ascending sections and the orange line marks descending sections.

The Haute Route is a high-altitude climbing and skiing journey for the ski mountaineering enthusiasts. It is long and difficult and should never be undertaken without a guide. There is a great deal of controversy about whether the start is at Saas Fee in Switzerland or Argentière near Chamonix in France, but whichever direction is followed the journey provides some testing terrain. The route can be made harder by adding peaks or easier by circumventing some of the harder climbs.

much argument about whether it is better to move from west to east or east to west, those mountaineers who are anxious to include the customary peaks – Allalin, Monte Rosa, Breithorn and Pigne d'Arolla – prefer to start from Saas Fee. Some tour operators and local tourist authorities organize group mountaineering holidays, taking a simplified line along the route.

The complete route takes between a week and fourteen days. The accommodation is in untenanted huts of the Swiss and French Alpine Clubs, and so all food has to be carried. It is customary to break the traverse at Arolla and Bourg St Pierre for re-supplying

The gentle climb up the Glacier d'Otemma is a good start to a very long day.

(continued on page 24)

23

It is downhill either way from the Col Valpelline.

and changing clothes and equipment.

As the entire route involves long and often dangerous glacier ascents and descents, a full complement of Alpine mountaineering equipment must be carried. There are no route signposts and, should the weather close in, considerable experience in map reading and navigation is essential. It is for these reasons that skiers who are not qualified mountaineers are advised to engage a guide.

The route should not be attempted before early May. By then the days are longer and the winter snows and storms have bridged the crevasses. The day starts very early, usually before first light at about 4.00 AM. The day's skiing is over by about two in the afternoon

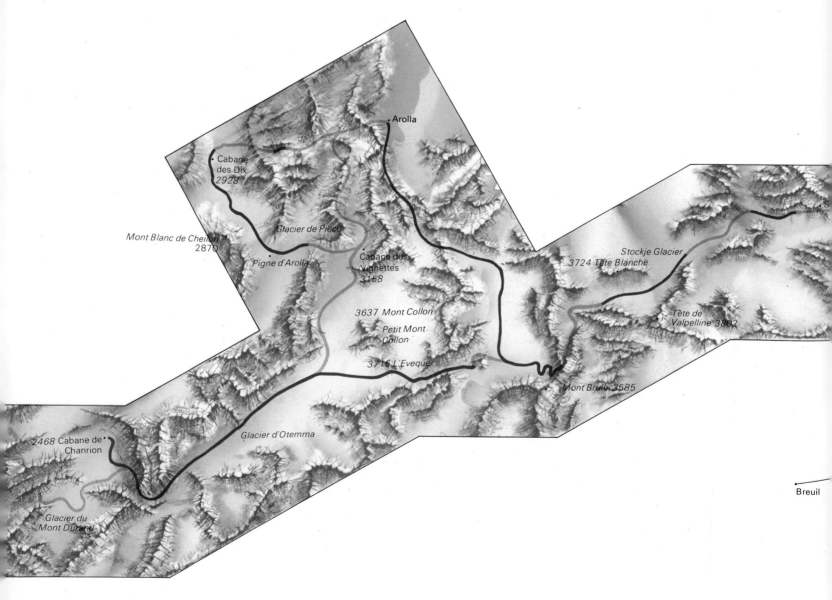

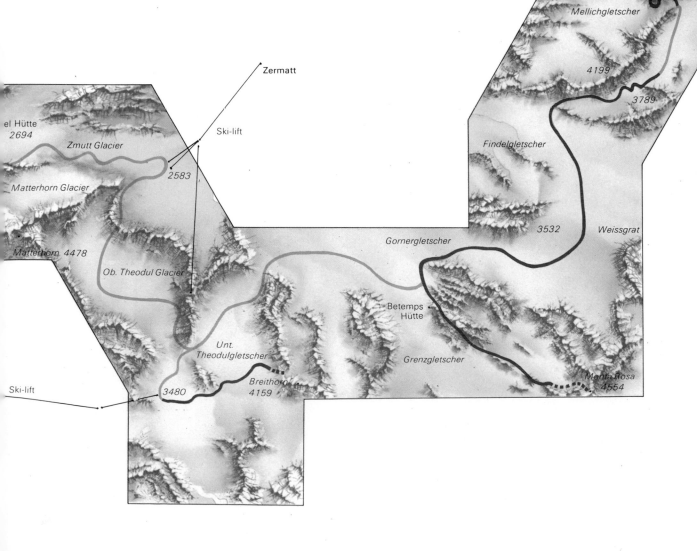

The first long day from Chamonix end is the trudge up the Glacier de l'Argentière.

by which time the snow is becoming slushy and the crevasse bridges are weakened.

The standard of skiing required is not very high as safety and the problems of a thirty-pound back-pack take precedence over sophisticated technique. Climbing, using skins, rarely exceeds four hours, though certain stages, notably between the Schönbiel Hut and the Chanrion Hut are exacting and exhausting having a series of sharp steep climbs interrupting the descents.

The Haute Route is the best known but not the only high-level hut-to-hut ski mountaineering circuit. Two almost equally famous but not so demanding routes are the Oetztal and Stubai circuits, both in Austria.

THE VASALOPPET

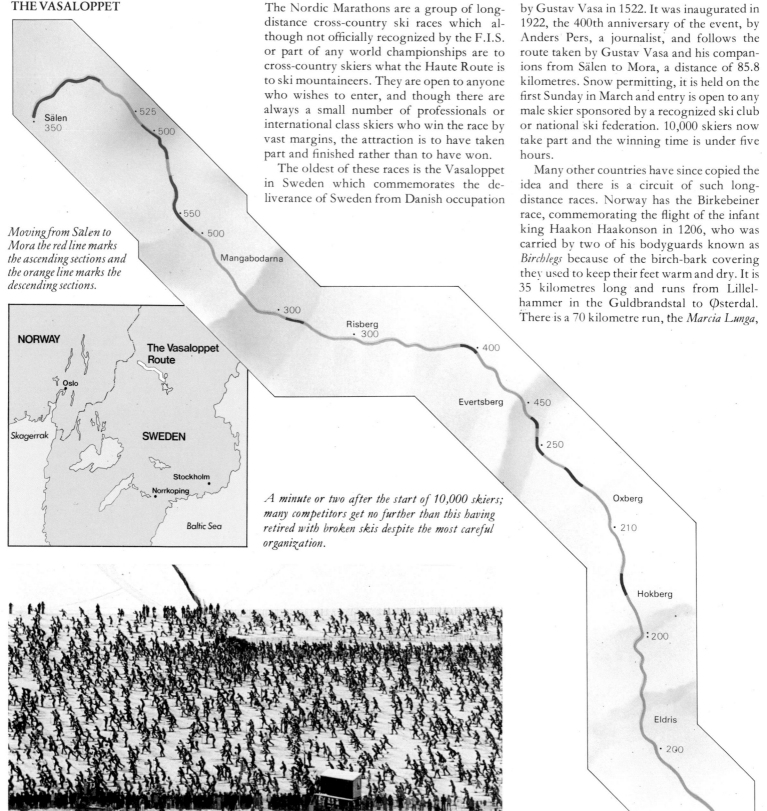

Moving from Sälen to Mora the red line marks the ascending sections and the orange line marks the descending sections.

NORWAY

The Vasaloppet Route

Oslo

Skagerrak

SWEDEN

Stockholm

Norrkoping

Baltic Sea

A minute or two after the start of 10,000 skiers; many competitors get no further than this having retired with broken skis despite the most careful organization.

Sälen
350

• 525

• 500

• 550

• 500

Mangabodarna

• 300

Risberg
• 300

• 400

Evertsberg

• 450

• 250

Oxberg

• 210

Hokberg

: 200

Eldris

• 200

• 250

Mora

The Nordic Marathons are a group of long-distance cross-country ski races which although not officially recognized by the F.I.S. or part of any world championships are to cross-country skiers what the Haute Route is to ski mountaineers. They are open to anyone who wishes to enter, and though there are always a small number of professionals or international class skiers who win the race by vast margins, the attraction is to have taken part and finished rather than to have won.

The oldest of these races is the Vasaloppet in Sweden which commemorates the deliverance of Sweden from Danish occupation by Gustav Vasa in 1522. It was inaugurated in 1922, the 400th anniversary of the event, by Anders Pers, a journalist, and follows the route taken by Gustav Vasa and his companions from Sälen to Mora, a distance of 85.8 kilometres. Snow permitting, it is held on the first Sunday in March and entry is open to any male skier sponsored by a recognized ski club or national ski federation. 10,000 skiers now take part and the winning time is under five hours.

Many other countries have since copied the idea and there is a circuit of such long-distance races. Norway has the Birkebeiner race, commemorating the flight of the infant king Haakon Haakonson in 1206, who was carried by two of his bodyguards known as *Birchlegs* because of the birch-bark covering they used to keep their feet warm and dry. It is 35 kilometres long and runs from Lillelhammer in the Guldbrandstal to Østerdal. There is a 70 kilometre run, the *Marcia Lunga*, which starts in Cortina d'Ampezzo in Italy, and the Koasalauf, run in two sections, from St Johann i. Tirol.

The longest of all is held every winter in Canada, called the *Coureur de Bois* (the wood runner) over a 160 kilometre track. This Canadian marathon was instituted in 1967 and to enter for the Gold qualification it is necessary to complete the course carrying a minimum 5 kilo pack containing food and tenting equipment for a night outdoors.

A ski marathon that is attracting increasing attention in the United States is the American Birkebeiner which is held at Telemark Ski Centre, Hayward, Wisconsin, over a distance of 55 kilometres. It is a particularly testing course as it has an almost constant rise from start to finish.

Among the most popular of all these marathons is the Engadiner Marathon, which is run over 42 kilometres from Maloja, through St Moritz and Pontresina to Zuoz. First run in 1969 with 900 competitors, both men and women, it is now limited to a maximum of 10,000 competitors. This number is now reached annually.

The popularity of this particular marathon can be found in the relatively easy ground which it covers. Until St Moritz is reached it is virtually flat which makes for an easy, well-preserved track. However the spirit-breaking climb to Pontresina and the rutted descents have made many a brave runner collapse before the last lap.

THE AMERICAN BIRKEBEINER

Moving from Telemark to Hayward the red line marks the ascending sections and the orange line marks the descending sections.

The Birkebeiner Route

At the island on Lake Champfer the Engadin marathon skiers are thinning out.

Weather, Snow and Avalanche

Weather, snow and avalanches make a trio which skiers throughout the world face in a relationship compounded of myth, ignorance and hope. The theses, textbooks and over-simplified journalistic articles would fill a library shelf but, despite satellite observation, computor analysis and electron microscopes, the sum-total of hard fact and demonstrable truth remains meagre.

Most elusive of these three aspects of the skier's ecosphere is weather. It is the micro-climate of a small section of a mountain range, of an Alpine valley or even a single hill which concerns the skier. This is where everything except luck, experience and a weather sense born of long observation and good memory is virtually valueless. The answers will always remain speculative in detail, though with a minimum of basic knowledge a trend can be guessed.

Reduced to the simplest of terms, weather consists of air masses of various average temperatures moving from one area to another in the form of wind. They are warmed or cooled by their altitude and absorb or lose moisture which they hold in suspension as water vapour as a result of increases or decreases in temperature and, to a lesser degree, pressure. These air masses move along predictable paths from a high-pressure area to a low-pressure area in a clockwise direction (southern hemisphere) or an anti-clockwise direction (northern hemisphere) more or less parallel to the lines of equal pressure called isobars. The closer these lines are together, indicating a steep pressure gradient, the stronger the accompanying winds perceived at ground level are likely to be.

When, in addition to a pressure gradient, there is also a definable temperature gradient then these air masses can be referred to as cold fronts (bearing relatively colder air) or warm fronts. As they pass over the countryside they produce a characteristic change in weather. This may or may not be associated with a marked temperature change. As a very rough rule of thumb, when a warm front creeps in, the warm air slides over the top of cold air. This produces a gradual increase of cloud cover and a steady increase in precipitation (rain, snow or hail) which can culminate in a severe storm followed by warmer, fine wea-

Temperature inversion with a trapped layer of cold air in the valley produces a dramatic and beautiful cloud ocean — the 'Wolkenmeer'. This one covers the Verwall Valley, Austria.

ther. A cold front, on the other hand, arrives violently, frequently accompanied by thunder, as the invading cold or very cold air impinges on the static warm air. The departure of the cold front is followed by prolonged periods of precipitation and a very slow clearing of the weather. Warm fronts are preceded by rain or snow and cold fronts are followed by rain or snow.

Clouds, the outward evidence of temperature changes in the upper air, are condensed water vapour. Their shape, movements and changes are good indications of weather changes but, although every kind of cloud is classified and has a name, their interpretation can be difficult. Warm fronts tend to be preceded by masses of small, fluffy clouds; cold fronts are visible as a solid mass of dense cloud on the horizon. Thin, wispy clouds at great heights are usually ice clouds and indicative of cold winds. Picturesque towers of billowing cloud, often called fine weather clouds may be stationary over a peak or lake or may grow alarmingly when there are signs of impending thunderstorms. A long, cigar-shaped cloud in a blue sky, often the only cloud visible, is a danger sign to any mountaineer or high altitude skier for it is the harbinger of sudden and violent weather change, which is often very local.

Of particular interest to skiers are the often disastrous incursions of warm, snow-destroying winds known variously as *Foehn*, *Chinook*, and by many other local names. They are characteristic of high mountain valley weather and belong to a class of air movement known as adiabatic. They are characterized by a sharp, often dramatic, rise in temperature and an extreme dryness. Given suitable topography, they can achieve hurricane force. Their origin is complex. Warm, moist air rises along the barrier wall of a mountain range. As it rises, it cools and deposits moisture as rain or snow. As it crosses the summit range, it becomes trapped below the high, cold air and is forced downwards. As it descends it is compressed, and consequently rises in temperature and expands. If it is then still trapped between the high walls of a narrow valley it has to force its way out and down the valley where it can explode with hurricane force. Higher up, on the wider, often flatter slopes below the range, this air movement can be so slight as to be barely perceptible. It is however so dry and warm that it will lick up snow at a phenomenal rate. This *Foehn* weather is frequently accompanied by cloudless skies on the lee side of the range though cloud will

often be boiling up along the summits. At summit level the winds can be exceptionally fierce, coming, as it were, from a cloudless sky. For many people this kind of weather produces considerable malaise and it is often blamed for anything from failure to pass examinations, to divorce and even murder. The collapse of this weather situation inevitably brings about heavy cloud and mild precipitation accompanied by a rise in temperature.

Temperature inversions are not uncommon in the mountains. These occur when dry warm air becomes trapped under colder air layers without any of the accompanying calamities such as *Foehn*. Not infrequently this will result in a kind of sandwich structure where cold air is trapped in the valley with a layer of warm dry air like the meat in a cold air sandwich. This may give rise to the dramatic sight of a *Wolkenmeer* – a cloud ocean – covering the valley floor leaving the mountains ranging out of the billowing clouds like islands. The ski fields will be basking in warm sunshine while the valleys are freezing.

Temperature in still air decreases about 1° centigrade for every 100 metre altitude. Warm air will hold more water vapour than cold air at the same pressure. The lower the pressure the less vapour can be held at the same temperature. A clear sky will cause a greater temperature drop at night than a cloudy sky because of radiation. Snow or ice, in order to melt, require heat which they will take from the immediate surroundings. Water has to lose heat to its surroundings in order to freeze. It may seem paradoxical but melting snow will cause air temperatures to drop and freezing water will make air temperature go up. These are the confusing laws of physics which govern weather, snow and avalanches.

Snow is formed when the moisture in the air is cooled below freezing point. It is generally believed that water crystallizes around minute specks of dust or salt. The first crystal is a simple, minuscule rod with six sides and the ends have six faces. These crystals become stuck to other crystals in a cloud and can combine in about 8000 different ways. The result is called a snowflake and meteorologists recognize 10 different basic shapes of solid, falling precipitation.

If the air is cold enough, the snow crystals will reach the earth in the form of snow. The colder the air, the smaller the crystals and, conversely, the warmer and moister the air, the larger the flakes as the half-melted small flakes will stick together and refreeze. Snow

falling at great altitude, such as on the Himalayas, or through completely dry air, such as occurs on the western face of the American Rocky Mountains, lands as very light, unspoiled crystals which, if sufficient fall, give rise to the famous 'Rocky Mountain Powder' or bottomless, wild, powder snow.

From the moment the flake reaches the ground, it begins a long sequence of changes resulting from the physical damage suffered on the ground and begins a cycle of melting and refreezing. Snow scientists recognize two fundamental changes, known as destructive and constructive metamorphosis. The destructive changes start with the breaking up of the fragile stars and result in a compacting and cohesion of the flakes. The colder and drier, the less the flakes will compact or settle. If fresh snow is physically moved, either for example by the wind (known as freighted snow) or by snow-ploughing or blowing, it undergoes a dramatic change because of the friction between individual crystals. The surface pressures and friction cause minute temperature rises and the subsequent loss of heat then causes immediate re-freezing. The result is that the snow can become a compacted, concrete-hard mass.

Within any snow layer there is a constant change, partly due to the snow settling under its own weight and partly due to a cycle of internal evaporation and re-crystallization, known as constructive metamorphosis. The temperature within a thick layer of snow is an almost constant $-1°C$, as natural snow consists largely of airspaces and very little ice.

A skier is largely concerned with the upper snow surfaces and the changes which occur here due to the action of wind, sun and temperature. These can be represented as a virtually closed circle which only terminates with the final dissolution of the snow cover into slush and water.

Directly related to both the constructive and destructive metamorphosis are avalanches. These are things that happen to other people in the resorts the sensible skier never visits. They are virtually always avoidable and predictable, but when they do occur they can be fatal. They are the result of the forces of gravity becoming greater than the friction and cohesion within the snow layers. Three fundamental types of avalanche are recognized. Wet snow avalanches, air borne powder snow avalanches and slab avalanches. Within this category further sub-divisions are made into weight, solidity, path, speed and destructiveness.

Wet snow slides or avalanches are characterized by their narrow V-shaped point of rupture, their entire snow thickness and the fact that they consist of water-logged denatured snow. Their paths are predictable and annually repeated and can be extremely destructive. They can start spontaneously, triggered off by the last final drop of water from an overhanging ledge. They move relatively slowly and do not ever become airborne, and are commonest in the spring or after a rapid temperature rise following heavy snow falls.

Airborne, true powder snow avalanches are released spontaneously after a very heavy snowfall during a period of little or no wind. They are the result of a build-up of snow on steep slopes and remain poised as long as temperatures remain low. They are characterized by a very high speed, a tremendously destructive wave of air and relatively little residual snow. Their great destructiveness is caused by the fact that newly fallen snow can contain up to 90% air. During the course of the avalanche fall, this is released explosively while the snow dust continues to displace vast quantities of new air. The airblast preceding a powder snow avalanche can reach speeds of several hundred miles an hour and will lay flat

an entire forest, blast down entire villages and kill almost all living things in its path by suffocation. After the passage of a powder snow avalanche it is surprising what a thin dusting of snow is left near the debris, though anyone even remotely within range of such an avalanche will find every pocket, crevice and seam of clothing filled with snow and it will even penetrate the closest of nylon fabric weaves. They are extremely rare and are often confused with the airborne front of a major ice or slab avalanche.

The most common, most lethal and most insidious of all avalanches is the windslab slide. It is to be found on any lee slope (direct or indirect) of any steepness after any snowfall, however thin, where there has been sufficient wind to transport snow. It can lie dormant under a number of subsequent fresh snowfalls and will only decay after long exposure to wind, sun and weather. The snow surface giving rise to this type of avalanche is the result of snow being freighted by wind and deposited in such a manner that the surface is consolidated and tensioned by the action of the snow movement. This results in a skin of varying thicknesses, from inches to feet, being formed which is, in effect, under

tension as it is occupying less area than it should. This tension is held at bay by the internal friction and locking-up of snow granules. Frequently such slab layers lie above a narrow air pocket or on a layer of finely powdered snow or recrystallized snow which will act as a lubricant should the slab begin to slide. Slab avalanches are never released spontaneously but always as the result of the surface skin being breached by some foreign agency, be it a skier, a frightened animal, an explosive charge or a lump of snow dropping onto it. The break-away area is characteristically angular and long. The slabs are large and to begin with slide freely, the higher ones riding up on to the lower ones. As the speed increases, the rear sections over-ride the front and may then become airborne.

Potential slab avalanche areas are to be seen on concave slopes or bowls, often below a corniced ridge. The snow colour is frequently dull grey, the surface easily broken by a skipole and the fracture of a slab area produces a dull, reverberating noise. The break-away crack travels at near-supersonic speed. Slab surfaces will eventually become weathered, when they collapse into themselves and leave a curious, orange-peel-like surface. This is then completely safe and will usually provide good skiing and it is often possible to pick a skiable line through bad wind crust by moving from one to another of these pock-marked areas.

Avalanche protection is afforded to trail skiers by the security patrols who release potential avalanches by means of explosives. Regular passage of grooming machines will reduce avalanche danger and clever positioning of snow fencing can reduce the danger.

An avalanche warning sign should never be ignored. If a party is caught by an avalanche help should be brought in immediately. Unless the party is numerous or equipped with electronic avalanche bleepers or has used ski mountaineers' avalanche cords and if the victims are not immediately visible, haphazard searching will not be effective and may spoil the scent for rescue dogs trained to work in snow. Survival time, unless the victims are sheltered by an overhanging rock, or in a river bed or under the remains of a building, can be measured in terms of tens of minutes. For any successful rescue time and experienced searchers are of the essence.

A long line of windslab avalanches released from the cornice above.

THE WORLD SKI ATLAS

WHERE TO SKI
Country by Country

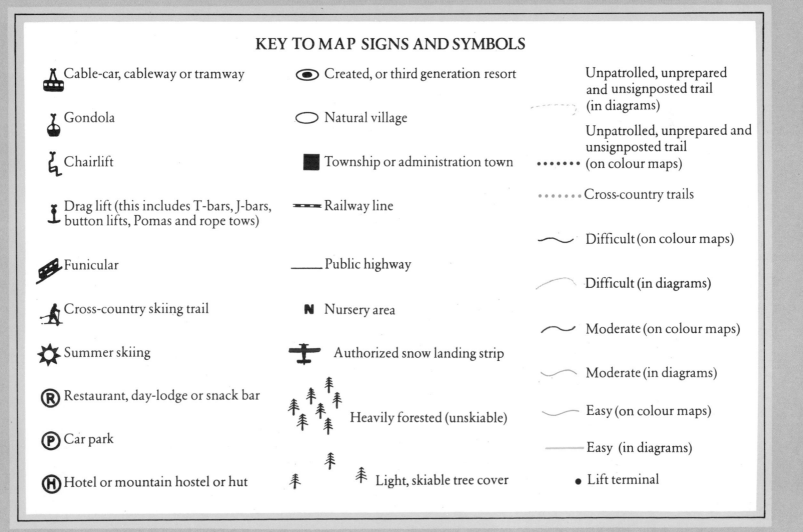

KEY TO MAP SIGNS AND SYMBOLS

Cable-car, cableway or tramway

Gondola

Chairlift

Drag lift (this includes T-bars, J-bars, button lifts, Pomas and rope tows)

Funicular

Cross-country skiing trail

Summer skiing

Ⓡ Restaurant, day-lodge or snack bar

Ⓟ Car park

Ⓗ Hotel or mountain hostel or hut

Created, or third generation resort

Natural village

Township or administration town

Railway line

Public highway

N Nursery area

Authorized snow landing strip

Heavily forested (unskiable)

Light, skiable tree cover

Unpatrolled, unprepared and unsignposted trail (in diagrams)

Unpatrolled, unprepared and unsignposted trail (on colour maps)

Cross-country trails

Difficult (on colour maps)

Difficult (in diagrams)

Moderate (on colour maps)

Moderate (in diagrams)

Easy (on colour maps)

Easy (in diagrams)

• Lift terminal

The United States

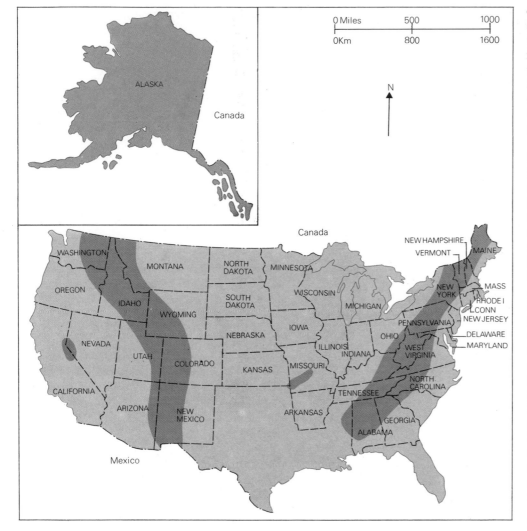

There are over 800 places to ski in the United States. Forty-eight states list at least one resort, and these include such disparate locations as Hawaii, Alaska, Illinois, Kansas, Missouri, Alabama, Georgia and Tennessee, with no fewer than 61 in Wisconsin. Their names range from the vernacular to the fanciful, such as Squilchuck and Inkpa-du-ta, Tannenbaum and Schuss, Hardscrabble and Golden-Gate-to-Fun.

Millions of Americans have learned to ski since the middle of the nineteenth century when Norwegian miners and lumberjacks first made their own equipment for winter transport and for racing. The sport in the United States has passed through three distinct phases. The first was a primitive, do-it-yourself, club activity by men and women who had fallen in love with skiing in Europe. A 'typical Tirolean village' phase

followed when wealthy sponsors tried to recreate the rosy memories of youthful *après ski* in Austrian chalet hotels. The picture was completed with ski instructors imported from Austria. In the final phase, the American skiing public took the imitation Alpine scene by the neck, shook it, and came up with a style of ski centre that is intrinsically American.

The timberline in the west can extend up to 10,000 feet (approximately 3,000 metres) or even higher, and in the east very few of the peaks are not covered with forest. There had been no medieval clearing of great areas of trees for farming and grazing, as had been the case in Europe, and every square foot of skiable land had to be cleared of forest and protected against erosion. Access roads had to be built, utilities fed in and each and every one of these preparatory

engineering activities was subject to scrutiny by the relevant authorities, which were subjected in turn to formidable ecological pressures, before the first hole could be dug for the first lift pylon. Individual ski areas are leased or bought from the land owners, and the whole operation is not renowned for its maximized return on invested capital.

The ski centres that have emerged fall into three basic categories. There are the European-style resorts which provide residential and service facilities in the form of shops, restaurants, hotels and apartment blocks all within easy distance of the ski slopes. These resorts are in a minority, and are found mostly in the west: names such as Vail, Aspen, Squaw Valley and Taos spring to mind. At the other end of the scale are the lodges at the bases of mountains where the majority of the accommodation and recreation must be sought in nearby townships. Many of these areas are very small, with little more than a couple of short chairlifts and a few hundred feet of downhill running. They are often very busy at weekends and come to a near standstill between Monday and Friday. During the years from 1950 to 1970, this style of resort was considered the norm, and skiers would make a journey of anything up to 20 miles (32 kilometres) from the nearest hotel to the ski mountain.

Increasingly, Americans adopted the habit of a winter vacation and this, plus the 1973/74 oil crisis, led to the third type of resort – the condominium block within easy walking distance of the ski slopes. Condominium in the strict sense is a misnomer and the European would class most of these developments as self-catering, furnished apartments let by the week. According to one respected American writer, who carried out an exhaustive study on the subject, this development was responsible for the final death of American *après ski* life – a lack most keenly felt by the visiting European.

The final rupture with the classic Alpine scene is visible to every visitor to New England. The trails had to be carved out of dense forestation and are now visible in winter from miles away like tracks left by the errant scavenging of a mad army of termites eating their haphazard way down from the mountain

summits. These distant untidy partings through the trees, running vaguely down the fall-line, can strike terror into any European skier's heart for, to him, they spell nothing more than narrow, scratchy forest trails – the sort that are the despair of many a tired skier as he nears home.

On closer inspection they are revealed as carefully planned routes, skilfully cross-connected and artfully graded from what is termed 'Top Expert' (unskiable for most) to 'Easiest'. Each centre plans its trails so that a percentage of the runs (geography permitting) can be classed as the steepest in the county, area, State, or even country. It is significant that the U.S. ski magazines list, from time to time, an analysis of which resorts have the steepest, the longest, or the longest-and-steepest trails.

More prudent skiers will find that the modest trails are wide, even very wide, perfectly groomed (except for those who

deliberately boast the biggest moguls in the world) and are a pleasure to ski.

'Lack of snow' is rapidly becoming an archaic expression for skiers in the United States. The development of the artificial 'snomaker', which produces a jet of snow made from compressed air and water, is now so perfected that entire mountainsides·are equipped with them. No serious ski centre has less than one major slope serviced by these machines.

Safety patrols and slope discipline is exemplary and lift lines, rare as they are, are an object lesson to the European skier for discipline, order, politeness and co-operation. Where in Europe can you hear the familiar liftline cry of 'single', when an American invites any other single skier to share his chair?

Ski rental in the base lodges is another aspect which European resorts cannot match either in quality or efficiency. It may well be a production line but in ten minutes skiers can be fitted with boots,

Aspen Mountain may look small until the hundreds of skiers are found, virtually lost in the scale of the mountain itself. There are four mountains at Aspen.

skis and poles, and bindings can be tested and adjusted.

American inventiveness and originality have revolutionized the art of ski instruction. The short-length ski was introduced and popularized in America, and free-style and professional head-to-head racing, the snomaker, and the chairlift were invented there.

The American ski ambience, East or West Coast, is a definable entity and for any European skiers who have experienced it, skiing can never be quite the same. What is fascinating is the fact that there is now, very slowly, a reverse of the old habit of importing the Alps to America and European resorts are copying some of the obvious efficiencies of the North American ski centre.

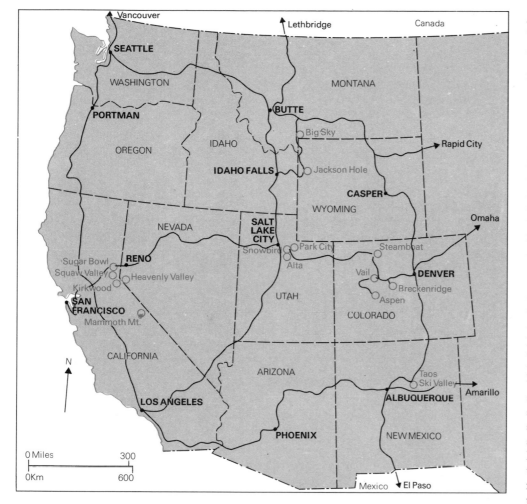

On the map: Vancouver, Lethbridge, Canada, SEATTLE, WASHINGTON, MONTANA, PORTMAN, BUTTE, Big Sky, Rapid City, OREGON, IDAHO, IDAHO FALLS, Jackson Hole, CASPER, WYOMING, SALT LAKE CITY, Omaha, NEVADA, Snowbird, Park City, Steamboat, Sugar Bowl, RENO, Alta, Squaw Valley, Vail, DENVER, Kirkwood, Heavenly Valley, Breckenridge, SAN FRANCISCO, Aspen, Mammoth Mt., UTAH, COLORADO, CALIFORNIA, N, ARIZONA, Taos Ski Valley, LOS ANGELES, Amarillo, ALBUQUERQUE, PHOENIX, NEW MEXICO, Mexico, El Paso

0 Miles 300
0 Km 600

WEST COAST

West coast ski centres are those located along the line of the American Rocky Mountains and the Sierra Nevada. There are 105 centres in the states of Washington, Oregon, Idaho, Montana, Colorado, Nevada, California, Utah, New Mexico and Arizona.

Although the very first skiing in North America took place in California, the area lagged far behind in enthusiasm compared to that developed in New England. The superficial similarity with the Alps as far as mountain scenery was concerned meant that the earliest centres were attempts to recreate Alpine-style villages. In the years to come the lodestone was to be not a facsimile but a climate and snowfall which have now made skiing in the west a unique experience. Because the mountains are effectively a coastal range with a desert hinterland and because the accessible ski fields are very high, the entire west coast enjoys not only quite unbelievable footages of snowfall but also a character of snow that unless experienced is unbelievable.

To speak of powder snow to a European skier calls up memories of unblemished snowfields with inches – at the most a foot or so – of new snow which is light, fluffy and delightful to ski in, but as evanescent as a passing shadow, ruined by the first breath of wind or the early touch of sun, becoming compacted cardboard that varies from difficult to impossible to ski. On the west coast, however, powder snow is lighter, deeper, fluffier, an almost bottomless covering of powderpuff down, renewed with unbelievable regularity each night as the onshore winds from the Pacific rise up over the mountains and deposit their moisture in the form of snow.

Alta in Utah was the first resort to be talked about. Later came names like Jackson Hole, Taos and the back bowls of the Vail skifields. They jealously preserved their trails from grooming machines and they vied with each other for still steeper, deeper, more magnificent powder-snow slopes. They set a legend on which an entire skiing industry has grown up. Distance, a sparse population and a reputation in the east of fabulous skiing has resulted in most of these centres becoming, to some degree, resorts in the traditional sense. It is probable that at any one time there are more easterners than westerners skiing there. Skiers from the east have profited from a well-organized and cheap tourist industry and travel more miles than they would have to for the European Alps for

It would be a mistake, however, to imagine that all skiing in these western areas is for experts only. Grooming the less steep slopes produces a surface of packed powder that, in some respects, is even more remarkable than this fabled powder for it packs down into a firm, very smooth surface that never turns to scratchy, unmanageable ice and provides a skiing surface which is as near to ideal as any skier could wish for. It is on these sorts of ski fields that places such as Breckenridge and Steamboat have built up a reputation for being safe, enjoyable, family resorts where everyone can learn to ski with pleasure.

The trails are, in general, high and the timber line is higher still – anywhere from 8000 feet (approximately 2500 metres) upwards – and consequently mid-winter skiing can be very cold. This is emphasized by the universal double, triple and even quadruple chairlifts which have no form of protection and which sway up interminably in sub-zero temperatures. The climate and geography combine to make spring skiing either powder or slush and there is rarely any transition through that most delectable of all surfaces, spring corn.

Although the famous names in Colorado and California do hog the limelight, spare a thought for the lonely, deeply forested lodges hidden in the wilder parts of Washington and Oregon, places where often only snowshoes are suitable for wending a lonely trail through the dense trees and where skiing has still much of the flavour and atmosphere of a bygone age.

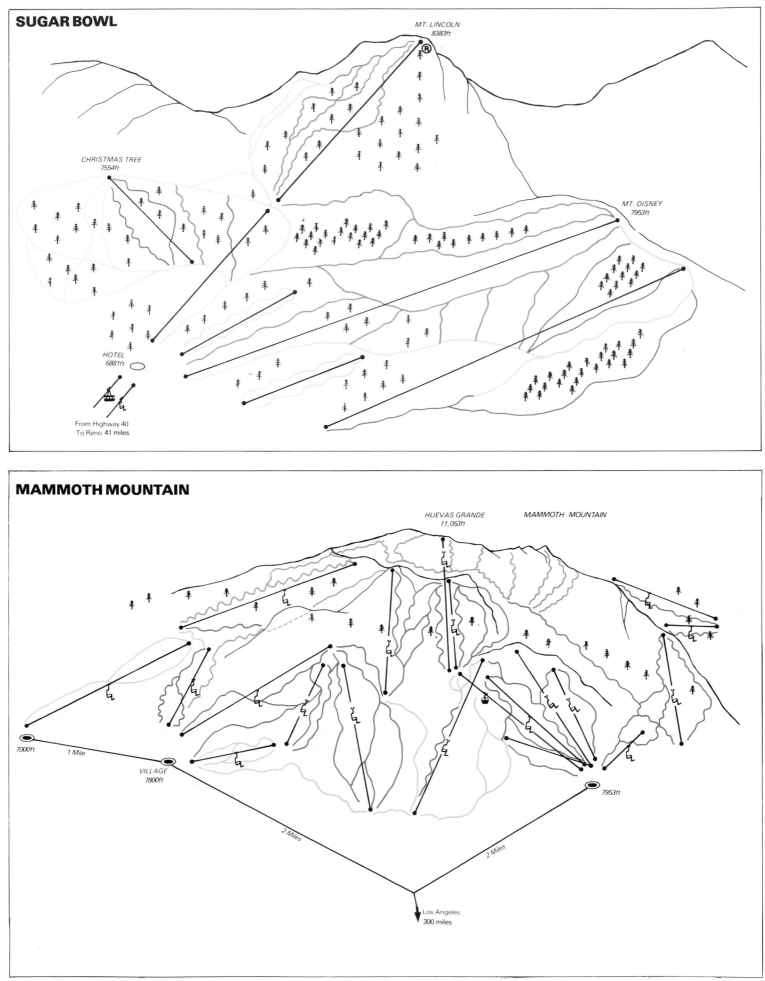

SUGAR BOWL

MT. LINCOLN
8383ft

CHRISTMAS TREE
7554ft

MT. DISNEY
7953ft

HOTEL
6881ft

From Highway 40
To Reno 41 miles

MAMMOTH MOUNTAIN

HUEVAS GRANDE
11,053ft

MAMMOTH MOUNTAIN

7000ft

1 Mile

VILLAGE
7800ft

7953ft

2 Miles

2 Miles

Los Angeles
300 miles

SUGAR BOWL *California*

A large lodge, a small mountain and a mass of private homes and condominiums make up Sugar Bowl. It would be indistinguishable from a long list of similar ski centres in the Sierras or Rockies were it not for one unique factor – it is completely automobile free and the only access is by chairlift or cableway from Highway 40, 41 miles (66 kilometres) out of Reno.

The skiing is relatively low, but the forest is not dense and although ski trails have been cut, there are sufficient lightly forested areas for any amount of free, tree slaloming.

MAMMOTH MOUNTAIN *California*

This resort is not called after any prehistoric behemoths that might have been found there, though the name might well refer to its size. In fact it is a corrupt translation from the Spanish who called this dormant volcano the 'big mountain'. It is high, it provides a fascinating zig-zag of interlocking lifts and some very big treeless skiing. There is also a hot springs pool which, in springtime, serves as the final landing place for the last run of the season, and it is fortunate that skiboots are now made of indestructible plastic.

It is a long journey to go to ski – 300 miles (483 kilometres) by road from Los Angeles – but there are L.A. skiers who have been skiing there for more than 20 years, which must prove something about the skiing.

HEAVENLY VALLEY *California*
Lake Tahoe

Lake Tahoe and the mushrooming vacation colony on its shores is an emotive subject among militant conservationists for this is an area of outstanding natural beauty, easily accessible from Reno, 60 miles (96 kilometres) away. The area has everything – mountains, lakes, a fun-city within striking distance, and, after the near financial disaster of the 1960 Olympic games in nearby Squaw Valley, a major skiing complex on the south shore of the lake.

Heavenly Valley is exceptional in North American skiing in that it not only combines two mountains, but two States, California and Nevada.

The skiing is good and the trails are preponderantly easy or moderate. It is difficult to find a natural black trail which is not a contrived short cut, and the majority of such trails will be found on Heavenly Valley West, in California, and, contrary to the general rule, they are the lower trails, while those from the summit wander gently over open ground and even the novice can have the pleasure of a long curving run from just over 9000 feet (2742 metres) on the Californian side to the base lodge at 6600 feet (2010 metres).

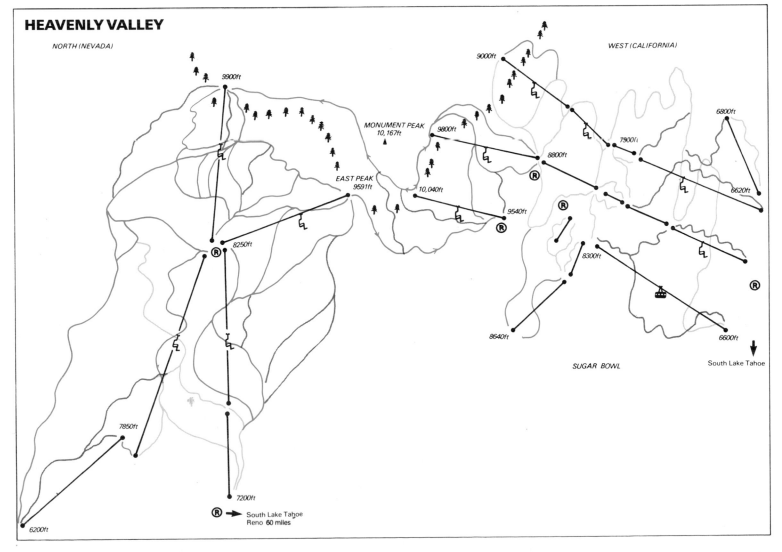

HEAVENLY VALLEY

NORTH (NEVADA)

WEST (CALIFORNIA)

9900ft

9000ft

6800ft

MONUMENT PEAK
10,167ft

9800ft

7900ft

8800ft

EAST PEAK
9591ft

10,040ft

6620ft

9540ft

8250ft

8300ft

8640ft

6600ft

7850ft

SUGAR BOWL

South Lake Tahoe

7200ft

South Lake Tahoe
Reno 60 miles

6200ft

SQUAW VALLEY *California*

Mark Twain was the first to write about Squaw Valley, in 1861 while he was staying in Carson City. He regarded it as '. . . the fairest picture the whole earth offers. . . helmeted with glittering snow.' The valley remained a private hideout for connoisseurs until 1946 when Alec Cushing had a mad dream to create a ski resort on the north side of the Donner Pass above Lake Tahoe. It was selected as the site of the 1960 Winter Olympics in arrogant defiance of everything that the High Sierras weather could throw at it. The years of preparation, 1950 to 1959, were a period of discord and disillusionment though in the end Cushing was proved right. The magnificent Olympic Village and the excitement of live television coverage proved to be the sparks which started the long-delayed growth of skiing in North America.

Reminiscent of many European third generation resorts, Squaw Valley is a model of what such centres should be. The three mountains over which the skiing ranges rise up from the village and the lift systems that serve four skiing areas are all within comfortable walking distance of the accommodation.

The valley is lightly forested and laced with walks and cross-country trails while most of the skiing is above the timber-line.

The lifts fan out from the village, the main traffic going to Elevation 8200 and the little collection of lodges and restaurants that lie in the bowl between Squaw and Emigrant Peaks. Unlike most North American mountains it is in this bowl that the best nursery slopes are to be found, and it is the natural meeting place for both easy and expert trails. It is busy, but the skifields are so extensive that there is little overcrowding – a feature of the earlier ski trail plans which Emile Allais, former French and World Ski Champion, designed both here and in Europe.

Squaw Valley has a very long ski season which starts in November and normally lasts until late spring. Unlike many western, powder-snow areas, spring corn snow is not uncommon.

Winter or spring, this is an area where the term trail is really out of place as there is not a glade or defile which is not skiable once the avalanche patrols have cleared the area. If the big moguls on KP22 are too much, a few steps to one side will open up a new natural slalom trail around an errant rock or lonely tree. If you are not an expert but enjoy powder snow the runs off Emigrant Peak should give pleasure for a long morning.

SQUAW PEAK 8900

EMIGRANT PEAK 8700ft

(8600ft)

GRANITE CHIEF 9050

8200ft

GOLD COAST

HIGH CAMP

SQUAW VALLEY EL. 8200

7540ft

SQUAW VALLEY VILLAGE 6200ft

KIRKWOOD *California*

Kirkwood is a good example of the newer type of ski centre in the general Lake Tahoe area. It is a typical condominium centre, very reminiscent of the smaller French third generation resorts, although the mountainscape is less friendly towards the timorous and the novice. Dominated by the massive rock face of Thimble Peak, a forest of gully trails drop down from the long ridge and, avalanches permitting, it is possible to ski a vertical 2000 feet (609 metres) in what is virtually an unbroken fall-line slalom. Hopefully named The Olympic, this run can become a mogul nightmare.

Competition is one of the hallmarks of American skiing. It is possible to ski for awards over slalom courses, like the skier on the right. The European habit of giving ski school proficiency badges is replaced by the NASTAR system where competitors race over standardized courses, and this is a feature of every serious downhill resort. The awards are sponsored commercially, and are based on the percentage time over a daily norm for all competitors.

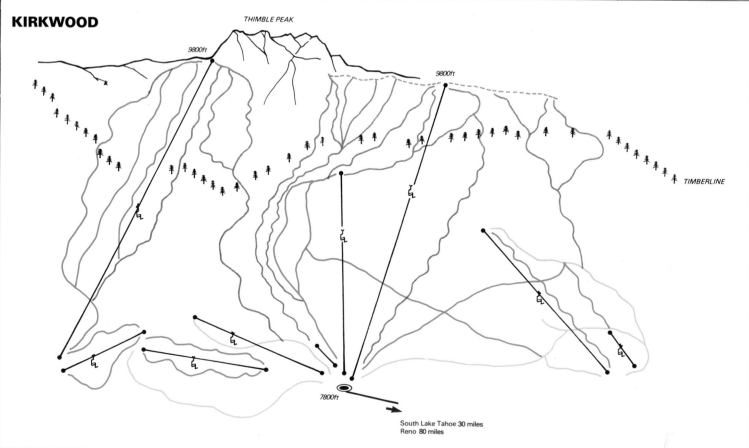

KIRKWOOD

THIMBLE PEAK

9800ft

9800ft

TIMBERLINE

7800ft

South Lake Tahoe **30 miles**
Reno **80 miles**

BIG SKY *Montana*

Big Sky, 58 miles (93 kilometres) from Yellowstone National Park, is not going to figure in any record book as having the highest, steepest, or longest of anything. But it is a good example of just what the United States can make of a year-round holiday area. The area devoted to summer activities such as riding, golf, camping, hunting, fishing or just wandering is considerably bigger than the downhill skiing area – which has been planned and directed so that it can provide a family with just about every kind of snow sport that they might wish to perform.

The skiing itself is good but has no great distinctions. There is ample cross-country trail skiing and snomobiling. The wildlife is interesting and there is a very active geyser that spouts out of a smooth snow field. This kind of ski centre is rare and Big Sky serves as a blueprint of just how well this sort of commercial enterprise can be run.

American ski hills must never be dismissed as insignificant from a distant view. This view of Big Sky should be compared with the trail map.

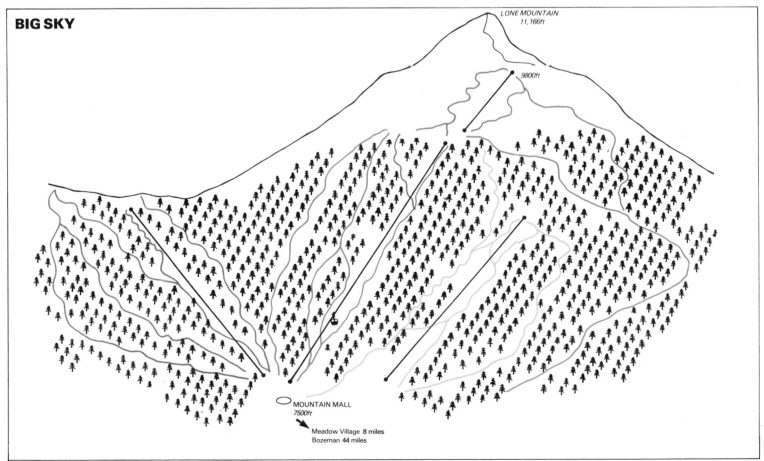

BIG SKY

LONE MOUNTAIN
11,166ft

9800ft

MOUNTAIN MALL
7500ft

Meadow Village 8 miles
Bozeman 44 miles

ASPEN MOUNTAIN 11212 ft

LOGES PEAK 11800 ft

10,000 ft

8,000 ft

TIEHACK

ASPEN HIGHLANDS

8912 ft

ASPEN

ASPEN *Colorado*

Far too much has been written about the life and times of this old silver mining town and far too much has been made of the beautiful life led by the beautiful people. This is the kind of publicity which, in the long run, can do such a magnificent ski area a great deal of harm. Much the same has happened to Gstaad and St Moritz and Megève and as a result they have nearly died as ski resorts, for the average skier has a horror of trying to ski surrounded by fashionable people who are more concerned with appearance than action.

Aspen is four separate mountains with four quite different moods (though one of these, Aspen Highlands, is an outsider and does not belong to the owners of the other three). Aspen Mountain, possibly because of its proximity to the not terribly attractive town of Aspen, is the least interesting and most conventional of the four. Aspen Highlands, the next in line, is comparatively small, much easier than Aspen Mountain but more enjoyable for the traffic seems less and more orderly even though variety is missing. Buttermilk, the smallest of the four, has the reputation of

being a beginner's mountain. However, there is a run there, Tiehack Parkway, with all its steep left-handed funnels and glades, that is anything but beginner's country and if the main fall-line routes are easy, what is wrong with that?

Snowmass is a very different story. I still dream about a day spent on Big Burn and still cannot believe that the skiing I did there on that bitterly cold February day was real. On a vast wide slope, 2000 feet (609 metres) high, quarter of a mile (400 metres) wide with a few trees dotted about just to give perspective to

BIG BURN 1750 ft

ELK CAMP

HIGH ALPINE

SAM'S KNOB

CLIFF HOUSE

TIEHACK

BUTTERMILK

CAMPGROUND

SNOWMASS 8250 ft

BUTTERMILK/TIEHACK

the size, there was a packed powder surface that was like velvet. As far as I could see there were only two skiers on that slope at a time, even though the chair back seemed to be full. I liked the little modern village and the well guarded nursery slopes.

The Aspen complex is a very good example of a basic problem that besets all American ski centres and areas. Any European ski planner would start by linking the four mountains so that each could be skied individually or all four could make a long, continuous and logical circuit. In America this is virtually a

Utopian dream. To begin with, any individual ski area has to be leased after lengthy negotiation, usually from the Forestry Commission. Very strict limits will be placed on the actual development area and the trail maps will usually show a black dotted line stating 'limit of ski area'. Crossing this line on skis can result in the immediate cancellation of a lift pass. To negotiate rights-of-way from one area to another becomes virtually impossible.

The second problem is the fact that ski areas are the property of one or more commercial companies; there is frequently one

enterprise owning the realty and another owning the lift installations and ski services. The companies are not necessarily equally motivated and the problems involved in assessing the utilization of each other's facilities could baffle a complex computer.

Superficial knowledge of the problem can however lead to very wrong conclusions. The conservationist would be the first to object to the obvious linking of resorts such as the four Aspen ski mountains; such a linking would inevitably bring with it a great increase of intrusion by lifts into the countryside.

43

STEAMBOAT *Colorado*

Just so that no-one should think that all Colorado skiing is Aspen and Vail, here is another truly family ski resort. It is in the Routt National Forest and is loosely based on the old mining town of Steamboat Springs, only two miles away. As a ski centre it is in many ways reminiscent of many Alpine resorts in so far as a majority of skiers are under some form of instruction and the number of enterprising children's classes is impressive.

Like many place names in Colorado, Steamboat got its name, or so legend has it, from gold-rush days when a steam-powered river launch was packed in small sections on mules and reassembled on the Colorado River. The wild mining days are still very much alive in this part of the country and though many of the original towns have disappeared there are still a number which have been skilfully restored.

The massive condominium block is rather an eyesore in this landscape but there is some good skiing here.

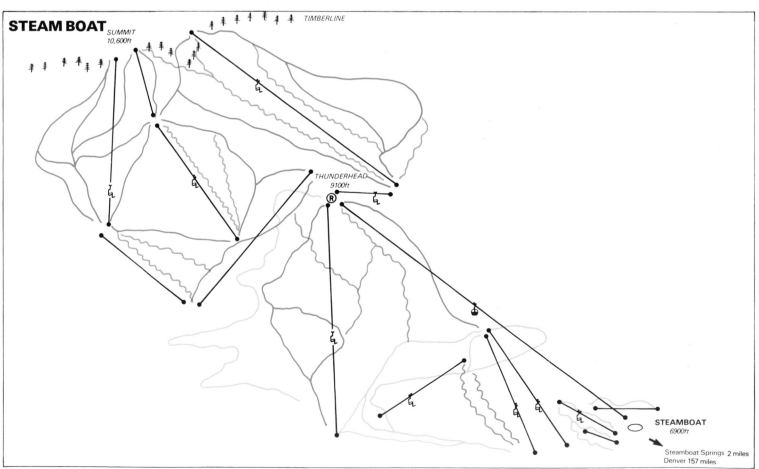

44

BRECKENRIDGE *Colorado*

This two-mountain ski centre is well-organized for family vacations. When I first saw this rather scattered residential area in a wide valley I was irresistibly reminded of Morzine in France – the same gentle hills for skiers, the same backdrop of glaciered mountains and, I suspect, the same happy mix of families of moderate skiing expertise. It is probably invaded every weekend by the young experts from Denver but that should not distract you – there is some very interesting skiing that can be put together after a careful study of the trail map. It is possible to do a there-and-back 10,000 foot (3000 metre) vertical run complete with two food stops at the two mid-mountain lodges, spend a happy half hour on the two 11,000 foot (3351 metre) summits – Peak 8 and Peak 9 – and be back in Denver in time for an early evening meal with very pleasantly tired legs and a happy glow.

The Telemark – 1970 not 1870 – is still the most elegant turn in the skiing repertory, Nordic or Alpine.

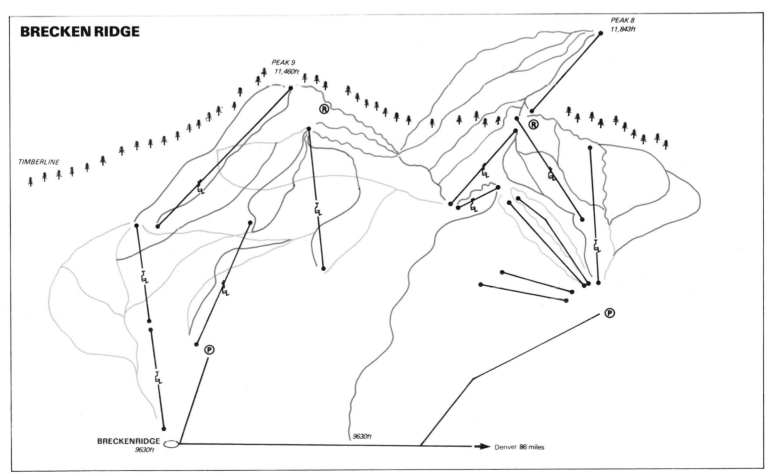

VAIL *Colorado*

Vail is based on Vail Village and Lionhead and it is from these two main areas that the wonder of Vail skiing can be experienced. This includes the famed back bowls which offer mechanized, ungroomed powder snow. Then there are the long, difficult and very varied trails that can be knitted together starting from the east, down the north-east bowl, up to Vail Mountain summit at 11,250 feet (3427 metres), and down all the way to the village. Then you can take the lift up to mid-Vail and some welcome refreshment. Go on up again to Wildwood for a long ridge run to the Eagle's Nest for lunch. After lunch tackle the bowls, and ski home down one of the trails, Born Free perhaps, for some delightful glade runs. That could amount to 20,000 feet (6093 metres) of downhill skiing, which is all in a day's work in this resort.

This is what one might call 'basic Vail'. The fabulous back bowls are far above and out of sight. These trails are the end of a day's skiing.

SUN-UP BOWL

CHINA BOWL

TEACUP BOWL

EL 11250 ft

PTARMIGAN PT 11

GAME CREEK BOWL

EAGLE'S NEST

TO SUN-UP AND SUN DOWN BOWLS
11250 ft

TO GAME CREEK BOWL

MID-VAIL

EAGLE'S NEST

LIONSHEAD

VAIL VILLAGE

LIONSHEAD VILLAGE

PARK CITY *Utah*
Alta/Snowbird

Forty minutes out of Salt Lake City is the present training ground of the U.S. National Ski Team, 7000 feet (2132 metres) up in the mountains, with Jupiter Peak offering a further 3000 feet (about 1000 metres) of mostly forested trails. Near neighbours are Alta, with its early powder snow, and Snowbird on the other side of the mountain from Alta. These two resorts are now linked. It is possible to stay in Salt Lake City and, with the aid of a hired car, visit the 11 ski centres that cluster around this major town.

If these centres suffer from anything it is from the fact that, unlike Jackson Hole or Taos, the skiing is in cleared trails through thick forest. Only the mountain tops provide open skiing and this is short, extremely steep and ranks as expert or top expert country. The quality of the snow, however, raises these resorts above the level of contrived centres.

JACKSON HOLE *Wyoming*

Jackson Hole, on the edge of Yellowstone National Park, is a near-perfect place to ski. It has an annual snowfall of 38 feet (about 13 metres) on a 10,000 foot mountain with just enough trees to help visibility and enough open ground to render any talk of trails a nonsense. It is a tight little village at the end of a 7½ mile (12 kilometre) run with a drop of just over 4000 feet (1218 metres). It has not tried to be an Indian Teepee, an Austrian Jodel Club or even a stetson-and-spurred snow ranch, and has little in the way of a fashionable in-crowd.

The nature of the skiing in this centre is very reminiscent of Zürs in Austria. It is a skier's mountain – not a beginner's, nor a speed hound's – just a very big mountain with an uncountable number of runs that are either moderate or extremely steep and which funnel down made-to-measure gullies, or turn round trees that appear to have been planted for that purpose. At the end, a cableway goes all the way up again.

It is possible to forego all the pleasure that is to be derived from just skiing this mountain and try for a badge that says you have exhausted yourself skiing 100,000 vertical feet. A rough calculation suggests that this will require 24 journeys on the cable-car; 4.8 hours spent just standing in the cabin with 63 other people and 63 pairs of skis and poles; and with four journeys a day, two in the morning and two in the afternoon, this should take care of a week's holiday.

TAOS SKI VALLEY *New Mexico*

Taos has become a legend quicker than any other ski centre anywhere. It is a kind of Valhalla for the skiers of the steep and deep with some nice novice slopes all the way down from the rather indeterminate ridge summit and from the lift that is the first stage of the new Kachina area. But for the moderate skier there is very little; from novice you jump straight into the top expert class with more than half the marked trails devoted to steep powder snow.

The joy of Taos is that this super-difficult skiing is no torture, no contrived piece of mogulled masochism, merely the logical exploitation by Ernie Blake, founder, planner and mastermind of the centre, of the ski ground that was available. He is a skier and takes a true skier's view that if there is snow – ski it.

The vertical may not be in the records, 12,000 feet down to just over 9000. Six lifts mechanize the mountain and you can choose between forest trails when light is poor or the great open expanse of go-anywhere country of the Kachina basin. The talk is of the runs that are open, the avalanches which have been safely disposed of by the trail patrols, the runs yet to be attempted, achieved or never to be tried rather than the vertical feet to be skied. The village life is tight, comfortable and quite surprisingly European with the best of the trans-Atlantic examples used and the worst discarded.

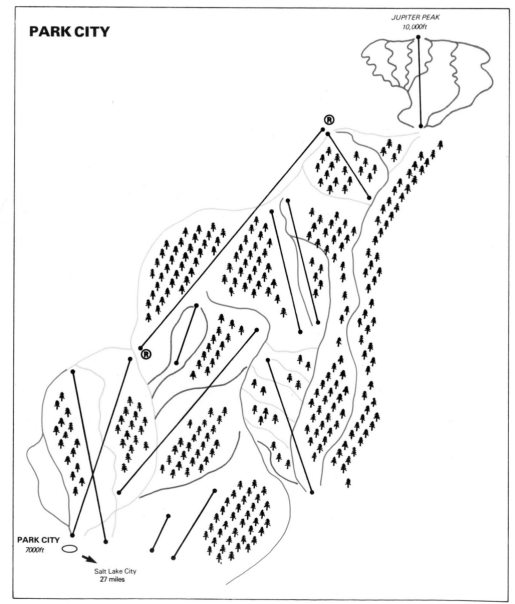

PARK CITY

JUPITER PEAK
10,000ft

PARK CITY
7000ft

Salt Lake City
27 miles

JACKSON HOLE

RENDEZVOUS MT.
10,450ft

Jackson 12 miles
Salt Lake City 250 miles

TETON VILLAGE
6311ft

TAOS SKI VALLEY

11,825ft

KACHINA BASIN

TAOS
9213ft

Sante Fe 144 miles

The aerial view of Gore Mountain should be borne in mind when looking at trail maps.

EAST COAST

The east and New England in particular must be considered the true cradle of American skiing, for it was there that the pioneers of the 1920s explored and discovered the possibilities of the wooded, rounded hills of the Appalachian Mountains that run like a great barrier from northern Maine to the north-east corner of Alabama, shielding the populous east from the wild west and mid-west. That is how it seemed to the early settlers of this area and for more than a hundred years these mountains served as a psychological barrier to any penetration into what was virtually *terra incognita* inhabited only by fierce Indian tribes.

What is truly surprising is that in an area where the climate is extreme, where winter cold is intense and snowfall was uncertain and alternated wildly with high winds and high temperatures, there should have been developed such a great network of ski centres, hewn out of the forest. These centres are often far from major population areas and, by comparison with Alpine skiing, they are superficially most unattractive. It is proof of the addiction which skiing can

produce. That circumstances were so difficult was, in the long run, of immense benefit to American skiing, for they produced styles, techniques, equipment and organization which can be said to have brought skiing into the era of modern technology.

Steep, narrow, extremely icy trails demanded hard, controlled skiing with equipment which would match the demands made upon it. The skiers, for the most part, were city dwellers who were prepared to travel considerable distances by automobile and train but on arrival expected to get their money's worth out of the facilities. Their knowledge and experience produced the now familiar base lodge – a kind of ski service supermarket. The concept of the mountain manager in charge of all aspects of activity on the mountain and directly responsible to the lessors of the terrain for the maintenance of rules and regulations grew up in the east. Forestry and National Park regulations made the creation of a village at the mountain foot difficult if not impossible and consequently visitors sought accommodation in nearby townships, in conveniently located motels and summer

lodges. The pattern has changed little though the number of huge ski centres has grown beyond anything that was thought possible.

East coast skiers may be slightly jealous of their west coast colleagues and the eternal boasts of even steeper powder gullies, but they draw comfort from the fact that they are harder, better skiers, instantly recognizable by style and the indisputable fact that they possess, for a week or two, the most magnificent spring skiing imaginable. Once winter has lessened its grip, the trails become idyllic spring ski slopes overnight.

The east coast has also discovered that it has one other great asset – the most perfect terrain for Nordic, cross-country skiing. Quite apart from the innumerable prepared trails radiating out from a hundred different tiny centres, there are the criss-cross tracks cut by the farmers on their annual sugarbush tapping expeditions and the often long-abandoned logger trails that all add up to a ski trail network that would take a lifetime to explore.

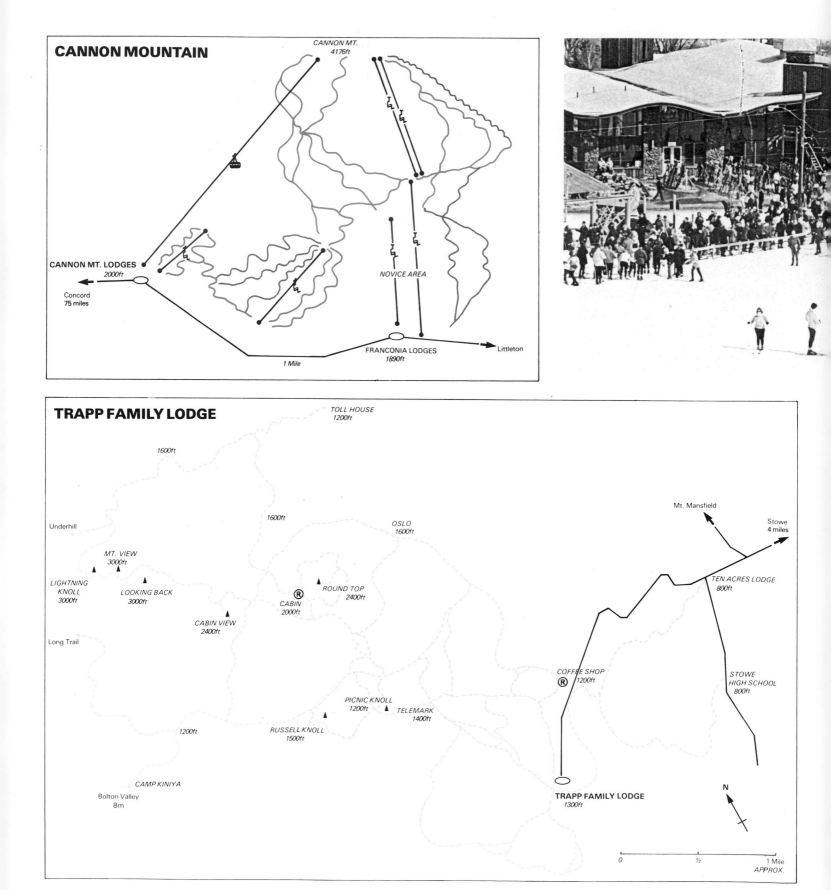

CANNON MOUNTAIN

CANNON MT.
4176ft

CANNON MT. LODGES
2000ft

Concord
75 miles

NOVICE AREA

1 Mile

FRANCONIA LODGES
1890ft

Littleton

TRAPP FAMILY LODGE

TOLL HOUSE
1200ft

1600ft

Underhill

1600ft

OSLO
1600ft

Mt. Mansfield

Stowe
4 miles

MT. VIEW
3000ft

LIGHTNING
KNOLL
3000ft

LOOKING BACK
3000ft

ROUND TOP
2400ft

Ⓡ CABIN
2000ft

TEN ACRES LODGE
800ft

CABIN VIEW
2400ft

Long Trail

COFFEE SHOP
Ⓡ 1200ft

STOWE
HIGH SCHOOL
800ft

PICNIC KNOLL
1200ft

TELEMARK
1400ft

1200ft

RUSSELL KNOLL
1500ft

CAMP KINIYA

Bolton Valley
8m

TRAPP FAMILY LODGE
1300ft

N

0   ½   1 Mile
APPROX.

CANNON MOUNTAIN *New Hampshire*

Driving over the Notch and dropping down into the long vacation area valley makes one all too conscious of the urgent need for environmental control and limitations to the size and wording of the hoardings advertising anything from dancing bears to super-burgers. The cableway that lifts skiers somewhat slowly up to the summit of Cannon Mountain, provides some rather limited skiing but, providing one stays above the level of the large and well-protected novice area, using the two parallel chairs, the skiing can, for a while, be quite entertaining.

TRAPP FAMILY LODGE *Vermont*

There can be very few people who have not heard of the *Sound of Music* and for whom the Trapp Family – even if only in terms of a Hollywood pastiche – is not a familiar name. Four miles (6½ kilometres) out of Stowe live the members of the genuine Trapp Family and it was there that they settled during the heyday of their world-wide musical tours. And it is there that Johannes von Trapp has created a ski touring centre that, however much you may dislike the ballyhoo of media publicity, is a delight.

It is possible to roam for miles over gently hilly, moderately wooded country, with well-prepared and excellently marked routes and enjoy a Nordic type of holiday and an Austrian type of living such as it would be hard to find in either Norway or Austria.

It is also expensive and, as they say in the trade, 'up-market'. So if you do not wish to wear a jacket and tie in the evening and conform to Maria von Trapp's quite relentlessly enforced rules of behaviour and decorum you can always stay in one of Stowe's motels and commute up to the ski area.

HUNTER MOUNTAIN SKI BOWL
New York

Hunter Mountain is the first, and possibly so far the only, ski area that is completely covered by snomakers. It is a tremendous undertaking and one shudders to think of the quantity of water, compressed air and fuel required to keep 200 acres permanently snowed up. However it is only 120 miles (193 kilometres) from New York on a very fast motorway, and if there were no snow guns on this mountain it is unlikely that the snow cover would last a busy weekend.

Hunter Mountain base lodge houses the mountain administration, shops, and restaurants.

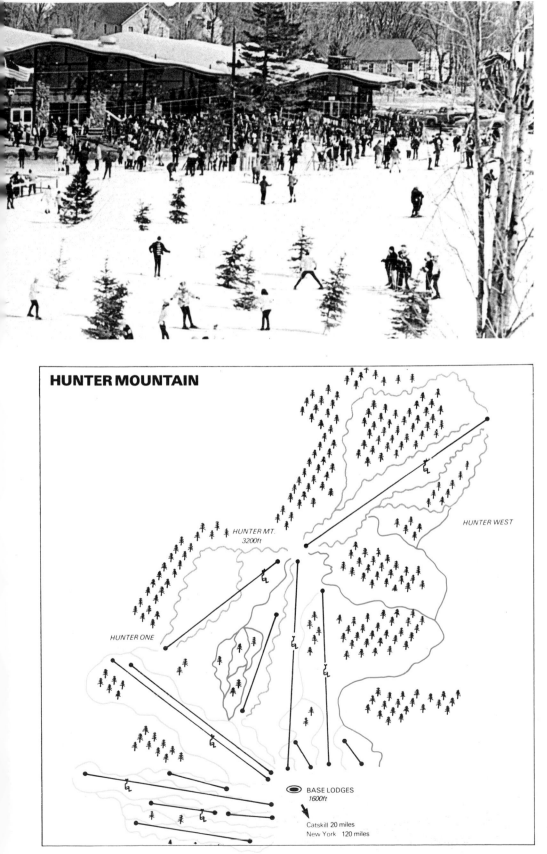

HUNTER MOUNTAIN

HUNTER WEST

HUNTER MT. 3200ft

HUNTER ONE

BASE LODGES 1600ft

Catskill 20 miles
New York 120 miles

A skier slides through the sugar maple trees.

STOWE *Vermont*

Stowe, a small, undistinguished little township, six miles (9.6 kilometres) from a small, forested pass called Smuggler's Notch, is an unlikely base for what must be considered America's fundamental ski centre. It was the skiing on Mount Mansfield that really proved just what skiing in North America can be like and the severity of the trails were such that they set a standard against which all other trails, east or west, are still measured.

I have my own views on that sort of skiing and must frankly confess that I no longer – if I ever did – enjoy it. Standing on the top of Nose Dive, seeing the icy, mogulled precipice disappear from under my skis, made me question the sanity of the sport and the mental state of those who professed to enjoy it. And after skiing it, Goat and Lifeline and a few other assorted pieces of concentrated masochism I had serious doubts concerning my own sanity. However time and a delightful day in spring skiing these same trails in ideal spring corn have softened the memories and, opportunity provided, I would undoubtedly ski them again.

There is of course a lot more to Mansfield and Spruce than black horrors and anyone learning to ski on the very adequate nursery areas will be capable of tackling any reasonable ski mountain after a week of modified Graduated Length Method instruction. What a pity that the accommodation is not more attuned to the skiing – a selection of motels with their uniform packaged food and packaged rooms is a poor finish to a day skiing this great trail collection.

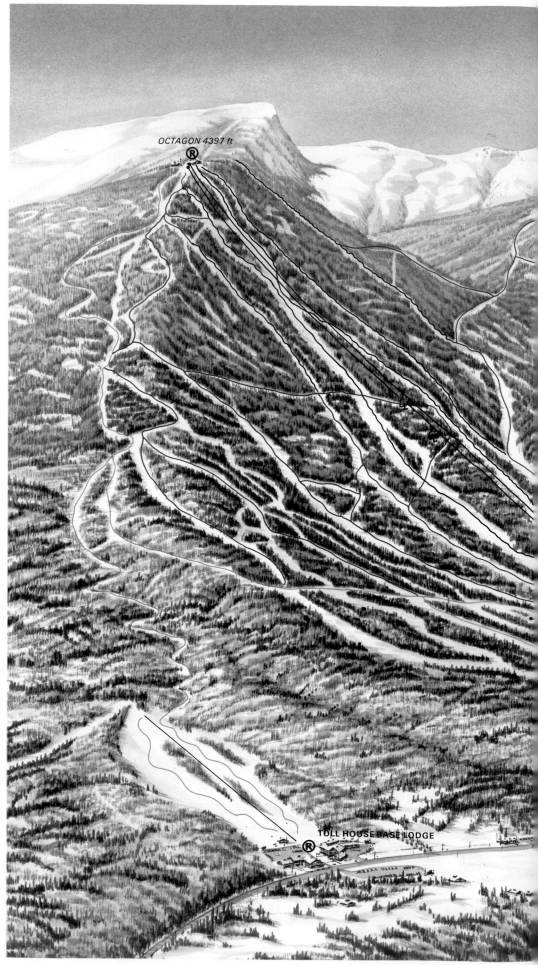

OCTAGON 4397 ft

TOLL HOUSE BASE LODGE

MT MANSFIELD

CLIFF HOUSE

BIG SPRUCE PEAK

SMUGGLERS NOTCH

MANSFIELD BASE HOUSE
1300 ft

MAIN STREET

SPRUCE HOUSE

MOUNT SNOW *Vermont*

This New England family ski area has moderate trails, good provision for children, and considerably more skiing variety than a first sight of this scarred hillside might suggest. Its proximity to Wilmington, make it an all-too-popular weekend terminal.

SUGARBUSH VALLEY *Pennsylvania*

The term *sugarbush*, for those unfamiliar with New England practices, refers to maple trees which are tapped in late winter or early spring for the sap which, when boiled down, produces maple syrup and, even more delicious, maple sugar, a brown, fudge-like delectable sticky mess now becoming almost as rare as caviar. The skiing here, and there is a lot of it for very little mechanization, is largely through maple forest and consequently the trees are not nearly as dense as pine forest.

Easily accessible from Burlington, with adequate accommodation adjacent to the ski slopes, Sugarbush has every right to considerable popularity, especially with families.

WATERVILLE VALLEY *New Hampshire*

There have been some very mixed opinions about this most enterprising development on the edge of the White Mountain Forest. It is, as far as I know, the first attempt to create a rounded, environment-conscious complex that will provide skiing interest for every aspect of the sport. Based on a nicely planned residential area, a large trailed area for Nordic skiing is only the inner ring of what can amount to day-long trails along the old logging roads that lead up and through the White Mountains. At the other end of the complex, rather too far away for walking, is the downhill area on Mount Tecumseh, a small mountain with a reasonable variety of trails on the fall-line. A much smaller, single-lift hill provides a good training area, be it for novices or for junior and even senior race training.

When one talks of an American character to a ski centre, Waterville Valley is just about the best example one could find to define this character. It is organized, efficient, with a strong purpose element in every development and a strong emphasis on environment with a sound and active environmental studies centre.

The accent is very much on youth and unstressed training. Mr Pfosi, a one-time Swiss ski instructor, who had so much to do with the development of Waterville, was killed in 1978.

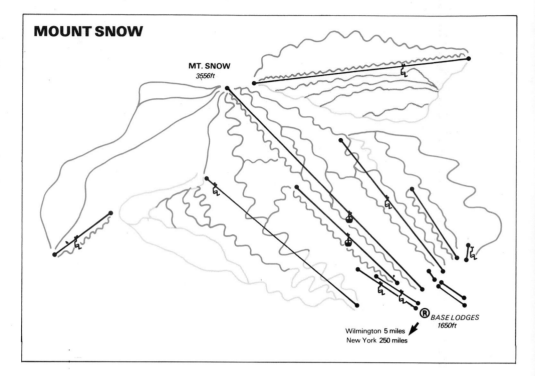

MOUNT SNOW

MT. SNOW
3556ft

®BASE LODGES
1650ft

Wilmington 5 miles
New York 250 miles

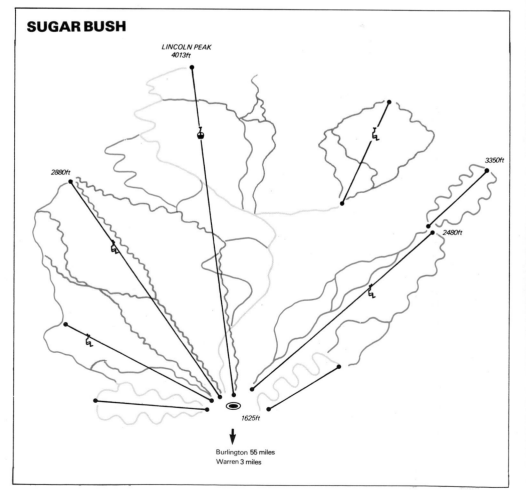

SUGAR BUSH

LINCOLN PEAK
4013ft

2880ft

3350ft

2480ft

1625ft

Burlington 55 miles
Warren 3 miles

WATERVILLE

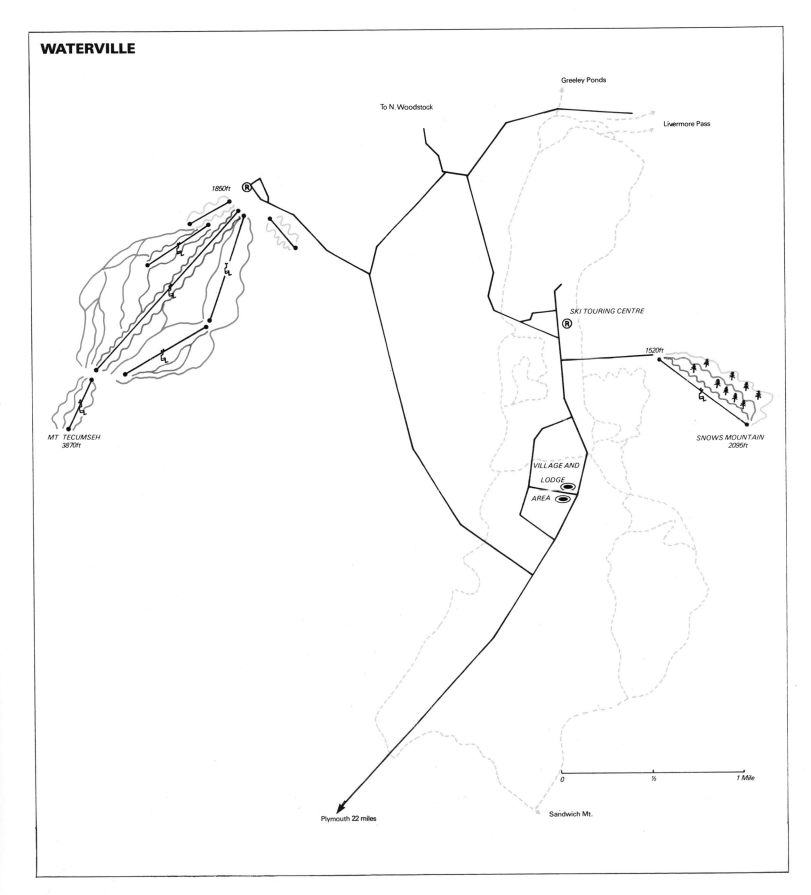

Greeley Ponds

To N. Woodstock

Livermore Pass

1850ft ℝ

ℝ SKI TOURING CENTRE

1520ft

MT TECUMSEH
3870ft

SNOWS MOUNTAIN
2095ft

VILLAGE AND
LODGE
AREA

0   ½   1 Mile

Plymouth 22 miles

Sandwich Mt.

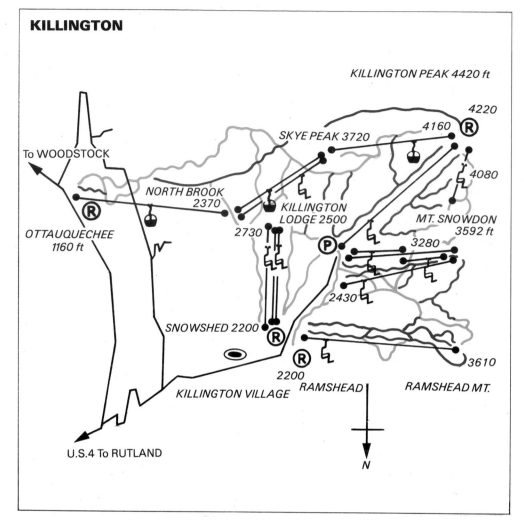

KILLINGTON

KILLINGTON PEAK 4420 ft

4220

4160

SKYE PEAK 3720

4080

To WOODSTOCK

NORTH BROOK 2370

KILLINGTON LODGE 2500

MT. SNOWDON 3592 ft

OTTAUQUECHEE 1160 ft

2730

3280

2430

SNOWSHED 2200

3610

2200

KILLINGTON VILLAGE

RAMSHEAD

RAMSHEAD MT.

U.S.4 To RUTLAND

N

KILLINGTON *Vermont*

Killington, 15 miles (24 kilometres) from Rutland, 21 miles (34 kilometres) from Woodstock (where the first ski tow in America was built on Clinton Gilbert's farm 40 years ago) claims to be the largest ski resort in the east. With 5700 beds within 11 miles (16.5 kilometres) of the slopes and more than half of these less than five minutes walk from the snow, there is no reason to doubt this boast.

It was in Killington that the controversial and extremely successful method of ski instruction known as GLM (Graduated Length Method) was invented and perfected. It is possible that this contributed more than anything else to the ever-growing popularity of the very large ski centre. They have never made any secret of the fact that they aim to please the casual recreational skier rather than entertain the specialists.

Traditional New England skiers, brought up on the demands of Stowe and Mount Washington's Tuckerman Ravine, may well look on Killington with a certain disdain, but the fact remains that nowhere else in New England can you find a trail to match either 'Four Mile' or 'Nameless' that run from Killington Peak in one continuous gentle line to the bottom of the Gondola at Ottaquechee. It is trails like this that have given such pleasure to the moderate skier. Nor is there anywhere else in New England where there is such a varied après ski life. What is more, there has been no attempt whatever to introduce simulated Tirolean folklore or pseudo-Swiss chalet life. It is an American ski resort and is efficient and entertaining.

For any skier looking for a more peaceful place to live and for a wider choice of cross-country skiing than is possible in Killington, the historic and beautifully preserved town of Woodstock is a delightful alternative.

For truly classic New England hospitality, Blueberry Hill Farm, a few miles out of Woodstock, would be my own personal choice. This is a cross-country centre.

LAKE PLACID *New York*

In any history of winter sports in America Lake Placid must take a leading place. The Lake Placid Club which was founded in 1895 first introduced winter sports to New England in 1905 and it was the son, Godfrey, of the founder of this club, Melvil Dewey, who brought the 1932 Winter Olympics to Placid. Since then, in contrast to many other Olympic locations, every one of the costly installations has been in constant use and has been updated.

Skiers are principally interested in two locations – Whiteface for Alpine skiing and Mount van Hoevenberg for Nordic and cross-country skiing.

Whiteface, 9 miles (approximately 14.5 kilometres) from Lake Placid, is operated by the Department of Environmental Conservation of the State of New York, which also operates Belleayre and Gore, two rather more distant ski mountains.

The skiing on Mount Whiteface is average for New England. As usual, the upper slopes present the greatest difficulties with the left-hand ridge claiming the expert trails while the central basin offers the moderate skier the longest continuous descent in New England (3200 feet).

The old, 1932, downhill trail is still just visible on the left-hand ridge but is now no longer in use as it is considered too difficult for racing and too inaccessible for recreation. The entire competition area, with the exception of the topmost downhill trails, is provided with snow-making machines.

The cross-country area around Mount van Hoevenberg, about 6 miles (9.5 kilometres) from Lake Placid, shares a car park with the bob run. It consists of two distinct areas. The closed loipes, the van Hoevenberg Loops and the North Meadow Loops, together give 30 miles (19.5 kilometres) of competitive, fully prepared trails. They are based on the car park and there are changing rooms for competitors and refreshment facilities at the bottom of the bob run.

For Nordic tourers, there is an almost unlimited mileage of marked and partially prepared trails based on the Adirondak Lodge. They can also be reached from the Van Hoevenberg Loops.

Accommodation in Lake Placid presents no great problem even though few would choose to stay in the vast echoing grandeur of the Lake Placid Club (for which guests are provided with a map but some have been known to become irrevocably lost).

WHITEFACE MT 4867

4436 ft

DOWNHILL

SLALOM & GS START

SLALOM

2564 ft

GIANT SLALOM

MID STATION LODGE

DOWNHILL

GIANT SLALOM FINISH

DOWNHILL

DOWNHILL

962 ft

BASE LODGE

Canada

For an American a visit to Canada from America is as foreign an experience as a visit to Europe. For a skier, be he a European Alpine skier, a Scandinavian concerned with cross-country or a devotee of either east or west coast slopes, skiing in Canada is as different in ambience, mood and quality as Italy is to Australia. To put this difference into words is a problem. To begin with the choice is limited, despite the long list of centres and resorts, mostly in British Columbia, Alberta, Ontario and Quebec. By American or European standards many of these locations are only facilities. Then, the sheer size of the country makes any generalizations impossible; it is further from Quebec to Vancouver than from Quebec to Dublin. A skier in Montreal will have to choose between Canadian and European skiing for it could be quicker and cheaper to go to St Anton than to go to Banff. It would be quicker and cheaper for him to visit Lake Placid than to fight his way through traffic and crowds to ski in the Laurentians.

Scenically there is a great resemblance between skiing the Canadian Rockies and skiing the Alps. An American west coast skier whisked into the Laurentians could be excused for thinking that he is in New England until he takes his first resort meal and meets French haute-cuisine rather than beefburgers.

Skiing came to Canada very early – to the Laurentians – but hibernated for 50 or more years. The climate was too vicious, the distances too great, the people too few and meanwhile ice hockey had become the major winter sport. The obvious skiing venue, the Rockies, were a summer vacation destination and the great resorts, Lake Louise, Banff Springs and Jasper Park Lodge, were closed all winter. The trans-Canada highway had not crossed the Divide and even the two great rail links, through Banff and Jasper, had their own problems keeping the link open. It was not until 1969 that Banff Springs opened for its first winter season and Jasper and Lake Louise did not open until 1975.

Banff had easy access from Calgary but accommodation limited the potential development to day lodges. Jasper was a very long drive from Edmonton and

Vancouver satisfied its few skiers with Whistler and Grouse Mountains, though the unreliable Pacific climate and very changeable snow conditions did little to encourage the sport there. The Laurentians had Mont Tremblant and Mont St Anne and the first chairlift in Canada but relatively few customers. Before the great Nordic boom started in the early 1970s Canada probably had less than half-a-million skiers.

The present total is probably less than a million out of a population of about 23 million. It is a population that inhabits a narrow belt only a hundred or so miles wide in a country of 3.8 million square miles, most of which is untamed and untameable. The small ski population has produced some of the world's greatest skiing in what is, by any standard whatsoever, the most magnificent mountain scenery in the world.

The potential locked up in inaccessible and unexplored ski territory or for ever forbidden by National Park regulations is greater than all the skiing of the rest of the world. Slowly, with the example of Hans Gmoser and his helicopter mechanization as a blueprint,

some of these magnificent high mountain areas will be developed for the more modest downhill skier. But skiing on the grand scale will probably remain very limited.

However for the Nordic, cross-country skier the potential is virtually unlimited. Already there are more cross-country centres in the four principle skiing provinces than there are mechanized, downhill resorts. But these places are catering for a captive variety of Nordic skier, one who limits himself to the prepared trails, manicured and signposted, and this is not the best kind of cross-country skiing to be done in Canada.

Skiing in Canada should be for the adventurous; for the ski mountaineer, the Nordic rambler and the lover of solitude. Canada could become the greatest conservationist ski country in the world and preserve, much as Norway is now doing, a heritage of real skiing values.

Space, snow and sun (above) are a summary of skiing in the Canadian Rockies. It is a sobering thought that most of the summits have not even been named.

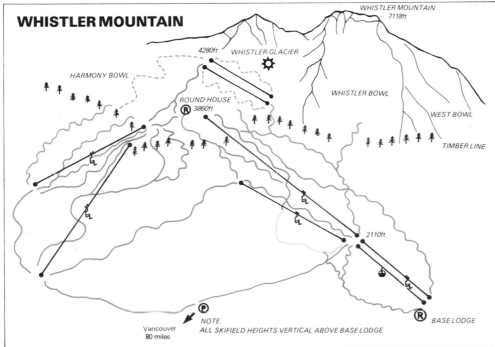

WHISTLER MOUNTAIN

WHISTLER MOUNTAIN
7118ft

4280ft   WHISTLER GLACIER

HARMONY BOWL

WHISTLER BOWL

ROUND HOUSE
Ⓡ 3860ft

WEST BOWL

TIMBER LINE

2110ft

Ⓟ

Ⓡ BASE LODGE

Vancouver
80 miles

NOTE.
ALL SKIFIELD HEIGHTS VERTICAL ABOVE BASE LODGE

WHISTLER MOUNTAIN *Vancouver*

Whistler has the reputation of having the greatest vertical skiing height in North America – 4280 feet (1304 metres). This depends on there being enough snow from the highest point at about 6000 feet (1828 metres) all the way down to the base lodge which is uncomfortably low for somewhere as close as this to the Pacific Coast.

The skiing in the three bowls above the Roundhouse (actually an octagon) is exciting, very large and mostly untracked. It can be a year-round occupation for in summer a portable tow is installed on Whistler glacier and regular skiing clinics take place there.

With Vancouver only 80 miles (128 kilometres) away and the alternative, Grouse Mountain, far too crowded and small, Whistler enjoys a popularity which its meagre facilities find almost impossible to digest. This is particularly the case when the classical weather pattern sets in which will guarantee powder snow at the Roundhouse when Vancouver is overcast and has rain.

MARMOT BASIN

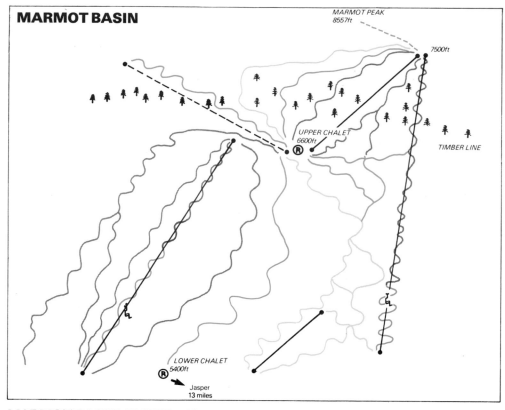

MARMOT PEAK
8557ft

7500ft

UPPER CHALET
6600ft

TIMBER LINE

LOWER CHALET
5400ft

Jasper
13 miles

Jet turns in badly tracked powder is one facet of skiing; a very different experience is alighting on the top of Zillmer for a steep, untracked gully (below) or linking countless turns on the long Vowell glacier.

MARMOT BASIN, JASPER Alberta

Marmot Basin, the ski area for Jasper, lies at the northern end of the classic summer excursion route along the Icefields Parkway that crosses the Banff and Jasper National Parks. Jasper is 235 miles (378 kilometres) from Edmonton in the middle of the Jasper National Park and consequently any ski development is very strictly limited. Nevertheless, 13 miles (21 kilometres) out of the small town, Marmot Basin has succeeded with an absolute minimum of lifts to open up some extremely entertaining skiing – though first impressions might not lead any skier to suppose so.

The lower section below the Upper Chalet at 6600 feet (2010 metres), is very heavily forested and the trails are the customary glades cut out of the timber. They are, for the most part, steep, rather narrow and strictly fall-line routes. However, once above the timberline, a great sparsely wooded bowl is revealed which can be skied along a hundred different lines from just below Marmot Peak, 1000 feet (304 metres) above the highest point reached by a T-bar from the Upper Chalet, 900 feet (274 metres) lower. A second lift, planned now for a number of years, should be completed soon and that will open up an equally large area on the far left of the bowl. It will be the best skiing in the area.

LAKE LOUISE *Alberta*

The Indians called it the lake of the little fishes. Tom Wilson, a young man of 23 on a hunting expedition, was the first white man to see it in 1882, the year before the Canadian Pacific Railway reached Calgary. The construction camp set up to build the next section of the railway was established three miles from the lake at a place then named Holt City after the engineer in charge of this section, Herbert S. Holt (though some historians claim it was after the brother, Tim). By 1882 the lake was renamed Laggan by Lord Strathcona. In 1883 Dr. G.M. Dawson renamed it Emerald Lake, but in 1884, Tom Wilson took Mrs. James Ross, wife of the chief construction engineer of the Canadian Pacific Railway to see the lake and, after this visit, Dr. Dawson renamed the lake 'Louise' after the first white woman to see it.

Since those early days, once the railway was completed, the lake became a scenic pilgrimage and in about 1920 the first skiers visited it. From then, though accommodation was primitive and the skiing arduous, the area has been continuously skied.

The incredible pile called Chateau Lake Louise replaced a simple wooden chalet which burnt down in 1924. It appears to have been modelled on a cross between the Suvretta Haus, the Kulm and Palace hotels in St Moritz by an architect with instructions to create the biggest residence in the world. It has been called many things, but beautiful it is not.

The setting is lovely – a sapphire lake, timbered slopes mirrored in the still water or shadowed on the white snow cover of the winter ice, and a great glacier tumbling down into the lake from a frieze of great granite peaks.

Ten minutes away is the ski area, in a huge forested bowl rising to two small summits, a bare 2000 feet above the base lodge. The trails are wide, so wide that they can hardly be called glades and the standard is as varied and big as the skill of the skier demands. You can amble down from Whitehorn past the midmountain lodge to Whiskyjack Lodge or across to Temple Lodge and up to point 7800 and all the way down along the five-mile trail without ever straining your technique. Alternatively you can take the same direction a few trails steeper and be very frightened by the long steep glades that funnel down the fall-line. This is good vacation skiing with enough variety and scenery and comfort to please the most demanding visitor.

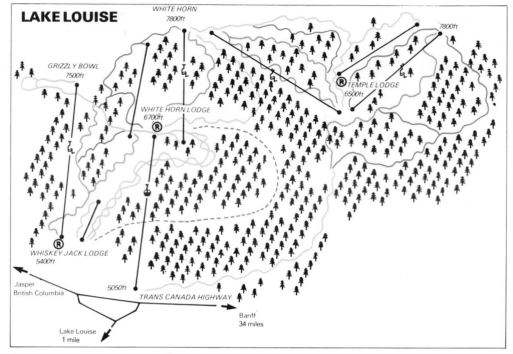

SUNSHINE VILLAGE *Alberta*

Sunshine, the third of the Banff area ski locations, is a completely created centre which started as a very primitive nucleus in 1936. It was not until 1963 that the 'village' began to take shape. It is a pity that such a lovely ski resort should have such a trite name. It is reached by a bus which shuttles the three miles (five kilometres) from the parking lot, 11 miles (18 kilometres) out of Banff, which is the only form of transport allowed in this lovely ski bowl.

The centre lies high, at the edge of the local timberline and only a lift away from the Rocky Mountain watershed – the Great Divide. With a minimum of lifts three sides of this bowl are mechanized giving a 1700 foot (518 metre) drop from the highest point,

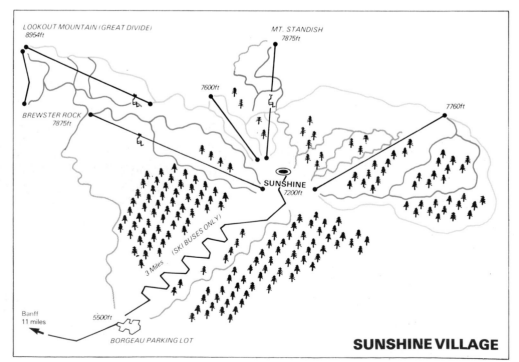

Lookout Mountain, which is just a few feet short of 9000 feet (2740 metres). A common complaint made against this area is that, being almost treeless, visibility and orientation become a problem in bad weather. The addition of a few trail direction posts would minimize the difficulties and it would be a very small price to pay for go-anywhere skiing – a rare commodity anywhere in North America.

Although weekends can produce some heavy crowds, access is limited to the ski bus, which means that the total number of skiers can be, and is, strictly limited to the maximum capacity of the uplift. It is a Draconian system but one that could, with advantage, be followed by other less organized resorts.

The skiing is moderate to easy with the exception of a difficult unprepared run down to the Borgeau parking lot that follows the river bed, and an unauthorized run from Brewster Rock through the trees down to the west side of the parking lot. The view is dominated by Mount Assiniboine, a complete twin of the Matterhorn, which is the centre of the panorama from Lookout Mountain.

Sunshine is a very good resort for a week's skiing holiday. Commuting from here to either Lake Louise or Norquay would be no hardship and would provide a little variety – and make Sunshine even more attractive.

NORQUAY/BANFF *Alberta*
Norquay must be almost the only mechanized ski hill that has no easy or moderate way down. It is also Banff's town mountain. Not that it is Banff's only ski resort, for Lake Louise is less than an hour away and Sunshine Village even less. This may account for the curious character of the town in that the main skiing is such a horror of a mountain and the best skiing is really in two other places. Not to be outdone by Lake Louise, Banff built itself a hideous and enormous hotel, called Banff Springs, which stands in curious contrast to the weird mixture of the wild west and the tourist trap that it has become. I was strangely reminded of Igls when first exploring the town, for here also was a resort that suffered from the proximity of a major city – in this particular case Calgary. Inevitably the majority of the skiers here commute from Calgary and the demand even for second homes is minimal and the residential populace must inevitably be made up of seasonal transients employed in one way or another by the tourist industry.

Fresh snow skiing in the Rocky Mountains.

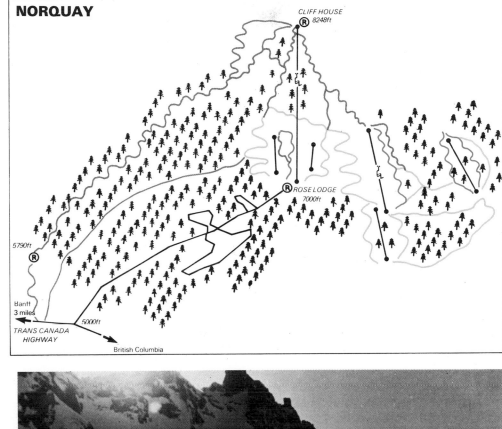

HELICOPTER SKIING/BANFF *Alberta*

If there is a skier's Valhalla then I am certain that it is located somewhere near the Bugaboos, the Monashees or the Cariboos in British Columbia and sitting on the throne will be Hans Gmoser who looked at the obvious, saw it, and made it real.

The concept of lifting skiers up a mountain by helicopter is as old as the first high altitude helicopter and was the natural successor to the glacier landings first popularized by the Swiss pilot, Hermann Geiger.

For Hans Gmoser and Leo Grillmayer, two Austrian emigrés to Canada who were fanatics about mountains, the idea was simple, logical and obvious. They made it work and proved that they were the true conservationists. No lift pylons, no clanking and squeaking, and no diesel fumes spoil the environment. No hideous architectural creations and tourist trap settlements disfigure the empty mountainsides but just two small wooden lodges, nestling among the uppermost trees. They are separated by more than a hundred miles (160 kilometres) and are surrounded by a few hundred thousand square miles of unexplored, untracked mountains and glaciers. The Bugaboos and the Cariboos are the two centres which can only be reached in winter by helicopter (and in summer possibly by jeep but more likely on foot). An isolated inn at Micah Creek in the Monashees, reachable by a four-wheel drive vehicle if conditions are good, completes the total of the bases for the greatest skiing in the world.

Forty people in each centre can spend a week on the most intensive skiing holiday of their lives. It has been described as the most expensive, the most difficult, the most testing and exhilarating skiing. It also entails communal living, military discipline and the inevitable discomforts of high-Alpine weather and snow. You pay for a minimum of 100,000 feet (30,000 metres) of downhill skiing, the best food I have ever eaten on a mountain and the most testing, exhausting, exciting high-risk skiing it has ever been my fortune to experience. Every run is through virgin snow, the great glaciers and bowls are untracked, and the silence is complete.

The beat of the helicopter vanishes within seconds of leaving you on your chosen peak or pass to reappear, as if by magic, 40 minutes later as you pack up your skis in some deserted valley, to lift you to the next summit. If you must use modern technology for skiing, then this is the ultimate, perfect solution.

McCARTHY GLACIER

CONRAD GLACIER

MALLOY GLACIER

VOWELL GLACIER

WALLACE GLACIER

○ Indicates Helicopter Landing Point

Switzerland

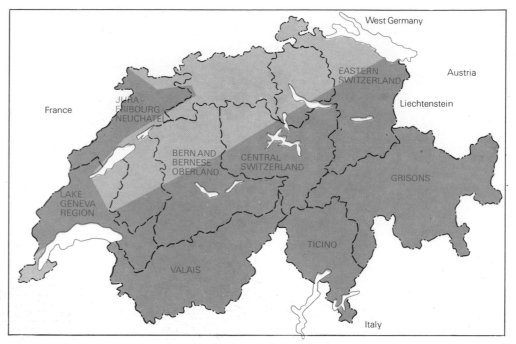

For the total ski fanatic, scenery, ambience and geography are becoming inconsequential sales gimmicks provided there is ample no-wait skiing over perfectly made trails or down equally perfectly preserved giant moguls. For these skiers, Switzerland is old-fashioned. How wrong they are and how they betray their incomplete mastery of the whole scene. Skiing is where the snow lies, be it downhill-only, cross country, high-Alpine moutaineering or just yo-yoing up and down a suitable snow slope. No other country in the world can provide any and every variation of the sport within easy access of only a few miles. In Switzerland there is a greater variety, a greater trail distance, a greater challenge to proficiency and a greater combination of high-Alpine and gentle pre-Alpine meadow scenery than the most competent propaganda professional could dream up in a year of media planning.

It is arguable whether modern recreational skiing originated in Switzerland or Austria, but two facts are incontestable – it was in St Moritz in January 1865 that the first ever winter-sports holiday group assembled; and it was in a group of Bernese Oberland resorts, Mürren, Wengen and Grindelwald, that the cult of downhill-only skiing originated and where the British created, from a curious eccentricity, a fashionable, socially acceptable, even envied sport and recreation.

It was no accident nor was it a lack of enterprise that, after the early boom in winter-sports in the 1920s, Switzerland did not become one vast, skiing service station. The winter-sports development is based on established summer vacation villages, villages often of great age and long traditions and which are still active mountain farming villages. The vast areas of Alpine pasturage and the glaciers and cliffs that surmount them are jealously protected by entrenched law and regulations governing mechanization.

The result of this historical and judicious background is that Swiss resorts have evolved rather than been developed. There are no forests of skilift pylons, no folksy après-ski and little chauvinistic derogation of other countries. In the place of these is a calm, almost cold, efficiency and value for money – and the greatest Alpine skiing in the world.

For the most part the ski trails navigate through the tree-less Alpine pastures between 2800 metres and the timberline at 1800 metres. The high levels of the permanent snowline, above 2800 metres and up to 3500 metres and higher, are sparsely lifted with open, moderate, go-anywhere trails and the glaciers, except for a few well-known exceptions, are left to the ski mountaineer. The home-runs to the villages are frequently steep, often heavily forested and still present the skier with many of the age-old problems of wood paths, steep traverses and tight trails for they follow the old hay paths trodden for generations by the farmers of the high pastures. But this is true skiing. To overcome these problems at the end of a long day's skiing provides a feeling of satisfaction that no simplified, trail can give. Long, fast, straight running such as can be found on the Parsenn above Davos or on the Diavolezza near St Moritz may seem unfashionable but only because nowhere else is there the open country that will permit such skiing.

Perhaps the most remarkable facet of Swiss skiing is the variety that can be found within such a small country. It falls sharply into three categories in three different areas: Eastern and Central Switzerland for pre-Alpine, low-altitude, mid-winter skiing which is very reminiscent of the greater part of Austrian skiing; Nordic, cross-country trails that stretch for miles along the spine of the Jura and across the rich farmlands of the Canton de Vaud from Neuchâtel to Lausanne; and the high-Alpine resorts and areas that stretch across the Grison, the Bernese Oberland and into the Valais where the skiing is big, hard, varied and as highly mechanized as any French super-centre.

There is yet another division which can be applied to the list of nearly 200 established Swiss resorts. There are well-known names, the places which can loosely be termed international. St Moritz, Zermatt, Davos, Flims, Gstaad, Crans-Montana, and all their lesser relations, are patronized by every nationality of the world. By contrast there are the small, almost unknown villages and centres which the Swiss consider their own and which, although they have been developed and modernized, have remained very much Swiss family resorts.

The Matterhorn (right) is a symbol for Swiss Mountain vacations. No matter how often it is seen, it exerts an irrisistable visual attraction.

CENTRAL AND EASTERN SWITZERLAND

Central Switzerland is that area which few tourists do more than pass through. It consists, roughly, of what are known as the Forest Cantons, the small group which in 1291 were first to pledge their allegiance to the newly born Federation. The group comprises Uri, Schwyz, Unterwalden. Included here, for the purpose of tourism, are Lucerne, Glarus and even parts of Zürich.

This is Swiss holiday territory and with few exceptions the resorts here will not figure in any tour operator's brochure nor will they receive heavy promotional support outside of Switzerland. The villages have a very special ambience common to them which is the result of straightforward demand by their Swiss guests. There is, on the whole, little night life and at about 11 o'clock in the evening the resorts close down. Less than half of the visitors are active skiers and most are family groups.

There are two important exceptions to this generalization – Andermatt and Engelberg. They began life as holiday resorts for the parents and relatives of the men restricted by their activities in the Army and the Church, which brought them there in the first place. Both have become international resorts and are still, respectively, a military garrison and a Catholic seminary and continue to enjoy a mutual benefit.

Skiing in eastern Switzerland is over a small area known as the Toggenburg and part of the Canton of Appenzell, and it lies behind the familiar vertical cliffs bordering the Walen See. Travellers from Zürich to Chur and the Arlberg see these cliffs beyond the dark water of the lake and they certainly do not encourage any thoughts of skiing. However, the country beyond is more hospitable even though the jagged outrunners of the Säntis appear to deny any potential.

The area serves Zürich, St Gall and even Basle and is best known for a quick day away from work rather than a week's vacation. The season is short, generally starting just before Christmas and finishing soon after Lent, though frequently this area can produce the best skiing in Switzerland as early as October and is a favourite seasonal first.

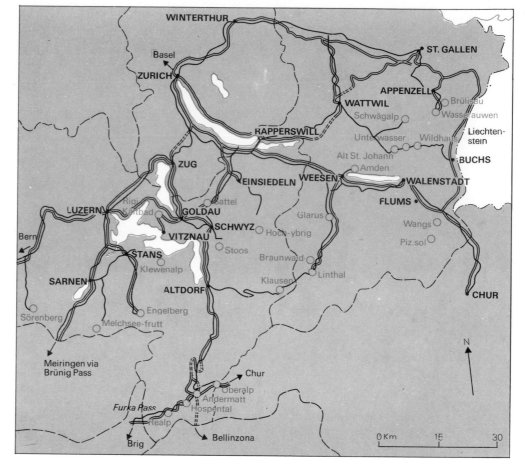

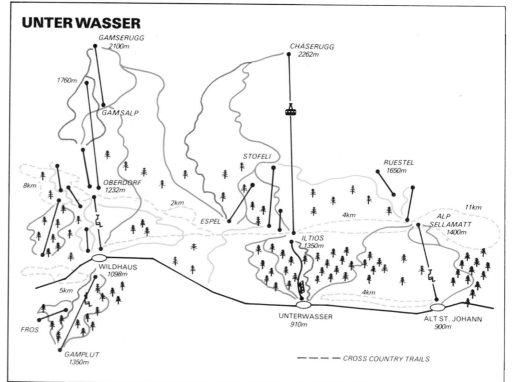

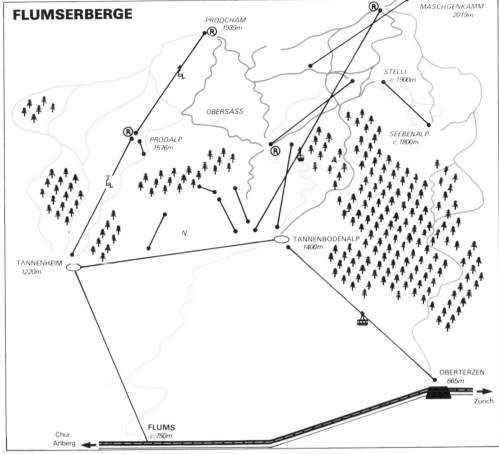

FLUMSERBERGE

Farmhouses, a church and the wide sweeping meadows are the hallmark of the Obertoggenburg.

UNTERWASSER
Wildhaus/Alt St Johann

These three road-side villages are almost household words to skiers from Zurich and St Gall for they are barely 90 minutes by automobile from town centre to skilift.

Although only separated by a mile or two, the three villages differ very considerably. Alt St Johann sees mainly cross-country tourers who prefer to live in the cheap bed-and-breakfast houses which surround the old village centre. For the downhill skier there is little joy.

Unterwasser is a different story. Now firmly lifted into the 1970s, it was always the traditional early season outing for Zürich families who, after the short funicular ride, started the long hogs-back climb to the summit of the Chäserugg with a fabulous plunging view across the Walen See into the Glärnisch. The run home was entertaining and not too taxing. Today there is a lift to the top and what before was a day's skiing for one run can now be done, top-to-bottom, in an hour. Hardly, I think, the village in which to spend an expensive week.

Wildhaus, in stark contrast to Unterwasser, is a busy family resort and hotels and holiday homes for banished children litter the wooded slopes. The skiing is appropriately easy except for the still incomplete link with the more challenging Unterwasser slopes. This link is a very draughty, and often icy, lift that struggles up to the Gamserrung. It offers a scratchy black run back home to Wildhaus or the mixed pleasures of a long red traverse over bumpy, wind-blown snow down to Iltios, the funicular terminal which is situated just above Unterwasser.

FLUMSERBERGE

Just after passing the Walen See by road or rail, on the journey to Chur, Davos or St Moritz or even the Arlberg, the landscape on the right suddenly opens up and the cliffs and shadows of the Glarner mountains give way to gently sloping meadows, speckled, like nuts on a cake, with tiny brown chalets that scatter up the slopes until they vanish in patchily wooded, snow slopes. This is the Flumserberge, time-honoured winter re-creation area for mothers with children while fathers continue to work in their home towns.

If you can forego a busy night-life and fashionable shops, this area is a high-winter paradise for children and mothers beginning to ski. There is even one super-black run which eventually leads down to Oberterzen on the Walen See and a cable-car goes back again, though few would care to repeat the run. In practice this cable-car is used as an access vehicle and the marked trail is rarely considered as skiable by contemporary skiers, even those searching for a challenge.

Gentle slopes, soft snow, fir trees and a blue sky are what Swiss families seek in Flumserberge.

BRAUNWALD

This is another Central Swiss family resort. It is on a sunny little balcony above Linthal, not far from Glarus where Catholics and Protestants share a cathedral – a happy compromise after religious massacres threatened to destroy the community. There is little to say about the skiing here except that it is the kind of place where you can chase the children out, armed with a liftpass, and cheerfully forget about them until hunger drives them home. There are not many places like that.

HOCH YBRIGG

Hoch Ybrigg is the third created Swiss resort. It is situated not far beyond Einsiedeln, a monastery and pilgrimmage town with a magnificent baroque cathedral. It is also at the end of a shallow valley that for many years has been one of the Swiss homes of Nordic skiing. With one longish black run and a collection of medium reds and quite a number of blues, it must also class itself as a family resort, and a very busy one, for it is only a bare hour away from Zürich and about the same from Zug. It is modern, it is efficient, a trifle soul-less and still very much in the course of development. What it will be like when the projected five lifts are finally built it is impossible to say. Great it will never be, but interesting, yes, and well worth a weekend away from Zürich.

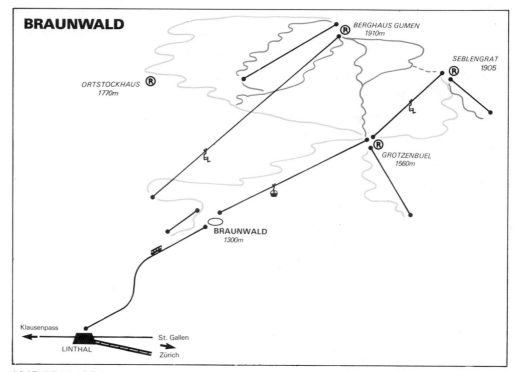

ANDERMATT

If you tell a Swiss person that you are going to spend your winter holiday in Andermatt he will either laugh or be appalled, for to him Andermatt means only one thing, military service. However, it is a delightful village of great charm and friendliness. It has an excep-

Andermatt and Urserental have always been underrated. The village is charming and very old.

tionally joyous night-life, the barracks are invisible and the military personnel are barely noticeable. The downhill and cross-country skiing are superb, and so is the Alpine touring. Families love it, experts revel in the technical problems and if you have had your skiing apprenticeship in Andermatt, there will be few trails which will frighten or deter you wherever you chose to ski in the future.

Those who like super-steep skiing should try the direct route from Gemstock to Gurschen, down the 'wall'. A fall on this section results in landing 300 feet further down with little contact with the snow. Powder-snow freaks can find their needs fulfilled on the ten mile run down to the Andermatt-Hospental road or even in the many little gullies that lead down from Stöckli.

The longer you ski in Andermatt, the more skiing you discover. There is only one disadvantage, and that is if you are not a skier and prefer to spend your day in the village you will find that, apart from it being totally deserted from ten o'clock in the morning until four o'clock in the afternoon, it will lack one essential commodity – sun. In the winter it only gets a bare hour in the morning before falling again into the shadows of the ranges that surround it for the rest of the day.

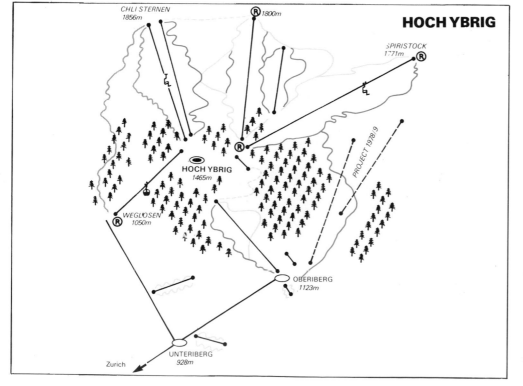

ANDERMATT

GEMSTOCK
2961m

ONLY IN SPRING

WINTERHORN
2000m

GURSCHEN
2212m

REALP
1538m

→ Brig
(Summer Only)

HOSPENTHAL
1453m

Chur
Disentis
Oberalp

ANDERMATT
1447m

NATSCHEN
1842m

→ Zürich
Milan

STOCKLI
2364m

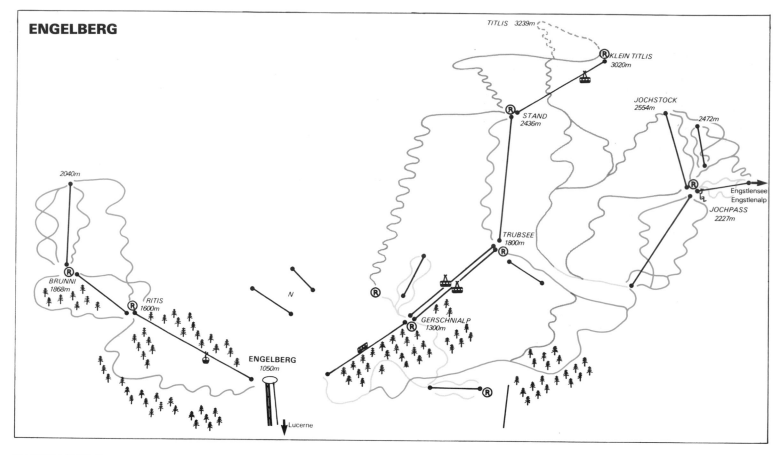

ENGELBERG

TITLIS 3239m

KLEIN TITLIS
3020m

STAND
2436m

JOCHSTOCK
2554m

2472m

2040m

TRUBSEE
1800m

Engstlensee
Engstlenalp

JOCHPASS
2227m

BRUNNI
1868m

RITIS
1600m

N

GERSCHNIALP
1300m

ENGELBERG
1050m

Lucerne

ENGELBERG

Engelberg is a monastery town that is still largely concerned with religious education. The Benedictine monastery was founded in 1120 and rebuilt in 1729 after a fire. It is still a place of pilgrimage and it became a ski resort by virtue of possessing an easily accessible glacier peak, the Titlis, and its popularity grew among the English during the golden age of skiing. Its proximity to both Lucerne and Zürich led to almost insurmountable crowds at the bottle-necks of the Gershnialp funicular and the Trübsee cableway. These have now been overcome and Engelberg should rank high among a skier's list of future visits and spring is the best season.

Two trails lift the skiing out of the class of ordinary into the superlative. Neither are prepared or signposted and both are difficult or very difficult. The Laub starts from the intermediate station at Stand and is a single 1000 metre drop to Gerschnialp. It is steep, open and excessively avalanche prone and consequently rarely skied except in spring. Then, however, if the snow is right, you will start your run in powder which will change imperceptibly into spring corn snow and if you meet it like this it is so good, you will

probably dream of it for the rest of your days.

The other run is known as the Grosser Sulz, which means the big, corn-snow field. It starts abruptly at the Jochstock above the Joch Pass and drops down a wide deep gully to the Trübsee. Neither as long nor as difficult as the Laub, it is one of the most atmospheric runs I have ever known. It is menacing, wild, silent and very exciting.

The Titlis itself is worth the visit even if the ski down is beyond your capability for the view from the moderately high peak is superb. The south-facing slopes of the Brunni lift system are disappointing and rarely provide good skiing.

There is a definite attraction between skier and slalom pole. No skier can resist it.

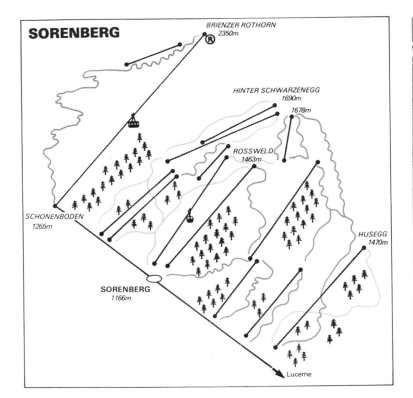

SORENBERG

Sörenberg is about an hour's drive south of Lucerne, and lies against the north flank of the mountains that border the Lake of Brienz. It follows the general pattern of the family resort with comfortable skiing through moderately dense patches of forest and a maximum height difference of about 600 metres. In addition there is the new cable-car that goes to the top of the Brienzer Rothorn. This peak, long known to Baedecker travellers and railway enthusiasts for its historic rack-and-pinion railway that pants up from the other side, was never seriously considered as a ski

The monastery and the associated seminary dominate the view of Engelberg. The baroque church is worth the short walk after a good day's skiing.

mountain until very recently. It now has a most interesting and testing run that drops some 1100 metres to the cable station only a mile away from the resort itself.

STOOS

Stoos cannot, by any standard, ever join the league of renowned ski resorts. On the other hand it still stands as a monument to what skiing was like 40 years ago. I have known it for about that length of time and it has hardly changed a brick or a tree.

Being only a few minutes from Schwyz and barely an hour from Zürich, it was a natural target for weekend skiing and even 40 years ago the crowds on a Saturday or Sunday were ferocious. Visit it on a week day and you will be charmed by the two mountains it has mechanized and amazed at the plunging view into the Lake of Lucerne from the summits. Even the skiing may come as a surprise for it is by no means easy and when, after a day skiing these slopes, you finally scratch your way down into the valley, you will have to agree that small and old-fashioned the village may be but it has been a great day's skiing.

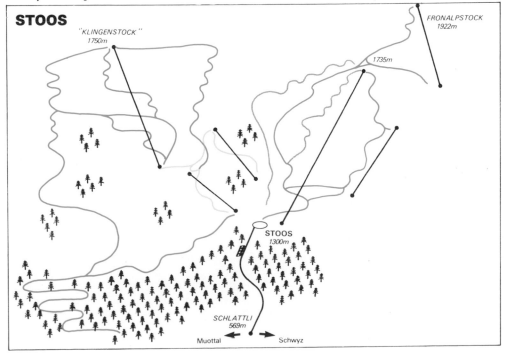

THE GRISONS

Grisons (Graubünden), the territory of the Grey League of 1442, home of the Rhaetians conquered by the Romans in AD 15, occupied by the Austrians, French and Spanish during the Thirty Years War, the 18th Canton of the Swiss Federation since 1808, is the largest of all the Swiss Cantons and has the lowest number of inhabitants. Large areas still speak their ancient Rhaetian language, Romantsch, and at every turn can be seen the remains of the fortifications that guarded the valleys and grazing meadows until well into the 17th century. In this Canton, Davos was the legal capital of all the territory to the east and south of Chur for 2000 years. St Moritz served as a rest and rehabilitation centre for the Roman Legions, Tiefencastel guarded the sanctity of the Engadin from incursions from power-hungry Chur and the Prince Bishops. Late in the winter of 1799, the Russian General Suvarow struggled down from the Panixer Pass into the Upper Rhine Valley and so to Chur, bare-footed, half his army lost through cold in the impossible flight from Andermatt, to rejoin his allies in Austria.

After this long and proud history it is only fitting that the Grisons should be able to claim parenthood of the whole scene of Alpine skiing as we know it today. St Moritz saw the birth of the

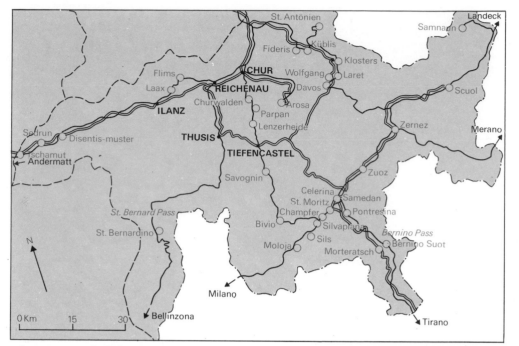

winter-sports holiday, and Davos witnessed the development of long-distance, Alpine skiing with the discovery of the Parsenn and its 18 kilometres of downhill running to Küblis, and the installation of the first public skilift, the ubiquitous T-bar, in December 1934. Strangely, perhaps, the Grisons cannot list many resorts – at least not in comparison with, say, the Valais. Apart from the great names, St Moritz, Davos, Arosa, Lenzerheide and

Flims-Laax, there only remain the expected number of small villages which have benefited from the explosion of the industry by the construction of a few lifts which serve more as adjuncts to the inevitable chairlift destined for summer use. So much of this large Canton is trackless, villageless mountain where the ski mountaineer and the high-winter tourer are more at home, wandering from hut to hut in any number of Grisons small *Hautes Routes*.

SAMNAUN

A quirk of geography and some rather doubtful politics resulted in this remote Lower Engadin valley becoming a no-man's land, free of taxes and duties, but definitely part of Switzerland. For the downhill skier there is nothing here, for this is the Alpine tourer's mecca where ski school notices still carry the nostalgic and evocative 'lunch-bag and skins' appendage to the day's programme. For Samnaun is the centre of the innumerable climbs in the Silvretta range that take tourers from distant Klosters through into Austria and half-way to Innsbruck.

The real pleasure of Samnaun lies in the fact that ski mountaineers can fully extend themselves during the day and return to hot baths, four-course meals, and, of course, whisky, gin and liqueurs at next-to-nothing for the bottle. The village itself is only a single street along which the few hotels are scattered in a haphazard fashion.

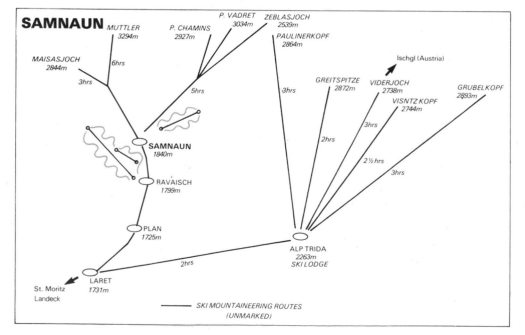

AROSA

Mention the name of Arosa in any of the internationally sought after resorts and the chances are that no one will be very interested. Talk about it to almost any German-speaking Swiss and you will be overwhelmed by a flood of reminiscences. Like Davos or St Moritz it is a complete winter sports centre but unlike either of those two it has never

The one disadvantage to Arosa is the fact that it is on a hill. Ski in the road at your own peril.

become a serious competitor for world renown, and the reason, if you view the place objectively, is simple. The skiing, by today's standards, falls neatly into the no-man's land of being neither small and homely nor big and exhilarating, but somewhere in between.

Arosa is scattered over a considerable distance with an irritating hill separating the old village, Inner Arosa, from the spread of Edwardian hotels in the lower village. It is perhaps this lack of cohesion which makes the potential visitor view the skifields as being equally scattered and he will be confirmed in this view once he starts to explore. The two principal mountains, the Hörnli and the Weisshorn both provide just short of 1000 metres of downhill running. They are only barely linked and although virtually all the skiing is above the timber-line the ground is sufficiently broken by deep gullies to make go-as-you-please skiing practically impossible. It is this topography which also limits the number of trail variants. Whereas once this was no criticism and skiers flocked in their thousands to this friendly neighbour of Davos the choice today is so much greater that Arosa has remained what it always was – a quiet, civilized winter-sports resort that can cater for families of any size and age and any skiing standard.

BIVIO

The road from Tiefencastel up the Julier Pass, just before the final steep climb to the desolate Hospiz, passes through a tiny village. Bivio is included in this collection of big and still bigger centres because it is so typical of so many Swiss villages where skiing is the meagre livelihood in the unproductive winter months. Three skilifts, some unimpressive slopes and not even a fine view are no recommendation for any ski centre. But it must suffice for Bivio, for this village has a character which can be discovered only by staying in either of the two hotels for a week's Alpine touring. If this is your kind of skiing, the chances are that you will be planning to return to Bivio, year after year. It is that kind of unremarkable ski village.

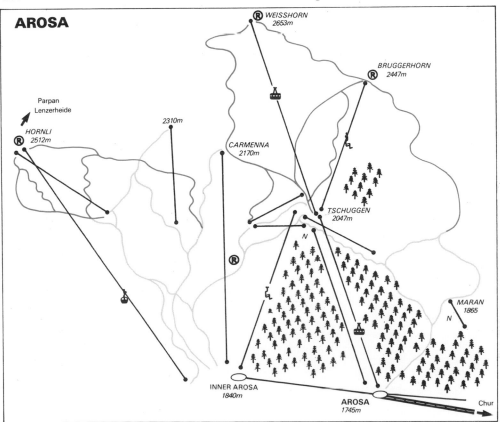

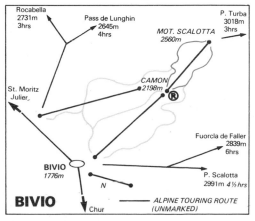

ST MORITZ
Pontresina/Sils/Sils Maria/ Silvaplana/Celerina

The Engadin has a very special ambience, a feel, a scent and a mood which are hard to forget and which even the heaviest of winter snow covers cannot remove. Each little village resort is so self-contained that it is easy to forget how dependent on each other they are by virtue of their combined skiing.

The magnet for everyone, sooner or later, is St Moritz, with its newer Bad and older Dorf, the former slightly less fashionable with large impersonal hotels and a Victorian shopping arcade, the latter a picturesque confusion of steep winding streets, the fashionable hotels, expensive shops and smart night-life. Probably less than thirty per cent of the visitors ski, though most will sun themselves on Corviglia or take the cable-car to Piz Nair. And, the truth be told, the skiing is not very special on the featureless slopes between Randolins and Chantarella. Even the link to Marguns and Trais Fluors does little to lift the complicated monotony of the numerous theoretical trails that all lead, sooner or later to Chanterella and the narrow drop down into St Moritz.

What keeps skiers coming to this region are the distant slopes beyond Pontresina that start and finish on the Bernina Hospiz and the long runs from Corvatsch.

Pontresina, sunless and uninteresting in winter, is the starting point for the skiing on the Bernina Pass which comprises Lagalp and Diavolezza. Most of the skiers will have come from anywhere in the Engadin by bus and train. Lagalp is a specialist mountain, one of the very few where there are no easy descents and where there are only black runs which never let up from start to finish and which test everyone's skiing technique. Diavolezza, on the other hand, is high-Alpine skiing for the moderate and from the summit there starts one of the great trails, the Isla Pers, the 'lost island', a long and testing glacier run that starts with a fearsome black from Diavolezza to the glacier, followed by a trudge and short climb onto the Isla Pers and from there a precipitous slope of at least 300 metres height difference decants skiers neatly for a eight-kilometre slide down the gently sloping Morteratsch glacier.

Corvatsch is a straightforward 3000 metre mountain that has been mechanized and cunningly linked to the Furtschellas skiing of Sils Maria. Access to these slopes is by bus, but good skiers descend into St Moritz Bad.

PIZ PALÜ 3905

BELLAVISTA 3895

PITZ BERNINA 4049

PIZ ROSEGG 3937

PIZ CORVATSCH

3303

FUORCLA SURLEJ 2755

2643

MURTEL 2702

FURTSCHELLAS 2800

2890

2536

2590

2226

2312

SURLEJ 1870

SILVAPLANA 1815

SILS MARIA 1809

PIZ NAIR 3025

2659

ST MORITZ BAD

SALASTRAINS 2040

CORVIGLIA 2486

2915

2452

ST MORITZ DORF 1822

TRAIS FLUORS 2762

MARGUNS 2284

CELERINA 1725

SAVOGNIN

Once there was a tiny hamlet on the main Julier Pass road to St Moritz called Savognin where every year a small band of ski mountaineers stopped for a last hot meal before setting off across the valley into what was virtually terra incognita, the Val Nandro, and a tiny hut in Tigia and a summer hotel in Radons. All around them were the most fabulous snow domes that cried out to be skied. But that was before the developers saw in this impoverished hamlet a great fashionable agglommeration of condominium blocks and a festoon of lifts. Part of this vision has certainly become bricks and mortar and Martegnas and Cartas have their lifts and the favourite powder-snow run has been christened Dream Trail. But, in the end, those wondrous snow mountains won, for if you should chance to be there the morning after six inches of new snow have fallen and before the ratracs have made it navigable, the trail from Cartas is a dream and more. The 32 kilometre trail from Martegnas over Ziteil, with its desolate, isolated monastery, to Tiefencastel still has not been mechanized.

Should you be in Savognin and should you wish to see a vestige of true, old Switzerland, ski to Riom and stand in the centre of this centuries-old village where the cobbled, icy alleys wind between the roof-touching barns and houses, and the scent of cows and wood smoke hangs like incense over the huddled

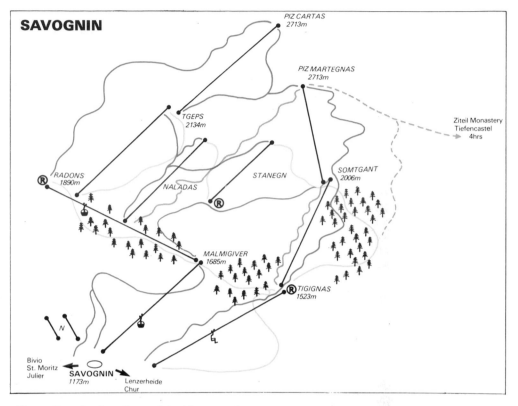

village. But don't talk to the old men who stump up the steep slopes with a hundred-weight of hay on their shoulders, for they will not understand a word you say. They only speak Romantsch, as their ancestors have for the past two thousand years.

The tight little huddle of Riom (below right) is only a few hundred yards away from the busy main road but life here is still in the old mountain farming tradition. Savognin could be miles away. St Moritz (below left and previous page) has a delightful centre of winding streets and shops.

LENZERHEIDE/VALBELLA
Parpan, Churwalden

The road from Chur to St Moritz over the Julier Pass climbs in steep bends through familiar grazing meadows and farming hamlets, through Churwalden which is an unremarkable village, past Parpan and its roadside stretch of car parks, country hotels, large houses dotted among the meadows and two ski lifts, before ascending abruptly to a heavily forested, long, wide and flat valley. A huddle of hotels marks Valbella before the road shoots through the trees, in a way more reminiscent of Canada or Washington State than Switzerland, to emerge into the busy, single-street resort of Lenzerheide. There is little to be seen of the skiing and most of the

Parpan can be charming or it can be nothing more than a traffic snarl. Lenzerheide is behind the woody ridge and Arosa over the mountains.

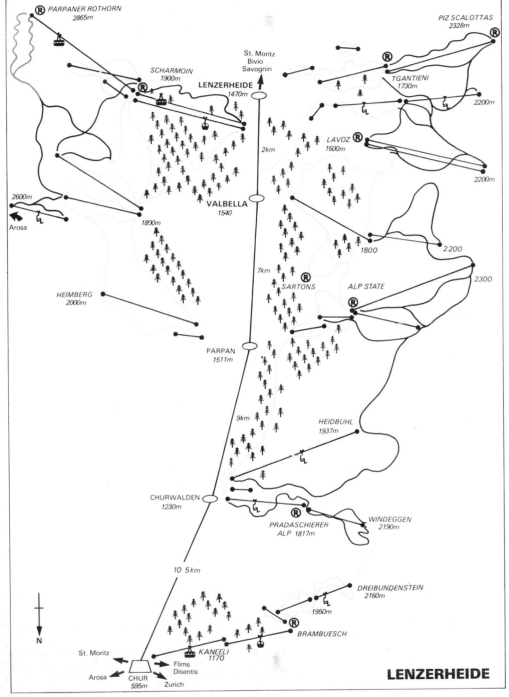

visitors appear to be engaged in taking long, marked walks through the woods.

Lenzerheide/Valbella is, by tradition, a place for quiet and rest. It comes as something of a shock to find that it is also the little known centre for some extremely testing — and for my taste extremely frustrating — skiing. On paper the ski domain is very large and of moderate to easy standard. In practice it is even larger and, unless you are extremely fortunate, can be extremely difficult, for the trails which face east and west have an unfortunate habit of being scratchy and icy with narrow, steep, forested end-runs.

The extent of the skiing is staggering. With

careful use of the comparatively few lifts, you start in Lenzerheide, after an annoying trek on foot to the first lift, and ten lifts and a very short, shallow climb later, find yourself skiing into Chur, which, by the map, is 23 kilometres away.

The west-facing slopes are less exciting. The Parpaner Rothorn serves summer walkers better than the skiers and the Scharnen lifts, designed to provide a direct skilift link

with Arosa, leave you stranded on the Parpaner Rothorn with a strenuous hour's climb to reach the Arosa Hörnli, though the return journey, either to Lenzerheide or Parpan, presents no such problems.

The journey to Chur alone is worth a few days visit to this most attractive valley. If you succeed in going there and back on skis, that is something you can write in red in your skiing diary for future reminiscence.

DAVOS/KLOSTERS

Several books have been written on the skiing in this fantastic snow arena. Davos, Klosters and the Parsenn have filled the ski journals of the world ever since the early 20th century and for any serious historian of the ski scene these mountains must take a key place in the development of Alpine skiing as we now know it.

In all the great ski centres of the world, the potential of the slopes is visible from the valleys and villages, but this is not so in Davos or Klosters where little is to be seen of the immense area except the uninviting slopes of Strela and the conical mound of Brämabuel and Jakobshorn. The remarkable thing is that all that is skied today was already fully explored by the early 1920s and there was not a winter's day when several hundred skiers were not wending their way up the climb to the Weissfluh and then skiing down to Klosters and Küblis, Jenaz and Fideris where they would take the train back to Davos.

Now a single liftpass serves on seven

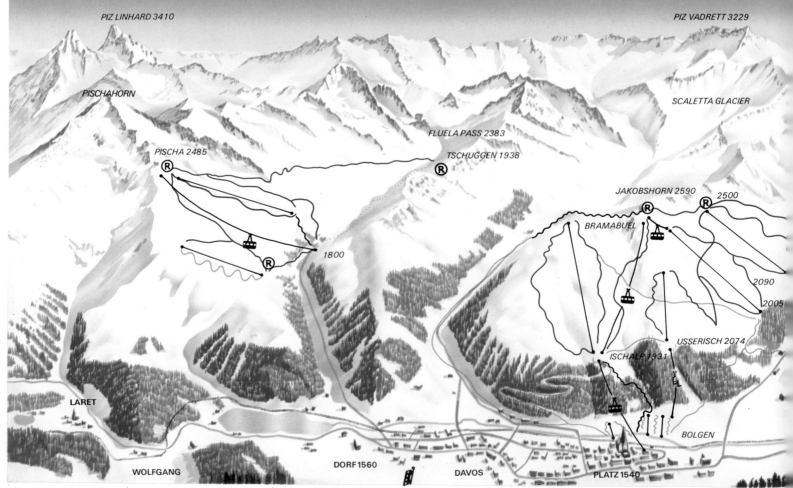

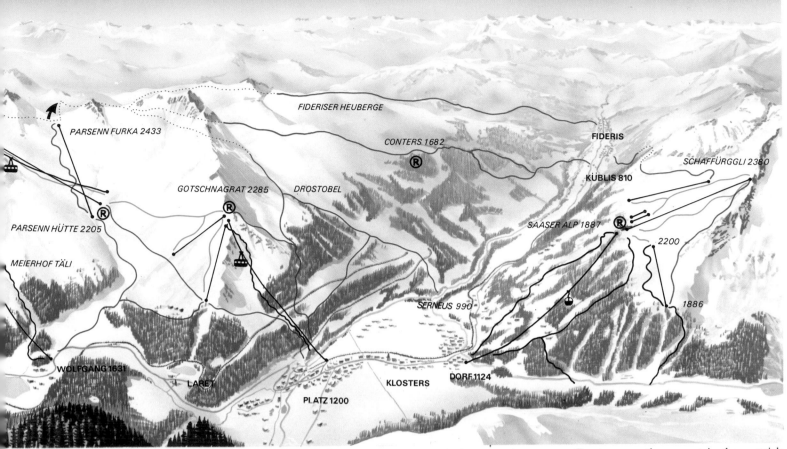

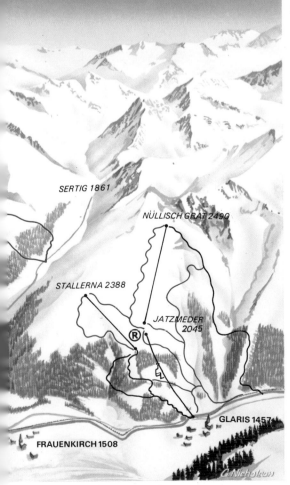

mountain systems, each of which any major resort would be proud to call their only skiing. Where today the senior resorts of the third generation boast about possessing the largest ski domains in the world, Davos and Klosters remain smugly silent, secure in the knowledge that within an area roughly 25 kilometres by 20 kilometres there is more distance to ski than at all the modern stations added together.

It has been argued that the trouble with this area is that it is either too difficult or too easy. This is a valid criticism if you base the classification on steepness and technical problems. The Dorftäli run from Weissfluh to Davos or the Drostobel from Gotschnagrat to Klosters are rarely pleasurable and always difficult. But to dismiss a run starting at 2663 metres on the Weissfluh and finishing at 813 metres in Küblis, some 18 kilometres away, as dull and easy simply because it is not one hideous icy mogul slope but a combination of fast straight running, tricky traverses and short bursts of steep twisting turns, displays a sad lack of comprehension of the sport.

It is a pity that Davos town, both Dorf and Platz, cannot live up to the magnificence of the skiing. By no stretch of the imagination can Davos be called attractive, atmospheric or even interesting. Sunday queues for the Parsennbahn stretch for hundreds of yards down the busy street and the 18,000 visitors the town can accommodate all move like flotsam on a lazy tide from one ski start to the next. But once on the mountain they vanish, swallowed up by the miles of trails. A visit, once in a lifetime, is a must for all skiers.

Klosters has a very different ambience. It is a small township with hotels, bars and restaurants scattered in happy untidiness about the centre and neat chalets stretching out into the former village grazing meadows.

The rivalry between Davos and Klosters has always been intense and the atmosphere entirely different. Where Davos was cosmopolitan and diffuse, Klosters was the place for the fashionable cliques. Before Gstaad became the centre for people in showbusiness, Klosters was their favoured hide-away and today there are still many famous names who spend much of the winter there in quiet and active anonymity. However Klosters has always suffered from the interminable queues for the Gotschnagrat cableway which is the sole entry into the Parsenn directly from the busy village.

Many people prefer to go to Davos where, on weekdays, the crowds are often less obstructive. This situation has improved recently since the new area of Saaseralp has been opened. It serves mainly Klosters Dorf, a satellite settlement about two kilometres from Klosters, and it provides the less advanced with a comfortable ski area much less daunting than the Parsenn. Scenically too it is preferable to the rather limited views which, should you have time between turns, you can see from the endless slopes of the Parsenn.

FLIMS-LAAX

Resort popularity is a strange, intangible quality which defies logical analysis. Flims is a case in point. For more than 40 years Flims and its near neighbour Flims Waldhaus enjoyed a quiet family-resort reputation where their clients returned year after year. And when lifts and cableways made their advent into the area, these same families came with their children and grandchildren to enjoy the easy, uncomplicated sliding around Foppa or the steep and testing *diretissimo* from Cassons. The scenery was magnificent and the potential enormous. Tentative moves were made to extend the skifields towards the gently sloped Vorab but violent objection stopped the plans in their tracks. Flims maundered on, more-or-less content, until entrepreneural acumen discovered a sleepy little village called Laax, drummed up the massive funds necessary, and, with a minimum of lifts, mechanized Crap Sogn Gion and Crap Masegn, linking the whole thing neatly into the Flims skifield

via La Siala. To the unbounded horror of conservationists and the eco-lobby, a lift was pushed close to the top of the inviolate Bündner Vorab.

Virtually overnight Flims-Laax, as it became known, jumped from being a comfortable little winter sports resort into the big league of major skiing. Tour operators from Germany, Holland, Sweden and Belgium fill all the newly created beds, the Swiss faithful still come to Flims and the weekend crowds from Chur and Zürich fill the lifts but it is still a ski resort looking for popularity, and no-one can explain it.

SEDRUN/DISENTIS

Disentis and Sedrun are so small that many road maps omit them and the guidebooks ignore them. Between them they can muster eight lifts and a dozen ski trails. They have no Grand Hotels, no great mountain, little publicity and at a push they could accommodate maybe 1500 visitors between them.

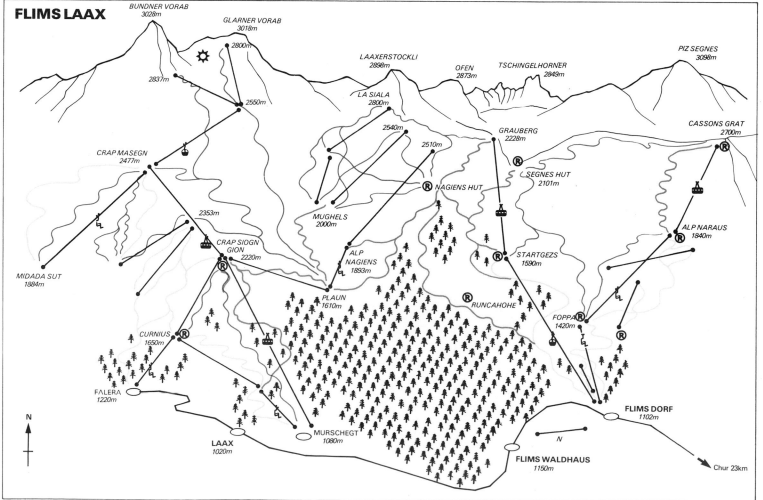

FLIMS LAAX

They are included in this summary of world ski resorts because they have character and ambience and invite intelligent exploration beyond the obvious confines of a skilift. Here, if you are a catholic skier, equally at home with Nordic skiing, Alpine skin-touring or happy trail-bashing, you could have the time of your life. If you can, find yourself sheet 5001 GOTTHARD or sheet 256 DISENTIS of the Swiss 1:50,000 Landeskarte, and feel the excitement and anticipation mount as you study all the routes and climbs and cross-country trails to be explored.

This is Sedrun, the whole of it. It will be many years before it ceases to be a perfect little Grisons village and becomes a ski centre.

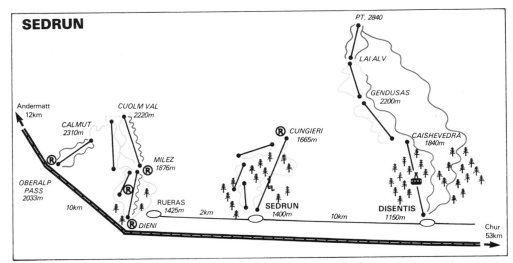

NEUCHATEL AND THE JURA

Nordic cross-country skiing is not new to this area, the New England of Switzerland, and the new breed of health-and-fitness loipe runner is regarded with a certain disdain. There are regularly organized, hut-to-hut cross-country weeks and even without being a member of one of the many clubs which operate lodges in the hills, there are sufficient convenient inns for skiers to set off with no plan and no time-table and go where the map and the inclinations suggest. You should make sure you are out of the area by the weekend, when, it would seem, the entire populations of Neuchâtel, Chaux-de-Fonds and even Payerne have set out on the trails.

The Swiss Ski Federation publishes a very useful booklet annually called *Skiwandern* which is obtainable through the Swiss National Tourist Office. It contains a complete list of all signposted and prepared cross-country routes in Switzerland with their length and exact location. They are divided into loipes and true cross-country trails. Their routes can be located with the aid of the 1:50000 or 1:25000 Federal Cartography maps.

THE BERNESE OBERLAND

The Bernese Oberland is not a political or administrative area – in fact it is difficult to define it in precise terms. It is within the boundaries of the Canton of Bern and starts at about Interlaken and stretches south as far as the mountain chain that borders the northern bank of

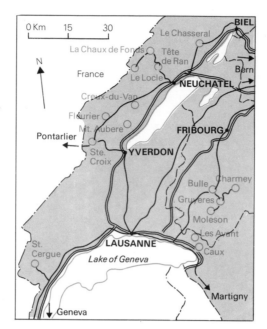

the Rhône. It extends eastwards as far as the mountains of Andermatt and trails off to the west at Adelboden.

Within these very general delimitations can be found the classic ski centres where tradition and intimacy are more important than vast ski fields and multi-lift complexes. Gstaad is hardly a skiing mecca. Saanen and Zweisimmen and Chateau d'Oex are where the theory of skiing turns was first worked out by Caulfield in 1911. Wengen is where 'downhill only' was born and a club of that name still rules the mainly British activities. Mürren housed the legendary Arnold Lunn in its Palace Hotel and the fearsome Inferno race is still held there down the original,

unflagged, unprepared course from Schilthorn to dark, sunless Lauterbrunnen. Grindelwald is a tidy chalet village under the menacing north face of the Eiger and the twin summits of the Wetterhorn. The famous Jungfraujoch train decants passengers panting into the rarefied atmosphere at 3454 metres to see the incredible view of the longest glacier in Europe, the Aletsch, where the ski mountaineering round-trip starts that takes in six 4000 metre peaks and provides some of the most challenging high-Alpine skiing, and ends, a week later, in Münster in the upper Rhône valley.

This high-Alpine area also includes a long list of barely known tiny hamlets such as Beatenberg above the lake of Thun, or Kandersteg, once a skating stronghold but now the haunt of get-fit cross-country fanatics. There is the hidden valley of Diemtig that nestles behind the northern hills of the Lötschental, a bare 48 kilometres from Thun, which is impossibly crowded by weekenders from Bern, but quiet and almost depopulated on a weekday when you can ski the lifts at Riedli, or climb up to the Grimmialp or over into Zweisimmen in snowy splendour.

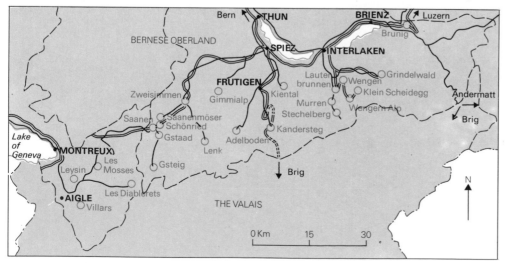

Winter in car-less Wengen has all the charm of old-time skiing holidays and all modern amenities.

LEYSIN/LES MOSSES

Leysin, the one-time residence of Catherine Mansfield and, more recently, the home of the International Mountaineering School, is one of the sanatoria villages that could have become a slum of decaying mausoleums. Skiing has, to some degree, rescued it but even with the most charitable intentions, it cannot be described as being a great centre. A competent performer might be occupied for a day or so but little more, for it offers no challenge and no great height differences.

Les Mosses grew out of the carriage trade. It lies on the main Aigle to Bern road in a gentle depression, the Col des Mosses, where a collection of roadside skilifts do a very busy trade at weekends. During the week, for the most part, they are closed. One relieving feature is the gondola to the Pic Chaussy which, given good conditions, can offer two quite exciting runs of nearly 1000 metres in height. Were Les Mosses ever to be linked with Leysin, the prospects might be very much more interesting.

VILLARS
Brettaye/Chesières/Barboleusaz

Just as Wengen and Mürren created about themselves a specialized group of holiday skiers, so did Villars. But where the Wengenites and Mürrenites were young and dash-

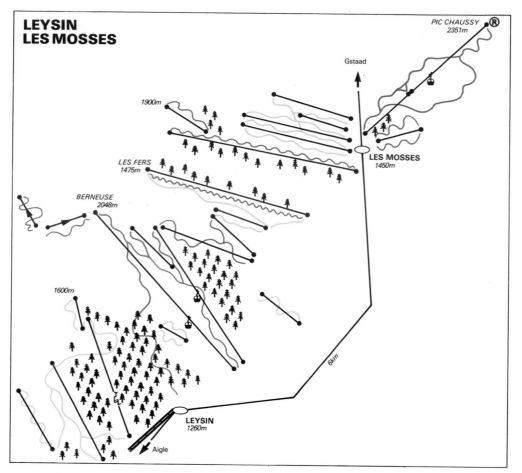

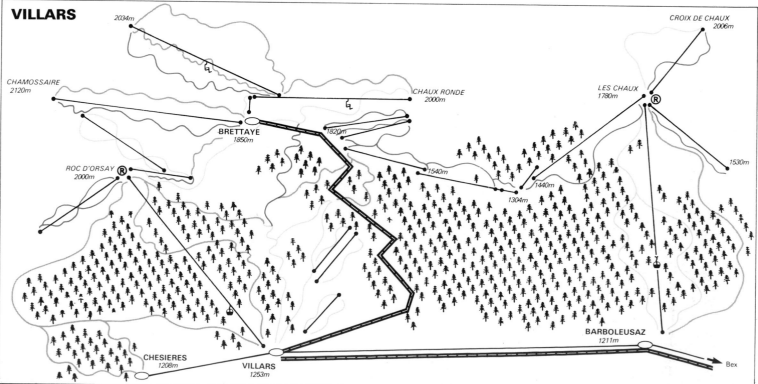

ing skiers, so the Villars enthusiasts were hard skiers, for they had on their doorstep some of the most difficult trails to be found in any popular ski resort. The masters of the steep, untracked routes have left behind them a tradition of hard fast testing runs which, with the passage of time, have been extended. The once slightly confined area of Brettaye is now linked to the new skiing in Barboleusaz, thus finally freeing Villars from the unavoidable dominance of the creaking railway service that dragged skiers up to Brettaye according to an inviolable railway timetable. Like St Anton, Villars has a way of putting skiers into their place and reducing bar-room parallels to the more realistic level of hopeful attempts.

LES DIABLERETS

Were it not for the Diablerets cable-way providing some very fine all-year-round skiing and a direct link into Gstaad, it is doubtful whether any list of major Swiss resorts would include this curious colony of second homes and childrens' convalescent establishments. Fortunately it is an easy ski over into Reusch and Gstaad on the Isenau gondola.

Gstaad (below), one of the traditional resorts in the Swiss alps has housed the famous on their winter holidays for many years.

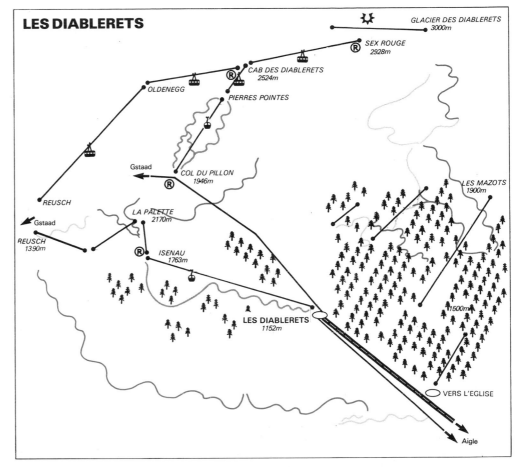

LES DIABLERETS

GLACIER DES DIABLERETS
3000m

SEX ROUGE
2928m

CAB DES DIABLERETS
2524m

OLDENEGG

PIERRES POINTES

LES MAZOTS
1900m

Gstaad

COL DU PILLON
1946m

REUSCH

LA PALETTE
2170m

Gstaad

REUSCH
1390m

ISENAU
1763m

1500m

LES DIABLERETS
1152m

VERS L'EGLISE

Aigle

WILDHORN 3247

WASSERNGRAT 1974

WISPILE 1935

RINDERBERG 2006

SEOBERG 1800

1900

HORNBERG 1800

HORNEGGLI 1770

EGGWELD 1455

REUS

156

GSTAAD 1051

SAANEN 1011

SCHOENRIED 1231

SAANENMOSER 1269

ZWEISIMME

HUGELIGRAT 1901

RELLERLIGRAT 1834

GSTAAD

If you sent all the filmstars home, blew up the neo-Gothic Palace Hotel, drowned the Eagle Club in its own ten-course meals, you would still find skiers flocking to this delightful pre-Alpine resort.

With cunning use of the Railpass that is part of the full lift pass to what is now euphemistically termed the White Highlands, there is varied and often very difficult skiing provided by seven different villages, each one an entity, each one quite as attractive to live in as Gstaad, and most of them are linked by signposted trails. It takes a little time to become accustomed to the place, but, once located, the Saanenmöser/Schönried/Gstaad link-up alone will keep you happy for a full

fortnight. Both the Lauenen and Reusch valleys are delightful cross-country areas, sufficiently wooded to be attractive, sufficiently clear not to be limited to pre-ordained paths. Rougemont and the Videmanette provide some testing high-Alpine skiing, and Chateau d'Oex has some equally testing, scratchy, wood paths. When the snow has melted in the valleys, the skiing from the top of the Diablerets down to Reusch or Oldenegg will be in full swing throughout the early part of summer until late in July.

Gstaad is a classic demonstration of the negative effect of publicity that fashionable resorts can acquire. For most skiers it is an unknown quantity but the Diablerets cableways have made it a place worth visiting, and

it is a considerable cross-country centre. The valley leading to Reusch leads to a number of deserted little re-entrants that are pleasantly forested and which are an open invitation to slide a pair of skis through the unblemished snow.. I have a friend, a fanatic ski mountaineer, who, whenever he is in search of a weekend of peace and quiet, goes to Gstaad and spends his days exploring this peaceful little valley. For non-skiers – if you like picking mushrooms try Gstaad in September when some particularly interesting and delicious varieties can be found if you know what to look for.

Gstaad is not all Palace Hotel and filmstars. A short walk up the valley leaves that all behind.

OLDENHORN 3122
LES DIABLERETS 3243
SEX ROUGE 2928
CAB DES DIABLERETS 2524
LDENEGG 1922
MONTS CHEVREUILS 1660
LA VIDEMANETTE 2156
LA MONTAGNETTE 1630
EGGLI 1670
1750
LA BRAYE 1215
QUOQAISE 1488
LES MOULINS 890
CHATEAU D'OEX 935
ROUGEMONT 1007

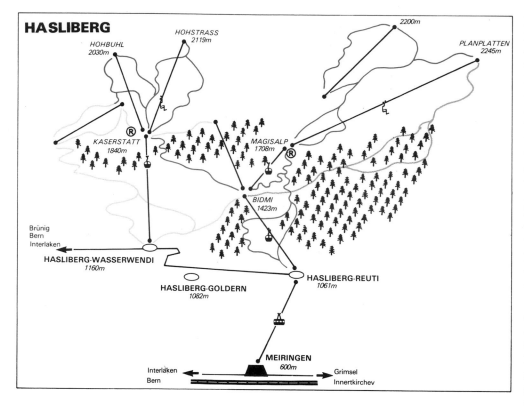

HASLIBERG

- HOHBUHL 2030m
- HOHSTRASS 2119m
- 2200m
- PLANPLATTEN 2245m
- KASERSTATT 1840m
- Ⓡ
- MAGISALP 1708m
- Ⓡ
- BIDMI 1423m
- Brünig Bern Interlaken ←
- HASLIBERG-WASSERWENDI 1160m
- HASLIBERG-GOLDERN 1082m
- HASLIBERG-REUTI 1061m
- MEIRINGEN 600m
- Interlaken Bern ← → Grimsel Innertkirchev

HASLIBERG/MEIRINGEN

Most people have heard of Meiringen, if only on account of Sherlock Holmes' final battle with the dastardly Professor Moriarty. Hasliberg, on the other hand, is probably only known to families of Zürich and Lucerne. Meiringen is a small town, more industrial than agricultural, which enjoys a very busy summer season. Innumerable tourists stop there briefly to visit the Aare Gorge before crossing over in their buses into the Rhône valley by the Grimsel pass and the Rhône Glacier. Hasliberg is a loose term for the four holiday villages, Hohfluh, Wasserwandi, Goldern and Reuti. It is doubtful whether there is any night-life here, or any luxury hotels. Nor will the skiing be too taxing for this is family holiday country of the kind of simplicity which the Swiss vacationer prefers.

ADELBODEN/LENK

Anyone searching for a traditional Bernese Oberland ski resort need look no further: Both these tidy little villages were important centres of pre-war skiing but, until very recently, it looked as if they would sink into obscurity for they had little to offer the

ADELBODEN LENK

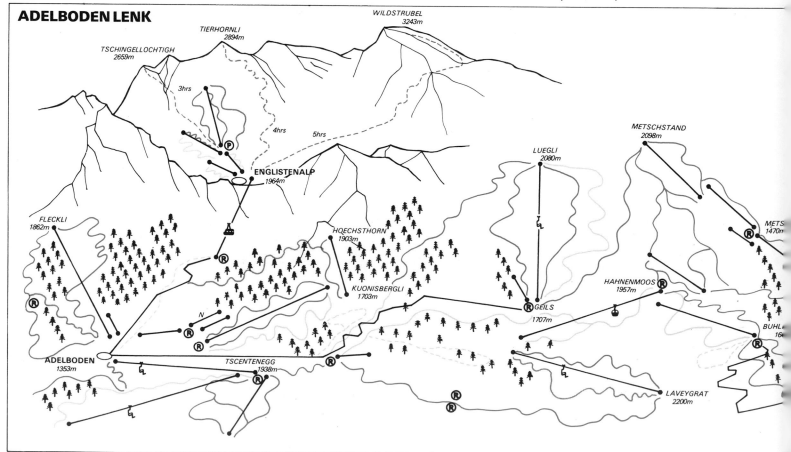

- WILDSTRUBEL 3243m
- TIERHORNLI 2894m
- TSCHINGELLOCHTIGH 2659m
- 3hrs
- 4hrs
- 5hrs
- Ⓟ
- ENGLISTENALP 1964m
- METSCHSTAND 2098m
- LUEGLI 2080m
- FLECKLI 1862m
- HOECHSTHORN 1903m
- METS 1470m
- Ⓡ
- Ⓡ
- KUONISBERGLI 1703m
- HAHNENMOOS 1957m
- Ⓡ
- N
- Ⓡ
- GEILS 1707m
- BUHL
- Ⓡ
- ADELBODEN 1353m
- TSCENTENEGG 1938m
- Ⓡ
- Ⓡ
- LAVEYGRAT 2200m
- Ⓡ

contemporary skier beyond a friendly ambience and easy access. The simple addition of two lifts, a gondola from Geils to Hahnenmoos and a chairlift to Luegli, joined these two villages and this virtually quadrupled the skiing area. Just what will happen to the quiet valleys if the long-discussed tunnel and motorway under the Rawil Pass above Lenk is ever built is a question which is certainly bothering the old friends of the area, for it will become the most important motorway link between Bern and the Rhône Valley and will inevitably produce major changes, not only to Lenk but also, possibly, to Crans where the road emerges.

However, none of this is likely to affect the tiny, roadless settlement of Engstligenalp above Adelboden from where you can comfortably climb the Wildstrubel and ski down onto the Plaine Morte and so to Crans-Montana. There are too few places like Engstligen where old ski values and quiet companionship, good food, and magnificent skiing provide a perfect holiday.

The view from Mürren is dramatic and impresses even the most blasé Alpinist.

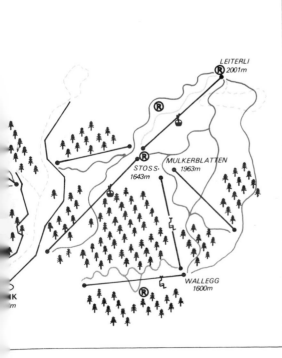

KRINNENBODEN 2260

OBERJOCH 2486 ®
FIRST 2200

WETTERHORN 3701

SCHRECKHORN 4078

EIGER 3970

MOENCH 40

SALZEGG 1990

EGG 1870
BORT 1570 ®

OBERHAUS 1350

GRINDELWALD 1050

BRANDEGG 1333 ®

ALPIGLEN 1615

ARVENGARTEN

HONEGG 22

BAERHAG 1715

2060

GRUND 943

ASPENHUBEL 960

LAGER 1800

WENGEN/GRINDELWALD/MURREN

Returning, after a long absence, to these familiar slopes, with my mind full of the super resorts of France, I was surprised at the confinement of what I had always thought of as one of the bigger skiing areas of Switzerland. It was a passing error, induced more by the presence, ranging high above the skier's head, of the mass of the Jungfrau Mönch and the Eiger. It is this very feeling of compactness, of knowing the whole skiing in intimate detail, that is part of the continued attraction of these three resorts.

Both Wengen and Mürren could be accused of being exclusive for they are small, with no automobiles. The British influence remains strong, particularly in the very limited ski area of Mürren where not being a member of the ruling caste, the Kandahar Club, makes you feel something of a second class citizen.

Wengen is less closely knit. The skiing is bigger and goes over the slightly forbidding cliffs of the Männlichen, down the long pleasant slopes to Grindelwald Grund and back again, or over the Kleine Scheidegg over Apiglen to the bottom of the same valley. It is possible to trudge the quarter of an hour up the hill to Grindelwald and the rather confined trails that drop steeply down through

94

JUNGFRAU 4158

EBNEFLUH 3962

BREITHORN 3782

TSCHINGELHORN 3577

JUNGFRAUJOCH 3454

SCHILTHORN 2970 Ⓡ

BIRG 2677

2404

EIGERGLETSCHER Ⓡ

SCHILTGRAT 2100

KLEINE SCHEIDEGG 2061

LAUBERHORN 2472

ALLMENDHUBEL 1908 Ⓡ

IWIXL 1830

WENGERNALP 1873 Ⓡ

MAULERHUBEL 2000

GIMMELWALD 1367

1800

BUMPS 1775

MÜRREN 1638

WINTEREGG 1578

867

ALLMEND

GUTSCHALP 1489

1460

INNER WENGEN 1260

MANNLICHEN 2372

WENGEN 1274

INFERNO

LAUTERBRUNEN 796

G. Nicholson

Bort. The rattling railway that gave birth to the concept of downhill only in the early 1920s may today be an anachronism, but no true Wengen enthusiast would ever suggest it should be replaced with a more congenial form of transport. Nor would they exchange the Wengen badges for all that the Kandahar could offer as they gaze across the deep Lauterbrunnen valley at their rivals and neighbours in Mürren with all the smugness

of the successful while they ski the lovely, powder-snow slopes from the Eigergletscher station to Wengernalp before reverting to the tamed moguls of the marked trails.

These three resorts are steeped in traditions and customs, though the origin of many of these is now lost. For example, Martha's Meadow in Mürren commemorates a win by a famous male skier entered for a race as 'Martha'. Or there are the infamous bumps

above Wengen that have now been softened in the interests of safety. The Palace Hotel in Mürren was where, in Room 10, Arnold Lunn spent his winters in an unbelievable confusion of paper. Despite several rebuildings, the hotel is still a Kandahar shrine. This may seem odd to the new ski generation, but it has a long history and an authentic atmosphere which has survived attack and erosion by modern ski ideas.

THE VALAIS

The Canton de Valais is the upper Rhône valley which runs from the river's source in the Rhône Glacier into the Lake of Geneva. The valley is a paradox for, although it is surrounded by the highest mountains in Europe, it enjoys for most of the year a sub-tropical climate more familiar to the Riviera than here, surrounded by glaciers. Historically the valley is fascinating. It served as a short-cut for countless invaders passing from northern Europe into Italy and as each invading horde pillaged its way up to the Simplon Pass the inhabitants retreated into the wild and inaccessible valleys. They still live a very private life despite the invasion of holiday makers, skilifts and twentieth century life. Despite the apparent prosperity which tourism has brought them, they are still, for the most part, subsistence farmers or work in the chemical and hydro-electrical industries of the Rhône Valley.

Skiing has played a relatively small part in the touristic development of the Valais. The attraction of the long scenically beautiful walks and the challenge of the 4000 metre summits combined with some world-class hotels spelled summer rather than winter vacations and apart from Crans-Montana and very much later, Zermatt, the Valais had little to offer the downhill skiers.

Within a very few years this changed dramatically as it became economically feasible to construct lifts and cableways into the territory of the ski mountaineer. Zermatt became a great spring skiing centre; Verbier joined up with Nendaz and Thyon; Val d'Annivier and the Lötschental hurried into the twentieth century; Champéry was linked with France and even the heart of summer vacation country, Belalp and the Alteschwald, joined the list of ski resorts.

The great joy for any skier in the Valais is the discovery that, despite fame, all these centres are still villages with very individual characters. Geography, conservation and conservatism will see that they stay unspoiled.

Verbier (right) has become one of the most popular resorts in the Swiss Alps for holidays spent with friends in a rented chalet.

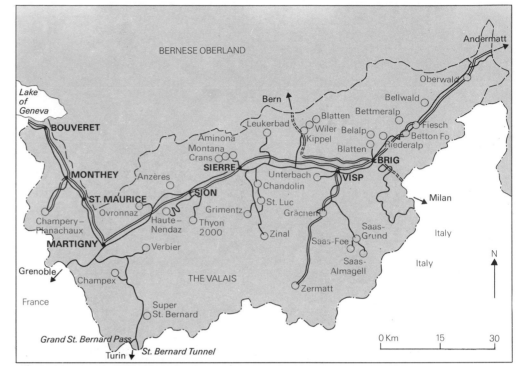

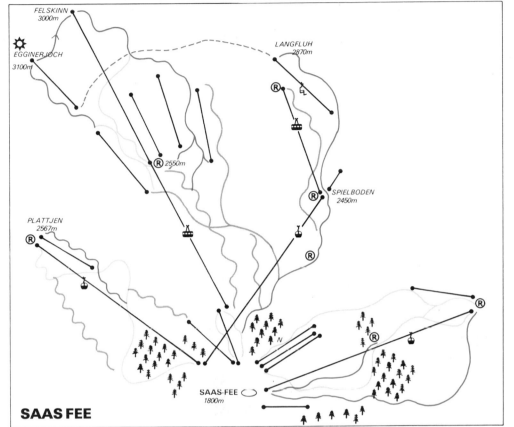

SAAS FEE

SAAS FEE

Less than ten miles (16 kilometres) from Zermatt as the choughs fly, nearly half-a-day's journey by train and automobile, lies Saas Fee in a shallow basin. It is a busy Valaisan village, car-less and dwarfed by a ring of 4000 metre mountains that lie so close you have to crick your neck to look up at them. Some find it claustrophobic and oppressive, others find it fascinating and a source of wonder.

The skiing hardly matches the scenery. It comprises a few shallow nursery slopes, a longer lift for novices up to the Hannig or a great leap into the expert class on the rather limited slopes around Langfluh or Felskinn or the scratchy steep run from Plattjen. It deserves a visit for a day or so, or a week learning to ski, but for anybody who is neither novice nor expert there is little pleasure, and for the expert even the most challenging run repeated throughout the day can become a bore. April and May are the best months to get the fullest enjoyment from these high skifields when the spring snow will make even the most dull trail a pleasure.

The old village of Saas Fee (below) is on the right while the new development extends up the valley.

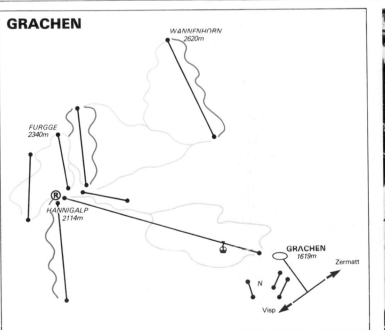

GRACHEN

GRACHEN

Grächen is a tiny lost hamlet high above the road and railtrack that leads from Stalden to Zermatt. At one time it was cut off from civilization for the winter months when the inhabitants struggled to survive. Now it is a flourishing collection of hotels and holiday homes with a surprisingly well-developed lift network. It is not the place for the expert, but for one who is in the intermediate classes it could be a near-ideal holiday centre.

Grächen also deserves to go into the

history of winter sport resorts for an extraordinary experiment carried out in the winter of 1977/78 when all the hotels left it to their visitors to pay just exactly what they felt their holiday was worth. All but a tiny handful paid the charges as advertised in the brochures.

MATTERHORN 4477

BREITHORN 4165

LUX 4091

KLEIN MATTERHORN 3883

TO CERVINIA

THEODUL PASS 3294

TESTA GRIGIA 3479

1979/80

FURGG SATTEL 3365

TROCKENER STEG 2939

3033

2891

2717

SCHWARZSEE 2582

2771

FURGG 2431

RIFFELBERG 2581

STAFFEL 2333

FURI 1864

WINKELMATTEN 1642

ZERMATT 1605

ZERMATT (*map previous page*)

Zermatt is without doubt the most famous, the most readily recognized and the most publicized of all mountain resorts. It has reached this status by virtue of a single mountain – the Matterhorn. That it has also become a ski resort of some renown is a less obvious development, and, truth be told, if the Matterhorn ceased to be, it is doubtful whether Zermatt could continue to hold its attraction for today's skiers.

The disadvantages are obvious. The lifts are too far away from the village and the bottle-neck of the Gornergrat railway, which carries the bulk of the moderate skiers to the only really satisfactory nursery slopes, is a constant irritant. Nor has the mechanization of the many, long slopes been entirely successful, for local considerations have frequently played a more important part in the planning than the eventual benefit to the skier. One particular sadness is the desecration of some of the greatest snow slopes in the Alps, such as the 1000 metres of uninterrupted single slope running from beside the Hohtäligrat above the Gornergrat

down to the edge of the Findelen Glacier above Grünsee, or, more familiar to present-day skiers, the so-called wall of death just below the Gornergrat. Even more irritating is the interminable wait for transport from Schwarzsee for all those whose technique is insufficient to master the often difficult and long run down by way of Staffel to Furri and then from Furri when the snow runs out. But these grumbles pale into insignificance against the incomparable advantages. Where else can you find such a village with an atmosphere that is the envy of all its competitors? Where else can you ski in such magnificent scenery, no matter which slope you choose nor which way you face? Where else can the gradual unfolding of the panorama as you grind your way up to Riffelalp or Gornergrat cause all passengers to watch and stare, be it their first or their hundredth journey?

The skiing can be easy, long, fast running from Testa Grigia or Theodul over the miles of smooth glacier, or undemanding journeying from Zermatt to Cervinia in Italy and back again, which even the first-year novice can master. There are a thousand variations

from Gornergrat to Riffelboden or Riffelalp, a 1000 metres run from Stockhorn to the little hut on Grünsee and still another 500 metres before going down through Blauherd and Tuftern to the entertaining path that finally ends at the foot of the Sunegga lift.

In the spring, if the glare of the snow has tired you, you can walk scented miles along the paths, through the larch, pine and bristle-cones, or sit in the thyme-scented meadows.

THE ALETSCH AREA
Riederalp/Bettmeralp/Eggishorn/Fiesch

The eight-kilometre shelf that lies above the upper Rhône valley just beyond Brig is one of the most beautiful landscapes of any mountain country. Facing south-west towards the mass of mountains that border Italy at this point, this might not, at first glance, seem to be a particularly auspicious location for any resort. But for some mysterious meteorological reason it attracts more than its fair share of snow and this, coupled with a magnificent sunshine record, makes it a perfect place for peace and contemplation and some not too exhausting skiing.

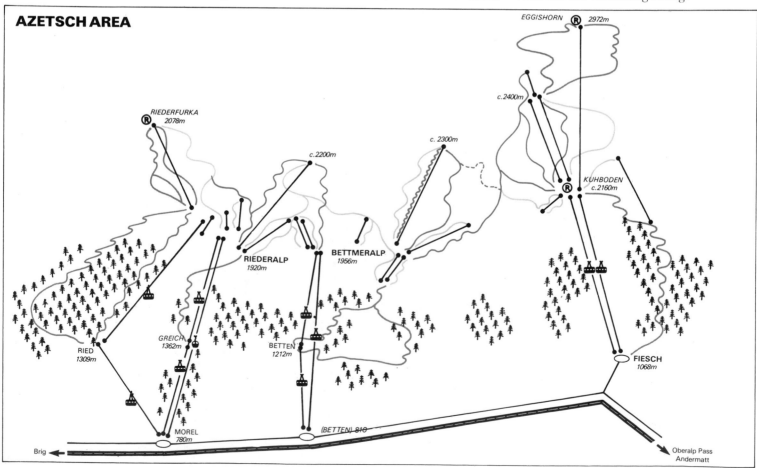

AZETSCH AREA

EGGISHORN Ⓡ 2972m

c.2400m

RIEDERFURKA Ⓡ 2078m

c.2200m

c.2300m

KUHBODEN c.2160m Ⓡ

RIEDERALP 1920m

BETTMERALP 1956m

GREICH 1362m

RIED 1309m

BETTEN 1212m

FIESCH 1068m

MOREL 780m

(BETTEN) 810

Brig ◀

Oberalp Pass Andermatt ▶

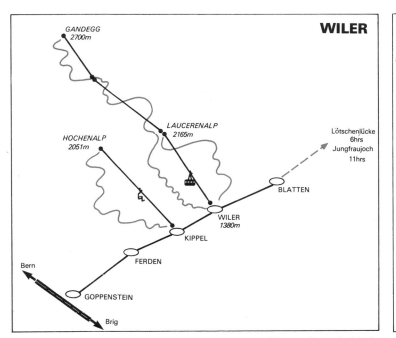

WILER

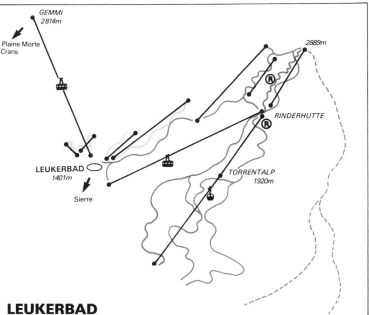

LEUKERBAD

WILER

Blatten/Kippel/Ferden

The Lötschental has often been called the lost valley. Accessible only from the exit station of the Lötschberg tunnel along a narrow road threatened by avalanche, this isolated valley is the home of many ancient customs, costumes and handicrafts which have survived almost unchanged since the middle ages. It is a fascinating place, and the end of the valley is equally fascinating because of the seven-hour climb to the ever-distant, perfect arch of the Lötschenlücke, the gateway to the Jungfrau district and the Aletsch glacier.

In Wiler and Blatten, the two principal villages, an attempt has been made to create a modern ski resort against embittered opposition from the conservation lobby. The result to date has been of mixed success and, despite six lifts which transport the skier close to the Gandegg glacier at 2700 metres, the skiing is still very limited except for the mountaineer. However, the days spent in this valley would not be wasted even if the downhill skiing were reduced to a minimum through poor snow conditions. It is rare to find a valley so picturesque and relatively unspoiled.

LEUKERBAD

Leukerbad owes its existence to the presence of a singularly unappetizing variety of mineral waters which you can either drink or swim in. They are said to cure most of the current human ailments. A long day's skiing on the limited but very testing trails of the Torrenthorn is likely to do a great deal more good. A 1400 metre drop on a solidly black trail, skied fast and fluently, will drop more pounds off you than a week of sulfurous water. Or perhaps you prefer to hoist your cross-country skis to the top of the Gemmi Pass cable-car and, not forgetting to pack your downhills on your back, skim across the ten miles of the Plaine Morte and swoop down to Crans-Montana for a day.

Verbier (map following page) is a sprawling village, and some of the many chalets occupy the area that was once the nursery area.

ROSA BLANCHE 3336

GRAPPON BLANC 2413

2350

(2100)

TORTIN 2050

R

THYON 2010

SUPER
NENDAZ
1730

(1700)

LES COLLONS 1800

1350

TRACOUET

PRARION

VEYSONNAZ 1233

HAUTE NENDAZ 1252

NENDAZ

SION

VERBIER/HAUTE
NENDAZ/THYON

Here is the proof that joining two or more neighbouring villages into one interconnected area can turn three moderate resorts into an accommodation base for a great ski centre. It is a pity that far too often petty politics and local jealousies have made this impossible.

Of the three, Verbier is by far the best known. It is the forerunner of the created,

third generation resorts, but carried out in a Swiss manner. Today it has a huge collection of small villas and chalets, a very few hotels and a considerable number of rather large, condominium-type houses which have spread and spread until they have engulfed the area which once formed the nursery slopes. Getting about in Verbier on a dark, snowy night can be a nightmare.

The skiing alternates between the two extremes of simple and very difficult. Once

upon a time the lift bottlenecks were unbelievable, particularly after spending the day around the Mont Gélé, Chassoure and Les Attelas. Now there is a great, lifted haute route that takes the skier from Verbier, down to Super Nendaz and over the Grappon Blanc, down to Thyon and back again. If you love your creature comforts and dislike crowds, living in Veysonnaz or even Thyon might well be preferable to an hotel in the featureless scatter of Verbier.

GRAND COMBIN 4314

MONT FORT 3328

MONT GELE 3023

2750

LA CHAUX 2200

LES ATTELAS 2730

LA COMBE 2460

LAC DE VAUX 2545

LES RUINETTES 2200

1525

2250

LES SAVOLEYRES 2354

LA TZOUMAS 1519

PIERRE A VOIR

VERBIER 1500

LE CHABLE 821

C. Nicholson

The most pleasant place to stay is in Sion, provided you own or have access to transport and can forego the expensive ambience of resort night-life. Sion hotels cost about 20 per cent less than the equivalent standard in the main resort.

Haute Nendaz and its satellite, Super-Nendaz, are the second example of Swiss third generation resorts. If you like concrete barracks in bare valley surroundings, Super-Nendaz could be acceptable. Haute Nendaz has regretfully failed to make a link with Verbier or even with Super Nendaz, and to commute to the big skiing you have to rely on the vagaries of public transport.

First impressions of this vast ski area could well be negative, particularly if your choice of residence has been faulty or you have arrived on a public holiday weekend. But the variety of villages and accommodation is such that you will, sooner or later, find exactly what you have always been looking for, and after only a week skiing here you will secretly be making plans to investigate the possibility of finding some barn or tumble-down chalet that could be renovated in order to spend the rest of your skiing days in this glorious area. For mountain ramblers it is as delightful in summer as it is for skiers in winter which makes it a very rare ski resort indeed. Most centres are likely to be a disappointment when visited in summer unless they have started life as a summer resort in the first place.

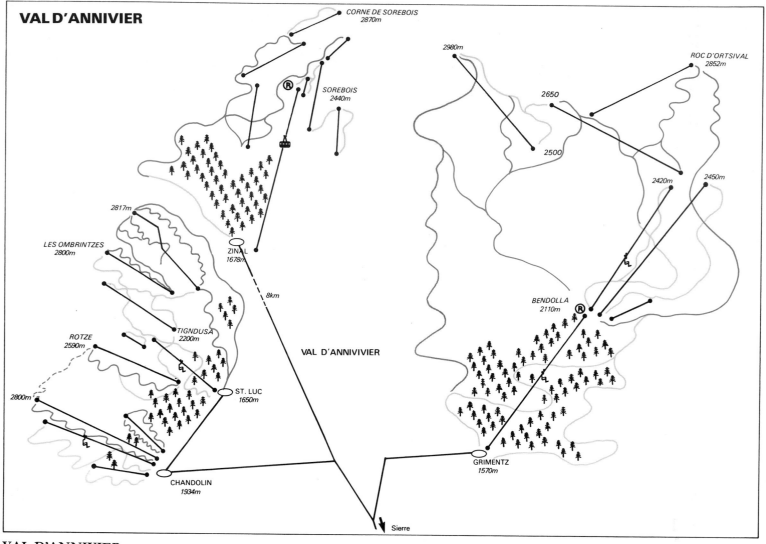

VAL D'ANNIVIER

CORNE DE SOREBOIS
2870m

2980m

ROC D'ORTSIVAL
2852m

2650

SOREBOIS
2440m

2500

2420m

2450m

2817m

LES OMBRINTZES
2800m

ZINAL
1678m

BENDOLLA
2110m

8km

TIGNDUSA
2200m

VAL D'ANNIVIVIER

ROTZE
2590m

ST. LUC
1650m

2800m

GRIMENTZ
1570m

CHANDOLIN
1934m

Sierre

VAL D'ANNIVIER
Grimentz/Zinal/Chandolin

The Val d'Annivier was one of the very last Valaisan valleys to receive the doubtful benefits of modern holiday traffic. Partly as a result of the work of the Dixence Hydroelectric complex, and partly to help the steadily dwindling population, these three delightful, picturesque villages lifted themselves into the twentieth century ski picture. The results are pleasant and for the moderate skier with transport at hand, the three resorts together provide very extensive skiing in scenically magnificent surroundings.

For anyone interested in genuine folklore, this is a valley worth visiting, though soon the only peasant costumes to be seen will be in shops and museums, and the traditional hard rye bread will be something grandmothers remember but grandchildren will not have the strength to eat.

ANZERE

Anzère, 14 kilometres from Sion, is one of only three genuinely purpose-built, third generation ski centres in Switzerland. Potentially it has much in its favour. It is small and well planned with good snow potential and it is very efficiently run. The skiing is moderate to easy and consequently well suited to novices and families with smaller children. Unfortunately, through the great choice of the French super-resorts with vast ski territories, the public has come to accept this as the norm and, failing to read their resort brochures with care, have arrived in Anzère and been disappointed, which is a pity for Anzère deserves a better fate.

Many people have wondered at the apparent failure of this Swiss third generation resort. Site, snow and planning cannot be faulted yet the second and later development stages have been postponed.

CHAMPERY

Champéry, at the head of the Val d'Illiez and within easy reach of Lausanne and Geneva, is the Swiss end of what the French term the 'Portes du Soleil' and for which there is a lift pass for both sides of the frontier. From Champéry this means a relatively simple ski switch to and from Avoriaz.

As a ski resort it makes up for restricted skiing by its charm and friendliness. The village itself has retained much old, pre-resort character with narrow streets, informal, unspectacular cafés and restaurants and an overall welcoming air that is as rare as it is pleasing.

For very many years this attractive village suffered from a complicated internecine war. Rival lift and ski school company quarrels caused the resort to suffer. Within a winter of these conflicts being resolved the village began to flourish.

ANZERE

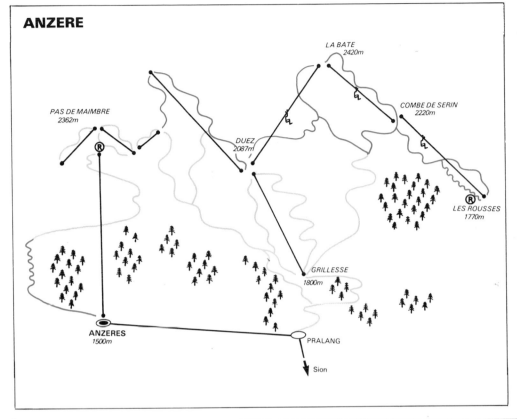

LA BATE
2420m

PAS DE MAIMBRE
2362m

COMBE DE SERIN
2220m

DUEZ
2087m

R

R LES ROUSSES
1770m

GRILLESSE
1800m

ANZERES
1500m

PRALANG

Sion

CRANS-MONTANA (*following page*)
Vermala/Aminoma

Like a vast balcony above the Rhône valley, gazing across to the high mountains of the Valais and Chamonix, this string of linked villages are one continuous vacation resort. A very fashionable agglomeration of hotels and vacation villas make up what is commonly known as Crans but whose official designation (after much argument among the five communities that govern it) is Crans-Montana.

The skiing is big and very varied, well divided into manageable sections both above and below the tree-line, and extends right up to 3000 metres on the Plaine Morte. Only one trail deserves very special mention and that is the 11 kilometre run from Plaine Morte into the village centre of Montana, a drop of nearly 1600 metres. To ski all the marked trails would be to cover the distance of 110 kilometres, and these are not just minor variants of a main trail. There is only one fly in this particular ointment, and that is the almost total lack of public transport from one end of the development to the other. The journey involves an expensive five-kilometre taxi ride or a very long trudge in skiboots.

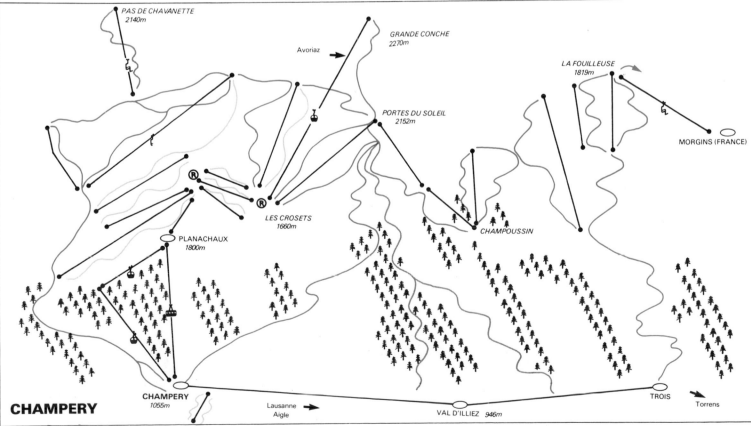

PAS DE CHAVANETTE
2140m

GRANDE CONCHE
2270m

Avoriaz

LA FOUILLEUSE
1819m

PORTES DU SOLEIL
2152m

MORGINS (FRANCE)

R

R

CHAMPOUSSIN

LES CROSETS
1660m

PLANACHAUX
1800m

CHAMPERY
1055m

CHAMPERY

Lausanne
Aigle

VAL D'ILLIEZ   946m

TROIS

Torrens

GLETSCHERHORN 2943

ROHRBACHSTEIN 2950

PLAINE MORTE 2927 Ⓡ

BELLA LUI 2543 Ⓡ

MONTAGNE DE RAWIL

2267

CRYD'ERR 2207 Ⓡ

CHETSERON 2120 Ⓡ

1960

PAS DU LOUP 2000

MERBE 1920 Ⓡ

VERDET 1883

GRAND SIGNAL 1715

ARNOUVAZ 1703

PLANS MAYENCE 1622

Ⓡ

1520

CRANS

VERMALA 1495

MONTANA 1470

CROSS COUNTRY AREA

WILDSTRUBEL 3243

ROTHORN 3102

MT BONKIN 2995

2465

⊛ PETIT BONVIN 2400

2570

LA TZA 2202

LES VIOLETS
2220
LA TOULA
1963

⊛

(1800)

1900

CABANE DES BOIS

PLUMACHIT 1750

AMINOMA 1437

HIGH LEVEL CROSS COUNTRY

LES BARZETTES 1500

1473

M.LYNN 78

West Germany

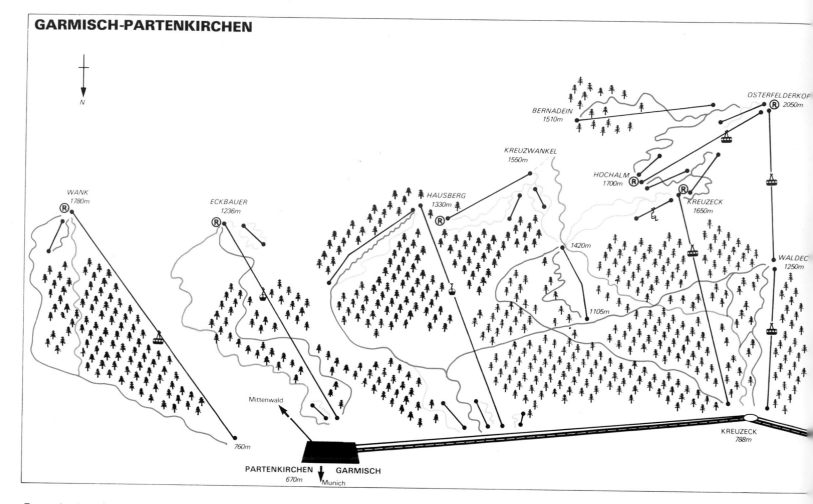

GARMISCH-PARTENKIRCHEN

Over the last seven years, West Germany has shown a greater increase in ski-associated industries than any other nation, and the majority of foreign visitors to the Alpine skiing grounds are German. This growth has been very greatly stimulated by the continued success of German skiers, both Alpine and Nordic, in the World and Olympic competitions and this stimulus has extended itself to the creation of a very large number of small ski centres in Bavaria, the Allgäu and, for purely Nordic activities, the Black Forest and the Eiffel Hills.

Many of these centres have little more than a few miles of prepared loipes or a few lifts installed on low, pre-Alpine hills. Snow cover is always doubtful as the hills lie well to the north of the main Alpine chain and consequently do not benefit from snowfalls engendered by the cooling of southern, maritime air. They have to depend upon major snow falls coming from the Arctic and persisting into the central plains of Europe.

There are about 45 resorts and ski areas stretching in a wide arc from the east of Munich to Frankfurt, and a few in the Sauerland lying between Dortmund and Kassel which are almost entirely devoted to Nordic activities. A similar area is the Bayerischer Wald, the frontier hills between Bavaria and Czechoslovakia and the Frankenwald on the northern boundaries of Bavaria.

The most popular of the Nordic areas is the Black Forest which, since the great resurgence of interest in Nordic skiing, is providing a wealth of facilities in an idyllic setting of gentle hills and deep forest where the snow lies longest.

Both the areas described here have shown an originality on their wintersports planning that could be an example to many a more famous resort and both can provide the skier with sufficient interest and variety for a week or a fortnight's vacation.

GARMISCH-PARTENKIRCHEN

Garmisch-Partenkirchen is a complete winter sports resort, providing everything from bob-running, through skating and curling, to high-Alpine skiing and long cross-country trekking. It was also the scene of the 1936 Winter Olympics and the 1978 Alpine World Championships.

The downhill trails are divided into three areas. The Zugspitze is certainly the most comprehensively exploited 3000 metre mountain in the world. Its tunnels, lifts, railways, restaurants, gift shops, terraces and maze of walkways would baffle a well-educated mole. To get back to the hotels skiers either take the train or cableway, or do the very entertaining Gatterle run into Austria. This involves a one-and-a-half hour climb and a taxi-ride home from the direction of Ehrwald. For those who like steep runs there is an exit from the tunnel at 1820 metres that, after the first very steep and unprepared 300 metres of slope, eases up and turns into a pleasant long run to Eibsee or Grainau.

The Hausberg/Kreuzwankel/Osterfelder-

108

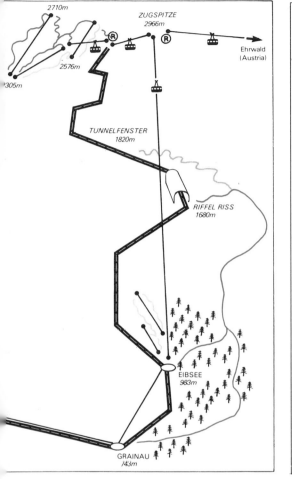

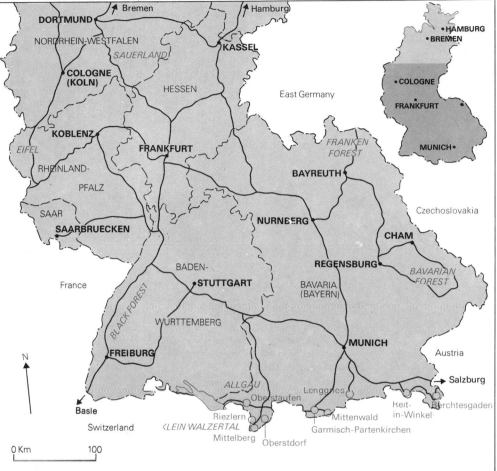

kopf group forms one cohesive area, well provided with lifts which are interlinked and which give the moderate skier a great deal of pleasure. The long black championship course from the Kreuzeck summit to the valley can be extremely difficult in poor snow.

One great asset of this area which deserves commendation is the provision of pedestrian paths along the sides of the main trails. These paths can be reached by chairlift or cable-car, and non-skiing friends and relatives can watch and be part of the day's activities and meet skiers at one of the many mountain lodges for a mid-day meal or mid-afternoon refreshment. The extent of these walkways is quite unique to Garmisch.

Two more, smaller areas complete the trails of this large and complex resort. Neither the Eckbauer nor the Wank offer very varied runs but are of greater interest to dryshod sight-seers and summer visitors.

The old Bavarian village character has not been lost in Garmisch-Partenkirchen despite the modern buildings and developments.

OBERSTDORF

Oberstdorf is an attractive village (*left*) which is small enough to give a feeling of unity but at the same time large enough to be able to offer all varieties of winter sports except a bobrun. Three ski areas, unlinked, provide moderate skiing and the wide valley floor has a good selection of cross-country trails. The ski-flying arena is only operative once or twice a year for the annual world championships. The Fellhorn provides the cross-over point into the Austrian Klein-Walser Tal.

The Nebelhorn and the Schönblick have followed the Garmisch example of providing pedestrian walkways parallel to the trails.

The Klein-Walser Tal is still a very under-developed area but one which compensates with a number of small, unspoiled villages and the essential Austrian ambience. Riezlern is the obvious place to stay as it provides the cross-over into Oberstdorf.

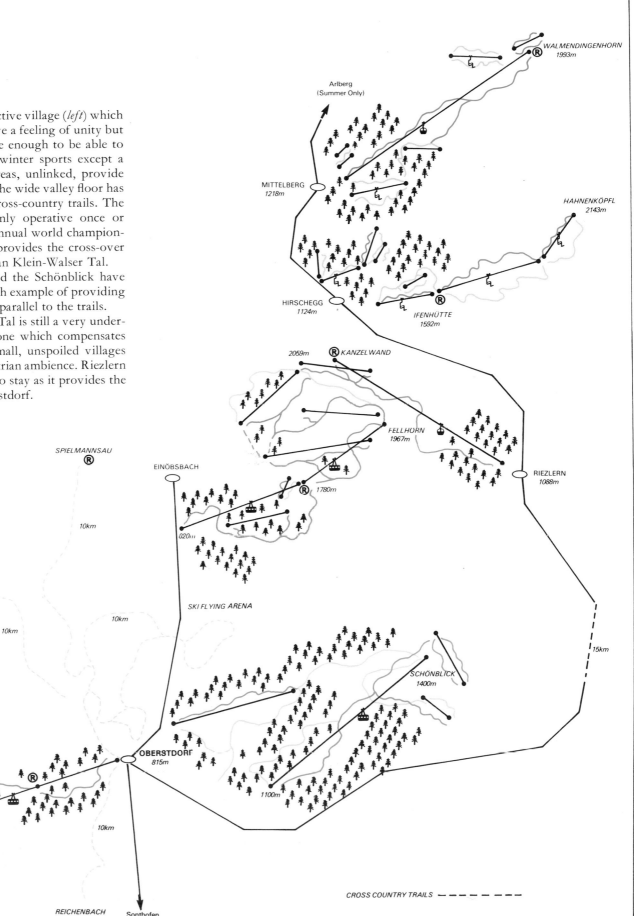

WALMENDINGENHORN
1993m

Arlberg
(Summer Only)

MITTELBERG
1218m

HAHNENKÖPFL
2143m

HIRSCHEGG
1124m

IFENHÜTTE
1592m

2059m

Ⓡ KANZELWAND

SPIELMANNSAU
Ⓡ

EINÖBSBACH

FELLHORN
1967m

RIEZLERN
1088m

OYTAL
Ⓡ

10km

Ⓡ 1780m

820m

10km

SKI FLYING ARENA

10km

10km

15km

SCHÖNBLICK
1400m

OBERSTDORF
815m

1100m

NEBELHORN
1929m
Ⓡ

10km

CROSS COUNTRY TRAILS - - - - - - -

2224m

REICHENBACH

Sonthofen

111

Austria

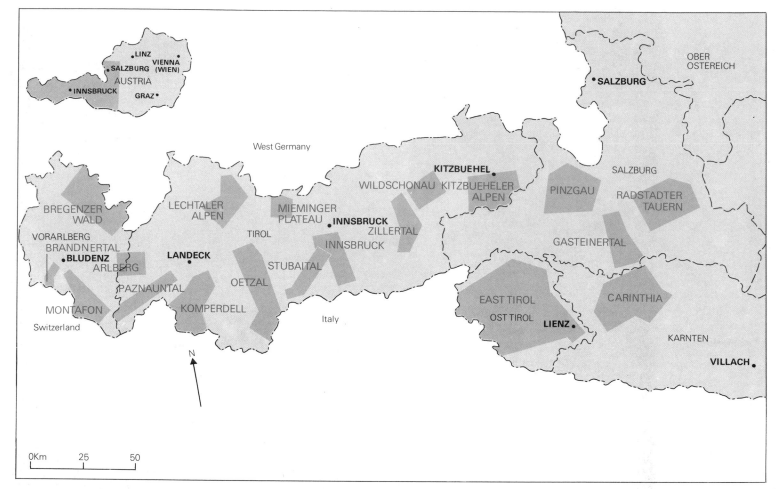

Skiing, for most people in the world, is synonymous with Austria. This is probably the result of the publicity arranged by tour operators who dominated the winter holiday industry immediately after the end of the Second World War, when travel was both restricted and expensive. A consistent run of Austrian ski racing successes, which received international media coverage, pointed sharply to the effectiveness of skiing in Austria, which in turn promoted an equipment industry that now dominates the world.

The traditional resorts created an expectation in the holidaymaker of friendly village life, and they have managed to retain this ambience of welcoming *Gemütlichkeit* despite the rampaging growth of modern ski service stations. The rustic atmosphere grew from the days when winter-sports holidays began in the 1930s. The fact that it is now artificially contrived is unimportant because it continues to

meet the demands of an insatiable public. The components of this atmosphere, such as rustic architecture and small friendly bars and restaurants, have been exported and cruelly copied and parodied by others who know it only by report. Yet today, when the price of an airline ticket buys a skiing holiday in Alaska or Courchevel, Zermatt or Mount Cook in New Zealand, Austria remains for most serious skiers an essential pilgrimage. When skiers arrive they find that the reality far exceeds the hopes engendered by the exports and copies. The attraction cannot be explained either by the excellence of the sport – for on an international comparison the skiing is moderate to poor with only one or two notable exceptions – nor by the superficiality of the 'Tirolean evening' (which in reality is Bavarian), nor by the purely commercial atmosphere which has been deliberately fostered as a sought-after top-dressing. The true reasons for both

fame and popularity lie much deeper in the origins of these ski villages: the gentleness of the pre-Alpine scenery, the small villages and their hidden valley groupings, and above all the fact that skiing seems as natural an occupation as it is in western Norway. The soft contours of the hills, the wooded glades, the inviting Alpine meadows all seem to have been deliberately contrived to please the eye.

The sport came to Austria with the skiing and ski school activity on the Arlberg. Zdarsky, Sohm and Bilgeri are the historical landmarks essential to the study of skiing's development, but immaterial to the modern ski resort. At a time when skiing in Davos, the Bernese Oberland and Villars was still something of an adventure sport, the Arlberg showed that it could be an organized and contained activity for the ordinary townspeople. The list of over 400 of Austria's resorts grew up because of this small, Arlberg beginning and it is to their eternal credit that they continue to prove to the world that the sport is not confined to the High Alps and that it is not necessary to find resorts above the timberline in order to enjoy a full day's skiing.

Skiing in Austria is essentially pre-Alpine. That is to say, it is restricted by geography to the hills and mountains that are the outlying slopes of the main Alpine chain that forms the southern boundary of Austria. In practice this means that the mountain tops are about 2000 metres high and the villages which have become the ski resorts are those same villages which were farming centres. They are located at around the 1000 metre level, and there is a sound reason for this. Until late in the 18th century it was considered to be impossible to live reasonably above 1000 metres. Consequently farmers working and living above this height were tax-exempt, and, in practice, also exempt from compulsory military service with the Ducal armies. The Tirol was an independent Dukedom under the protection of the Kings of Bavaria until the rebellion in 1809 led by Andreas Hofer.

Tradition, initially, and later careful conservation and building restrictions have kept virtually every one of these villages visually untouched, neat, charming, hospitable and unique. The hotels are, for the most part, extended versions of the original inns and date from the late fifteenth to the late seventeenth centuries. Modern additions have kept to the original architectural lines and it is not uncommon to find the *Alte Post* to be a hundred years younger than it neighbouring *Neue Post*.

There are serious drawbacks to this attractive rustic picture. Ever since the completion of the motorway network which links Bavaria and Austria, these once isolated villages have been brought within commuting distance of Munich. The result is that the villages are drowning in a sea of motor vehicles. It is easy now to say that provision should have been made for this foreseeable eventuality, that parking areas should

Bad Kleinkirchheim in Carinthia is a modern spa and sports resort. The pleasantly wooded, pre-Alpine countryside favours both skiers and walkers, summer holidays as well as winter-sports.

have been provided outside the village squares, that relief roads should have been constructed to channel the automobiles away from the narrow alleys. For the most part geography has made these solutions impracticable and even where they could be carried out the cost would have been so immense to be totally beyond the meagre finances of the village. The hordes of day-visitors that beseige the more popular villages every weekend are not a great source of income. They spend little beyond their lift pass and possibly a glass or two of beer or a coffee. They frequently scare away the holiday-maker who is the real money source for such small resorts.

There is a further disadvantage to the village-based resort. It is not uncommon to find neighbouring villages with adjoining territories to be quite incapable of arriving at any common ski planning so that what could be a large and attractive ski area is artificially limited owing to internal politics and personal feuds. This situation is very slowly being overcome, but it will remain an irritation to the serious skier for many years yet.

The sport itself should not be disparaged simply because the indicated heights appear low and, by comparison with say Val d'Isère in France or Zermatt in Switzerland, 'minor skiing'. A more attentive examintion of these apparently poorly mechanized, wooded hills will show that most, if not all, provide at least a 1000 metre drop and sufficient challenge to satisfy the most demanding technical expert. But the most enjoyable skiing will be found by the moderate, vacation skier. The schools are, for the most part, good and entertaining, the skiing is difficult enough to challenge but never frighten and nearly always there is a comfortable escape route. Snow cover, except in the most extreme cases of snow drought, is adequate despite the low altitude. Avalanches are rare and the general maintenance of trails, though not up to the super-perfection of Courchevel, is satisfactory. All-in-all it is good, entertaining, natural skiing.

Seefeld, Tirol is a most attractive holiday town which has gone out of its way to entertain non-sportsmen as well as every category of active skier.

THE VORARLBERG

The Voralberg is the province literally 'infront of the Arlberg'. Surrounded by Germany to the north, and by Switzerland and the glacier-hung Silvretta range to the south, it is the long flat alluvial plain which leads into the heart of Austria.

For the skier there is not a great deal of choice, but what there is is magnificent. To the north of the old market town of Bludenz lies the Bregenzerwald, an isolated, little-known area of deep forest, astonishing gorges and entertaining skiing.

To the south of Bludenz is the Montafon, which burrows into the tortuous valleys that lead up into the Silvretta range. Close by is the Brandnertal, a long narrow valley which is undistinguished except for Brand which has a long single road linking its various components.

It was in the Montafon that the earliest fully comprehensive ski tourist parties were organized by Erna Low during the 1930s. No one, least of all the few innkeepers of Brand and Gargellen, could have foreseen just what Miss Low had started.

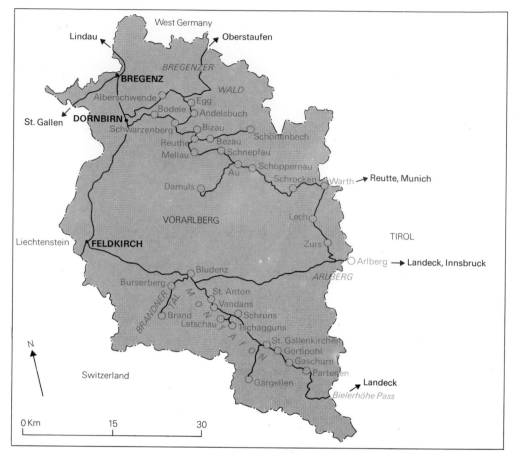

BREGENZERWALD

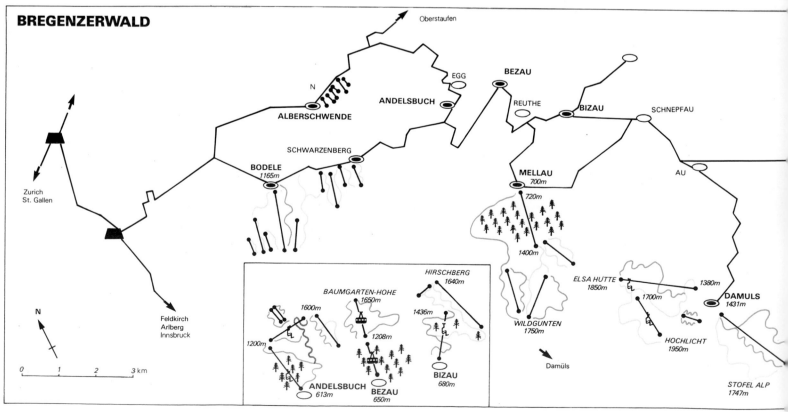

THE BREGENZERWALD

The Bregenzerwald was virtually uninhabited until late in the eleventh century when it was systematically colonized over a period of 200 years by peasants from the Lake of Constance. They built large communities with widely spaced houses and broad streets, and this pattern has survived. The effect is to give the area an atmosphere of prosperity and continuity. By the fifteenth century a farmers' republic had been achieved and to this day the area retains a degree of political independence unique in Austria.

The country is heavily forested with wild, deep gorges and strange rocky peaks that seem to dominate the valley like sentinels protecting the gentle slopes and fields on their far side. The valleys run diagonally across the compass, reaching their highest points in the south-east where they cross over into the Lechtal.

Coming up from Dornbirn, the traveller first passes Alberschwende and Bödele where a collection of nursery lifts give playing space to every known form of snow vehicle on fine Saturdays. Serious skiers stay in Bezau, 'the capital', or in Bizau, Andelsbuch, Mellau, Schoppernau, Schröcken or Damüls. At present the whole area still has the quiet, contented air of a 1930's ski resort, with virtually

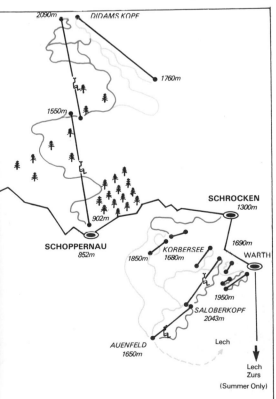

no night-life, but good hotels, excellent food and exceptional friendliness. It also boasts the resort, Schröcken, that has the highest annual snowfall in the entire western Alps which is a reputation worth having.

Bezau is the hub of the Bregenzerwald skiing. Although it has virtually no skiing of its own (the Baumgartenhöhe is essentially a summer walking area) 30 minutes by car will take the skier to any of the better-equipped little villages and it is therefore a very good centre for motoring.

The main mountain for Bezau is Bizau's Hirschberg where even a very moderate skier can enjoy an exhilarating 1000 metres of open skiing. There is more fun to be had here than the map would suggest. The Hotel Gams in Bezau has been in the same family for four generations and is the place to stay, for not only can it provide transport to all the other villages but has enough expertise in the family to be able to offer truly sound advice. Like other places in the Bregenzerwald, ski school is uncommon and those who come to ski here have come to have a holiday, to relax and to ski – not to learn to ski but to practise skills already acquired.

Schoppernau is not really a village, any

more than its near neighbour Au. They are scattered settlements of farms and guest-houses. But Schoppernau does have the Didamskopf, 1100 metres above the village. This is the longest and most enjoyable run in the Bregenzerwald. The skiing is so open and the variations so numerous that it deserves an above average rating.

Damüls is quite different to the other Bregenzerwald villages – a fact that is realized as soon as the church tower can be seen peeping over a steep ridge. It lies on the edge of the Bregenzerwald and was colonized from the Walsertal at the time of the great religious migration from the Rhône Valley during the 14th century.

The skiing in Damüls is moderate and in theory a great deal more could be made of the slopes available – and perhaps will be now that there is a tenuous link over into the Mellau area.

Mellau is the nearest to a third generation ski resort that the Bregenzerwald is ever likely to see. It is an attempt to rush this sleepy area into 1970s skiing, but its success remains to be seen. It has the only discotheque in the whole valley which, if precedents are anything to go by, will be filled by local youths rather than dance-hungry vacationers.

An ambitious lift programme for Mellau has been halted in mid-stride but a gondola does take the skier on his way to Damüls and a further T-bar to the Wildgunten will allow him to slide down into the Damüls ski fields. To get back takes a bit of a scramble for there is no direct connecting lift from the Damüls side.

Schröcken lies at the foot of the Hochtann Pass which leads to Warth and, in summer, to Lech and Zürs.

Warth, geographically part of the Lechtal, is however part of the Bregenzerwald Development Committee since in winter it is completely cut off from Lech. Warth's skiing, based on a tight little huddle of hotels and houses, is rather messy and incomplete. Pending the eventual construction of a lift from Schröcken to the Körbersee the only approach is from the Tannberg Pass by means of a rather complicated scatter of lifts. It is possible to ski from the top of the pass down into Warth, but the return journey requires a few minutes foot-climbing. The traverse to Lech on skis is a very entertaining spring journey as is the return, but it should not be undertaken except under very safe conditions. It requires climbing on foot for about 30 minutes.

There is fast, open skiing on the upper slopes of the Hirschberg above Bizau in the Bregenzerwald.

VERWALL RANGE

KALTENBERG 28

TRITTKOPF 2722

ALBONAGRAT 2358

VALLUGA 2811

2423

HEXENBODEN 2327

STUBEN 1407

SEEKOPF 22

TRITTALM 1944

ZURS 1720

1870

RUFIKOPF 2350

WIESELE

1570

WOESTERTALI

LECH 1445

STUBENBACH 1440

SILVRETTA RANGE

FLEXENSPITZE 2623

MADLOCH 2423

ZURSERSEE 2150

OMESHORN 2543

STIERLOCH

ZUG 1511

KRIEGER HORN 2178

ZUGER HOCHLICHT 2377

2131

1800

OBERLECH 1730

C. Nicholson

THE ARLBERG I
Lech/Zürs/Stuben

Although the term 'Arlberg' should strictly only refer to the mountain and pass itself, in other words to the hospiz of St Christoph, it is now universally regarded as being the general name for the five major resorts that use the mountains in the area around the Arlberg. It has become a kind of mecca for every serious skier and for many it remains the world's finest ski ground. There has been skiing here since Colonel Viktor Sohm started his own school in 1901 at St Christoph.

The area divides naturally into three skiing categories: Lech for novices and moderates, Zürs for advanced steep-slope skiers and St Anton for advanced pilgrims to the home of Hannes Schneider and the Arlberg Kandahar race course.

Stuben, lying at the fork in the roads to Zürs and the Arlberg Pass, safely ensconced behind its high avalanche protection walls, is really nothing more than a large car park, a couple of hotels and some very old, mountain farmers' huts. But it possesses a run which is possibly the longest sustained, difficult trail in the world. The Albona direct face is 950 metres of continuous black steepness over ground which can never be groomed. It takes a hardy enthusiast to brave the bitterly cold, two-stage chairlift to the start of this incomparable *Steilhang*, and woe betide the careless skier who finds himself on it when the snow is wind blown or sun crusted.

Zürs will make the advanced skier stop and wonder as he breasts the Flexen Pass from Stuben and gazes down on this most perfect of all ski valleys. Zürs was created by skiers, for skiers and there is no compromise for walkers or loungers.

For the deep-snow experts the Trittkopf cable-car opens up the fantastic variety of Alps called Ochsenboden. Above all, the Himmeleck, which no map will ever indicate for only once or twice a season is it safe to ski, will keep the skier dreaming even after he has visited all the resorts in the world.

Lech, which can be reached by ski from the Madloch or by road from Zürs, was once a beautiful medieval village. It has the blackest of black runs from the Rüfikopf down to Lech which is never prepared or even marked. Also running down towards Lech from the Zürsersee are the Wiesele runs, the black untracked powder routes which some connoisseurs rate even higher than the Albona Steilhang.

BRAND/BURSERBERG

Brand stretches nearly three kilometres along both sides of the road so it can hardly be called a village. But it is one of the oldest winter vacation resorts in Austria and it has earned a remarkable reputation for good ski holidays. The night life is uninhibited, even if you do have quite a walk to reach it. The scenery is magnificent and the skiing is just difficult enough to be a challenge to the average performer and yet easy enough to flatter his skiing. The main nursery area is around and below the Niggenkopf and can be classed as one of the most delightful nurseries anywhere in the Alps. The area is served by two T-bars. It is dotted, quite haphazardly, with a variety of fir trees, any one of which can be used as a slalom pole. Even the worst weather cannot stop the skiing here.

Bürserberg is little more than an additional nursery area for Brand. The small cable-car to Tschengla is for local inhabitants only.

THE MONTAFON

A great deal has been written about the Montafon, not least by Ernest Hemingway who spent a number of winters there in the 1920s, though he seems to have done little skiing and a great deal of drinking and card playing with the local policemen.

For most tourists, the Montafon is merely the way into the Silvretta toll road that leads in summer to Paznaun. For ski mountaineers it is the beginning or the end of a week or more spent climbing the many Silvretta summits. The arrival of the hydroelectric engineering complex of Illwerke GmbH tur-

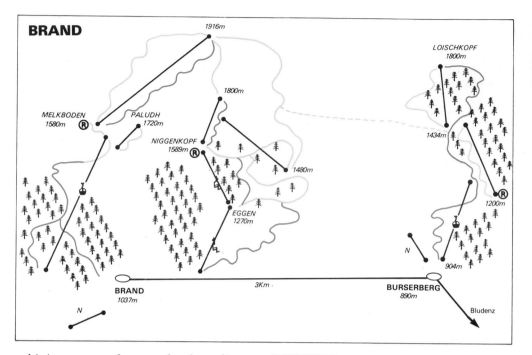

ned it into a gem of an area for the ordinary skier, for the company built and improved roads, set up mountain transport and made possible the subsequent ski tourist development.

The tourist organization provides a single lift pass to nine villages and enough skiing to keep anyone occupied for a few weeks. The Silvretta Nova circuit has proved to be almost too popular and, for the first time in its ski history, Gargellen is not the only Montafon village to boast of being sold out for two and more seasons ahead. The villages below will soon have merged into one large dormitory.

SCHRUNS

Schruns is neither a village nor is it quite a town. Whatever the niceties of classification are, it deserves its record of being the first Austrian resort to make the old centre free of cars. The atmosphere of this otherwise undistinguished place has improved dramatically as a result.

Skiing from Schruns is strictly a one-mountain affair served by a cable-car and a collection of T-bars and a chairlift. Kappell, the cable-car terminal, is a magnificent viewpoint and the restaurant also deserves a star or two as a mountain restaurant. But skiers should beware of the long red run that dives off down into Schruns, particularly if lunch on Kappell has fortified the courage a little too much. Like many such runs it starts very innocently but once the skier is committed, it shows its teeth with a vengeance. The route can be abandoned at a half-way stage but if the skier continues the attempt, and the conditions are even slightly icy, the long, left-hand traverse will shoot him unmercifully and completely out of control to a grandstand finish under the cable-car wires.

TSCHAGGUNS/VANDANS

These two villages, really suburbs of Schruns, have been able to develop as very satisfactory, small, winter-sports centres, as a result of the activities of the hydroelectric works being carried out in the area. From Tschagguns village the chairlift and T-bar to the Hochegga provide 900 metres of moderately dif-

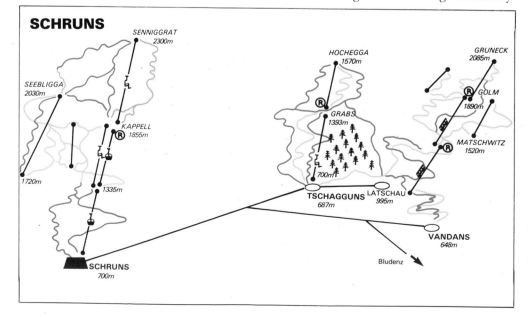

ficult skiing while the rather primitive funicular from Latschau, above Vandans, and a further T-bar open up a surprising drop of 1400 metres to Vandans. The skiing is easy to moderate and a shallow traverse across grazing meadow connects this area with the lift at Tschagguns. The run from Latschau to Vandans is parallel to the soft-snow, competition luge track that is also open to non-competitive visitors.

GARGELLEN

Gargellen ranks with the two or three most delightful skiing villages in Austria. It has no particular architectural merit, the skiing is average to difficult, but it will be impossible to get a hotel room at less than twelve months' notice. The answer probably lies in one single hotel, the Madrisa, that has become a legend among Austrian holiday skiers. The ambience envelops the visitor from the first moment he walks in and the memories it

leaves are ineradicable. The memories are not just mine, because of some trick of circumstance, but thousands of skiers from all over the world remember the Madrisa as the nucleus of all that a skiing holiday should be.

They may also remember skiing down from the Schafberg after an ample lunch and mistakenly embarking on the innocent-looking trail home rather than risking the humiliation of chairlifting to the Gargellen Alpe. This black trail is what the Austrians call 'interesting'.

THE SILVRETTA NOVA
St Gallenkirchen/Gortipohl/Gaschurn

Three villages make up the dormitory area for the circuit known as the Silvretta Nova, though it is already difficult to decide where one stops and the next starts. Skiers can enter the circuit from either end, though for most Gaschurn is the first choice for from here they can ski all except the Garfrescha slopes and

return to Gaschurn. However a more careful study of the topography would show that this is a mistake for the natural flow of the trails is from Garfrescha to Alpe Nova and this route is closed by the shallow run of about 2 kilometres back from Alpe Nova to the bottom of the first Gampinger lift. The slopes here are completely open and any trail mark is little more than a suggestion – a fact that can be a problem if the visibility becomes bad. The return down to Gaschurn is the most testing of the skiing here unless you choose the circuitous blue trail that follows a widely bending summer road.

The very steep, heavily mogulled slope from the Berg Restaurant down to Alpe Nova is one that should not be attempted light-heartedly even though it is comparatively short. Once committed there is no escape – the effect of which entertains the long queues waiting at the bottom of the lift and causes the unfortunate skier acute embarrassment.

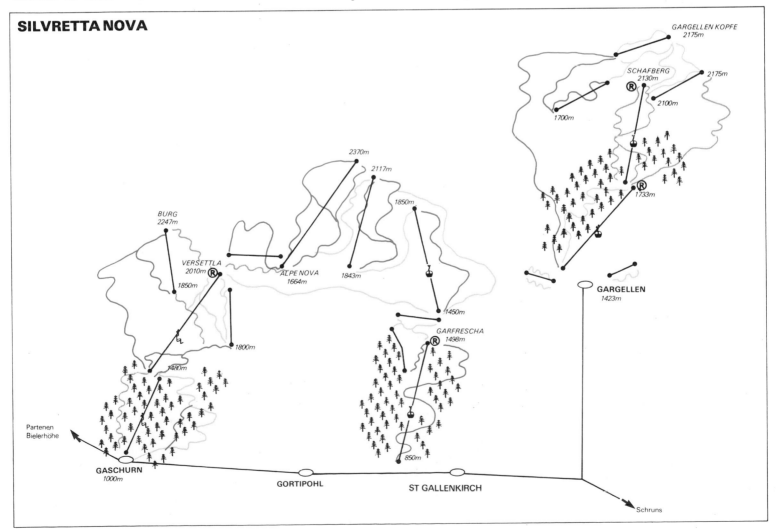

THE ARLBERG II
St Christoph/St Anton

The Arlberg, less of a mountain than a mountain pass, divides the Province of Vorarlberg from the Tirol and neatly divides the Anton skiers from the Zürs variety. It is a distinction born of history with the creation of the Arlberg ski school on the Tirol side of the Pass and, to this day, more than 70 years later, the distinction is still valid. Even the skiing country looks different and where Zürs lies open to inspection the drive to St Christoph from Stuben reveals nothing of the glories to come.

St Christoph, at the top of the Arlberg Pass, is an ungainly collection of ugly hotels. A chairlift and a cable-car link it into the main St Anton ski fields at the Galzig and it is a not uncommon starting point for those with transport who wish to avoid the impossible and unruly queues for which St Anton has never been able to find a solution. It is also the seat of Professor Stefan Kruckenhauser's ski laboratory where much of the finesse and idiosyncracy of Austrian skiing were, and still are, developed. People who learned to ski in Austria during the heyday of the Austrian methods have a very distinctive style.

St Anton is a place you either hate deeply or worship senselessly. It is an overcrowded town which, despite the main road by-pass, is always choked with cars. It is a place where you are always finding yourself at the wrong end – for whatever purpose. And it is a place with the odour of skiing sanctity. Whatever you may think of it, it remains the ultimate goal for most serious skiers. It does however present hazards to the most expert of skiers. The skiing is difficult to extremely difficult and the ski school has a standard higher than anywhere else in the world. Many a pride has been severely punctured by ski class allocations. Some, insulted by such behaviour, have gone off to ski on their own on the great classic trails of the Galzig and Valluga – and have discovered to their chagrin that what they believed to be faultless technique was little more than amateur fumbling when confronted by these gigantic, mogulled steepnesses. Perhaps discouraged by this ground they move over to supposedly easier territory on the Gampen to ski there the competition runs – and to discover that their road to ski perfection has lengthened.

It is to the credit of the Hannes Schneider ski school in St Anton that it has the ski instructors who can handle this élite with confidence.

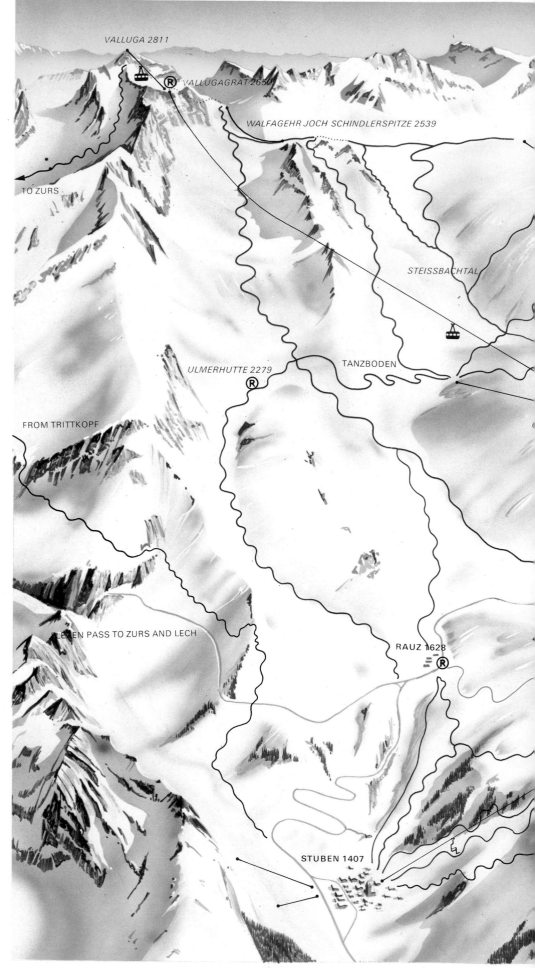

2326

GAMPBERG 2401

GAMPEN 1845

Ⓡ

BRANDKREUZ 2100

ST JAKOB 1295

1700

NASSEREIN 1286

85 Ⓡ

ST ANTON 1304

MAIENSEE 1840

1350

ST CHRISTOPH 1795

Ⓡ 1840

Ⓡ
ALBONAGRAT 2400

TO LANGEN

G. Nicholson

THE TIROL

More than three-quarters of the 400 ski resorts in Austria are in the Tirol and it is these resorts which have created the image of Austrian skiing. This is due less to the business acumen and drive of the Tiroleans than to the accident of geography which placed them in direct contact with the major urban population of Munich. The Tirol is predominently pre-Alpine and is an ancient farming area where forest clearing of Alpine meadows has been part of the agricultural heritage of the country for about 2000 years.

The architecture, which is partly Bavarian in style and partly indigenous, is characterized by the exterior of the ground floor of the buildings being of plastered, white-washed and often decorated stone blocks while the upper floors are faced with pine and have heavily carved and filigreed balconies. Careful conservation and rigid planning regulations have seen to it that any new buildings conform to the pattern set by previous generations. One unusual aspect of virtually all the Tirolean parishes is the fact that all the churches are of a design and architectural style peculiar to the Tirol. A Byzantine cupola surmounts a slender spire in place of either the square Roman tower or the slender Gothic spire more usually seen in the Alpine countries. This is because until the early 18th century the Tirol was virtually pagan. The Jesuits made a concerted effort, starting in 1725, to convert the inhabitants to Roman Catholicism. They built the churches to a standard design but were unable to locate them in the centre of the village or make them the gathering point for the village people as is usual in most Christian communities. The churches are found to one side and frequently on raised ground. Archaeological investigation seems to point to the fact that they were built on the site of ancient places of worship, dating back to before Roman times.

The East Tirol has some very ambitious plans for ski tourist development which, if the plans are adhered to, are going to make it an extremely popular ski area.

THE KOMPERDELL
Serfaus/Fiss/Ladis/Nauders

The Komperdell leads from Landeck into either Switzerland and St Moritz or Italy and Merano. It is a deeply cut valley which has left a quite remarkable shelf on the west bank of the river. It is on this shelf that Serfaus, Fiss and Ladis sit enjoying a degree of sunshine that bodes ill for any skiing.

Serfaus, on the other hand, is lucky for the skiing there is on predominantly east-facing slopes. The village itself has a very special charm which brings visitors back year after year and which has nothing to do with the comparatively limited skiing. Much of it is due to the fact that, despite the disastrous fire of 1942 which destroyed many of the original farm buildings, the village has kept much of its original atmosphere of mountain farm life, and a walk around the winding alleys will bring with it the scent of cows and hay. Before the fire, it was an area of special study of medieval farming life, and the village has served as a research centre for archeologists.

The hallmark of skiing in Ischgl is the very open skifields. With a minimum of mechanized uplift there are over 8000 metres of downhill running.

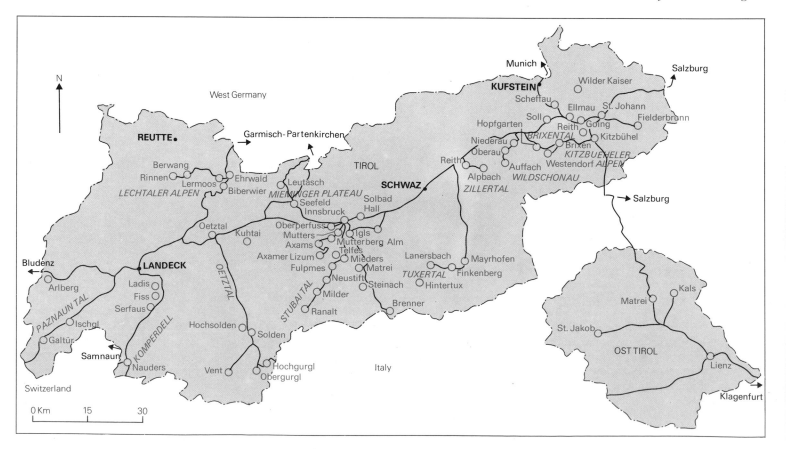

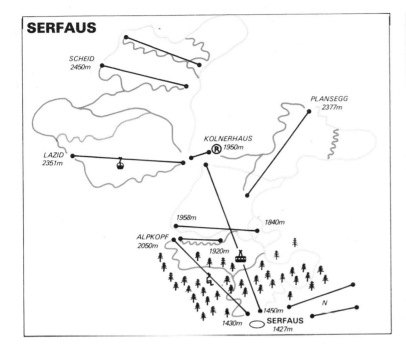

PAZNAUNTAL/ISCHGL/GALTUR

The entrance to the Paznauntal is dramatic, over a frighteningly high bridge and into a forbidding gorge flanked by sheer cliffs and apparently totally inaccessible little chapels. It leads directly into a broad shelf and winds from there to the Bielerhöhe and down on the far side to the Montafon.

Ischgl is the first major village on this road and at first sight does not promise much skiing. A tight huddle of hotels and houses causes problems for arriving guests who can rarely reach their front doors by any form of vehicle. Nevertheless there is a friendly atmosphere and the inviting alleys with discreet signs of restaurants and discotheques augur well for a week spent here. The skiing will amply repay any transportation problems the arrival may have caused.

Erwin Alloys, once Guardian at the Heidelberger Hut and now a Director of the lift company, was responsible for developing Ischgl. With a minimum of essential uplift in three linked areas, he succeeded in opening up more than 8000 metres of unrepeated downhill skiing in virtually treeless terrain which reaches up to the highest points of this part of the Silvretta Range. Although trails are marked and well made throughout the area, it is in fact go-anywhere country and suitable for any moderate skier. The ski school and nursery slopes are all on the Idalpe and the more advanced skiers spend much of their time around the Idjoch and the Paulinerkopf. It is from the Idjoch that a route leads into the

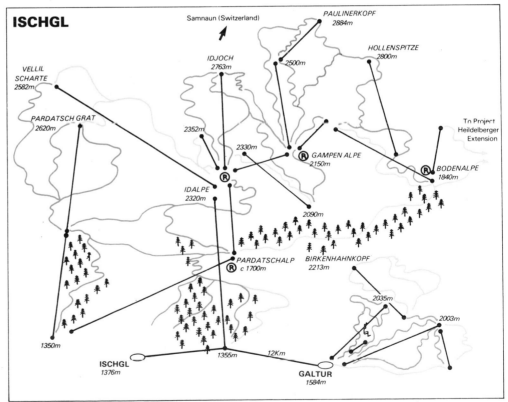

Samnauntal in Switzerland and the duty-free delights that can be found there. The return journey, however, is either by expensive snocat or a long three-hour climb with skins which can be tiring.

A long string of featureless houses in a bleak valley is very lovely on a hot summer's day but can be cold and cheerless in January or February and the very limited skiing, which is a long walk from the hotels, is no compensation. Galtur is however quite popular with Ischgl visitors who have their own transport and do not relish the crowded traffic which is that village's one drawback.

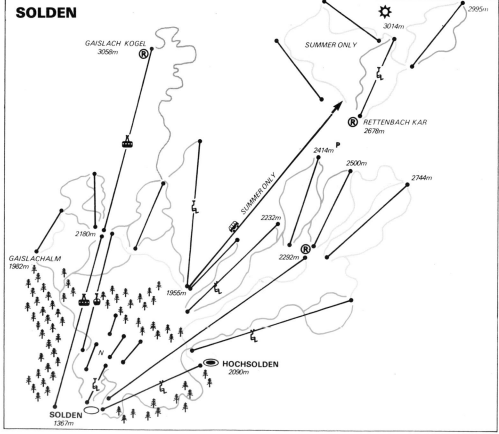

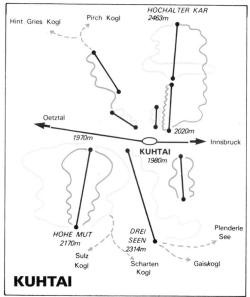

THE OETZTAL
Sölden/Obergurgl/Hochgurgl/Vent/ Kühtai

KUHTAI

The Wildspitze (left) is the highest point on the classic Oetztal high-level route. This last hour of the ski-mountaineering journey is over the only large and crevassed glacier on the route.

The Oetztal, running almost due north-south from the Upper Inn Valley, has assumed a skiing importance equal to the Arlberg or the Kitzbüheler Alpen. It achieved its fame as the entrance to one of the great spring touring areas of the Alps which, for accessibility and comfort, far excels the classical Haute Route and for those reasons tends to be looked down on by the hard men of ski mountaineering. It is from Vent, Obergurgl that ski mountaineers start the Oetztal round trip and from this has developed the habit of holidaying in the valley. Inevitably the skiing potential of Sölden and Obergurgl led to the creation of a mechanized ski-drome.

Kühtai lies outside the main traffic stream and is a dormitory area for guests who come to do serious day touring. The ski school is concerned almost exclusively with Alpine touring with skins, and as a result it is a very specialized resort.

Sölden, with its satellite Hochsölden, is about three kilometres long and the old village centre can best be located by the permanent traffic jam around the tourist office. Three main lifts travel into the ski country (for there is none in Sölden) and the beginners have their own completely isolated nursery which is reached by chair lift. The cable-car to the Gaislachkogl has a middle

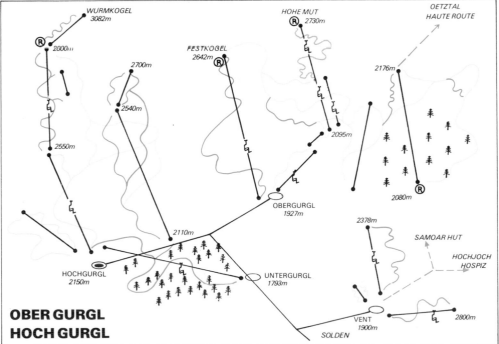

OBER GURGL
HOCH GURGL

Hochgurgl is the highest ski resort in Austria though the term resort is perhaps a slight exaggeration. The two hotels in the picture are exactly half the entire village.

Austria and the second highest in the Alps. It must now be the tightest huddle of hotels and carless alleys in the Alps and for very many skiers it surpasses all other resorts in Austria. Children, novices and rather timorous moderates will find an infinity of trails that dodge in and out of stunted fir trees or sweep down in a long gentle traverse from the Rosskarschneide, known as the 'Festkogl'. March and April are the months for this resort and there is frequently skiing on the Hohe Mut and gullies around the Sattel lift until late June.

Hochgurgl is an attempt by developers to go one better than Obergurgl and it is very doubtful if they have even touched first base with their ugly square hotels and nothing else. Bleak and exposed in winter, it comes into its own from March onwards when the main occupation is sunbathing with perhaps some leisurely skiing to keep cool.

Vent is nothing – the end of the road, a cattle gate, an ancient well and two hotels. But it is the arrival and departure point for any of a dozen or more ski mountaineering trips and for this alone it deserves a mention.

station for moderate skiers as the only run from the summit is a testing 1000 metre unmade black trail. Communication with the main Hochsölden ski fields are one way from the Gaislach side, a fact that has its irritations for those living at the top end of the village.

Sölden has also developed a summer skiing area which can be reached only by automobile in the late spring and during the summer months. It is located at the head of the Rettenbachtal.

Obergurgl was once the highest parish in

THE STUBAITAL
Mieders/Fulpmes/Telfes/Neustift/Stubai Glacier

Known throughout the world for its ice axes and climbing aids, the Stubaital stands equal to the Oetztal among ski mountaineers and climbers. Only minutes away from Innsbruck and linked directly to Munich by the Brenner motorway, it is surprising that so little enterprise has been shown in developing the considerable potential for holiday skiers. Possibly under the pressure of conservationists, perhaps on account of the reputation the mountains have for testing mountaineering problems, the valley has remained something of an unknown quantity except to the initiates.

The construction of the lift system at the end of the valley, which takes skiers and tourists into the high glaciers of the Stubai mountains, caused the three communities, Mieders, Fulpmes and Neustift to form an informal valley committee whose avowed aim was to preserve the character and seclusion of the valley. They appear to have succeeded. An indirect effect of this action has been to revive the centuries-old tradition and craft of cold forging which, since Roman times, was the staple industry of the valley. Now that the demand for swords and plate armour is minimal, they have turned to iron sculpture and lattice-work. There is a museum devoted to the craft in Fulpmes.

Fulpmes, a kind of fortress village high above the valley, is the gateway to a virtually secret gem of skiing territory – the Schlick. Small and scantily mechanized, it provides, completely hidden from the village and even from approaching skiers, a dream of a north-facing bowl where the snow comes early and stays late. Accommodation in Fulpmes is limited and the neighbouring village of Telfes is regarded as part of the Fulpmes dormitory area.

Neustift, the 'capital' of the valley, is an agglomeration of settlements lying along both sides of the Ruezbach. It looks like becoming increasingly scattered as more and more small houses occupy the flat ground of the valley. The local skiing is a classical example of bad planning. It may have looked good on paper and pleased the forestry

There is an irresistible fascination to place a turn round a tree or a slalom pole. The Schlick above Fulpmes is where almost every famous racer has practised far away from the public and journalists.

authorities but it does nothing except scare any skier of almost any degree of expertise. The ascent in the chairlift reveals the most hair-raising trails through forest that can be found in the entire Alps. The problems arise at each 180° turn where the ground drops to a near-vertical angle before resuming its steeply-angled traverse to the next wall of death. However, as a base for skiing on the Stubai Glacier Neustift provides all the comfort and entertainment required.

The Stubai Glacier development comprises two gondolas, one from the valley end to the Dresdener Mountain Hut with a second stage to a glacier col rises to 2850 metres, and two further T-bars breach the 3000 metre line. The skiing, as in all glacier areas, is simple and open and unlimited, though in practice skiers should stick closely to the marked trails for the glacier is quite heavily crevassed. The run home to the car park is nothing more than a snow-covered, rocky, narrow path and can become virtually unskiable. Most people pre-

fer the queue for the downhill gondola. The season is from the end of February to late summer and from October to November.

The slalom side, the Birgitzkopf, is a very different story and is also a lesson in relative difficulties. Normally a cold and scratchy slope, it is rarely skied for pleasure and most skiers go up to the Birgitzkopf in order to ski the interesting, and usually unprepared, trail down to Götzens – a journey which is infinitely preferable to waiting for a bus in the cold and crowded car park.

Steinach, on the Brenner Pass road, is an uninteresting, sunless village engulfed in an orgy of development covering an area of about six square kilometres. The skiing is quite extensive and, except for a wind-blown summit, it is all within the dense forest where a number of trails have been cut.

Skiing packed powder behind a trail groomer can have problems. A test-turn first can avoid trouble.

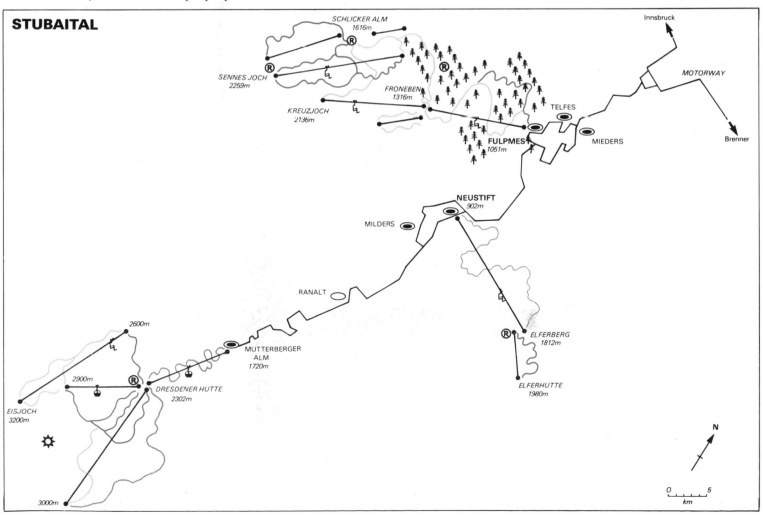

STUBAITAL

SCHLICKER ALM
1616m

Innsbruck

MOTORWAY

SENNES JOCH
2259m

FRONEBEN
1316m

TELFES

KREUZJOCH
2136m

MIEDERS

FULPMES
1051m

Brenner

NEUSTIFT
902m

MILDERS

RANALT

ELFERBERG
1812m

2600m

MUTTERBERGER
ALM
1720m

2900m

DRESDENER HUTTE
2302m

ELFERHUTTE
1980m

EISJOCH
3200m

N

3000m

0   5
km

INNSBRUCK

There is no other major city in the world – except perhaps Oslo – which can call itself a ski resort, and Innsbruck is historic, beautiful and most accessible. It was not always so and it took two Winter Olympics to seal the compromise with local parish politics which enabled Innsbruck to offer a universal lift pass and transport from the city centre to five distinct village centres and easy access to Seefeld and Steinach. Except for these two, no village is more than 30 minutes away and for those for whom even this is too much, the city itself has its own mountain, the Hafelkar, which is reached by cable-car from the city centre. However the people here make the best of the proximity, which is of little interest to those who do not like extreme gully skiing.

The centres of Steinach, Igls, Mutters, and the Axamer Lizum lie on a wide erosion shelf, on either side of the Brenner Pass gorge. It is thought that they were settled in prehistoric times by Illyrian farmers who moved to escape flooding, the unhealthy marshes and the passage of armed raiders which flourished in the Inn valley.

Tulfes is a small, unspoilt village above the spa town of Solbad Hall with little to offer except peace and a magnificent view. It is a paradise for children who can ski the entire 1100 metres drop, virtually straight down without risk except an excess of their own skill. Timid or elderly skiers sedately stemming their way down these wide, smooth trails should beware.

Igls is the classical Edwardian resort and the main centre for Innsbruck skiing. Very early in the history of holiday resorts, Igls was sought out by wealthy inhabitants of the lowlands who fled to escape the malaria and heat which the summer brought. In winter they visited the town for their asthma and for rest and quiet. The hotels in their shingle coats are beginning to look a little time-worn and the atmosphere is redolent of lounges with cane chairs occupied by whispering gentlefolk. You either love it or hate it.

The skiing is good and takes place on the Patscherkofel. The men's Olympic run starts here and is the normal red run home. More timorous skiers can take a long backwards and forwards journey through the forests from the Patscher Alm and experts can exhibit their skills on the steep and difficult black ridge run from the mountain summit (it is in full view of the restaurants – so the technique has to be perfect). For skiers who like a long challenge, the Ostabfahrt from the summit, avalanches permitting, will take them a full 16 kilometres to Sistrans where a bus runs back to Igls.

The long flat shelf between Igls and Tulfes is ideal Nordic touring country though, as yet, there is little prepared track available.

On the east side of the Brenner gorge are Mutters and the little hamlets serving as dormitory areas for the Axamer Lizum. Mutters, once a prize-winning village in the

The skiing on the Hafelkar is limited but the plunging view of Innsbruck is quite unforgettable.

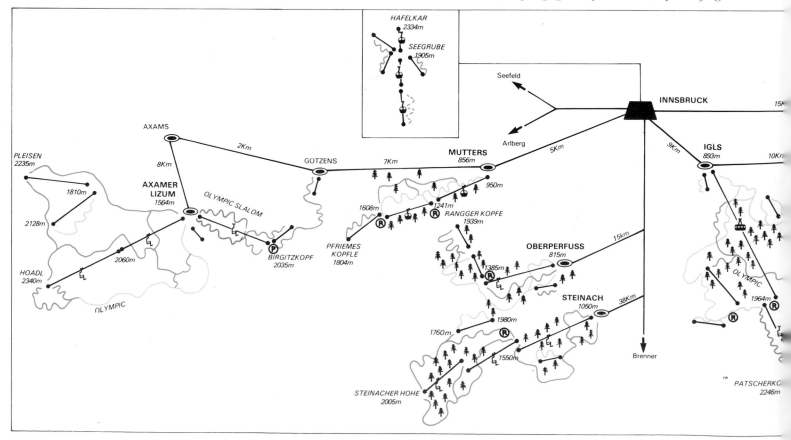

Austrian village beauty competition, has not
yet fallen prey to developers and remains a
most attractive place. The skiing on the Alm
and the Pfriemesköpfllift is unspectacular but
deserves a visit if only to ski the course of the
1935/36 World Championships. It is a lesson
to modern skiers for it is still in its original
state. Narrow, bumpy, not particularly steep
and by present-day standards not even fit for
weekend skiers, it proves what we have to be
thankful for.

The Axamer Lizum is served by the villages of Axams and Götzens, neither of which
have any skiing of their own, and lies a
considerable distance from either village. The
official list of runs in this Olympic downhill
area totals 20 but any skier looking for 20
different trails will realize that, quite acciden-
tally, he has probably skied three or four of
them in one run. This is not to say that the
skiing is dull, only that planning theory and
practical skiing are not necessarily the same
thing. It may come as something of a surprise
to find the ladies' downhill course from the
Hoadl shown as a blue run — which indeed it
is until it has been prepared for a race.

*Powder snow is rare here but these slopes on the
Ostabfahrt from the Patscherkofel are a delight.*

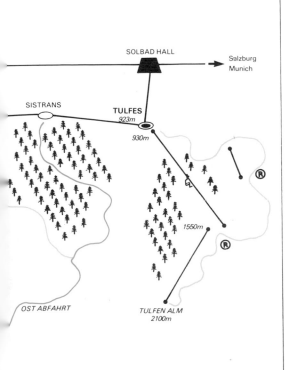

SEEFELD

Seefeld is a holiday town, just far enough away from Innsbruck to avoid crowds but close enough to permit an afternoon's sightseeing when the weather closes in. It is the site for the main Austrian Nordic competitions as well as two Olympic Games. A skier's town it is not and the downhill opportunities are limited to what can only be called a beginner's hill, the Gschwandkopf, and an intermediate's warm up, the Seefelder Joch. Both are a good walking distance from the town centre, which is an uncomfortable process in today's boots, and both can be-

come uncomfortably crowded at weekends. One run deserves mention and that is the Härmelekopf trail down the Reither Kar which is only practicable either very early in the season or in spring. At both times the route is ungroomed and demands a standard far above that customarily found in a place like Seefeld.

The area is ideal for Nordic skiing however. There is an extensive nursery close to the foot of the Gschwandkopf and a selection of loipes that cover everything from five to fifteen kilometres.

For all those who prefer not to have their

cross-country activities too highly organized and who like to find their way other than by following the tramlines of a track-making machine, the Mieminger Plateau, roughly 20 by 10 kilometres, is a small paradise. With only gentle gradients and a vast selection of signposted routes (summer walks, for the most part) it is quite feasible to do 50 kilometres a day for several days without repeating more than small sections of routes. For those who prefer simple accommodation, Neu Leutatsch, Unter Weidach, Kirchplatz, Obern and Moos can provide comfortable and quiet country inns nearby.

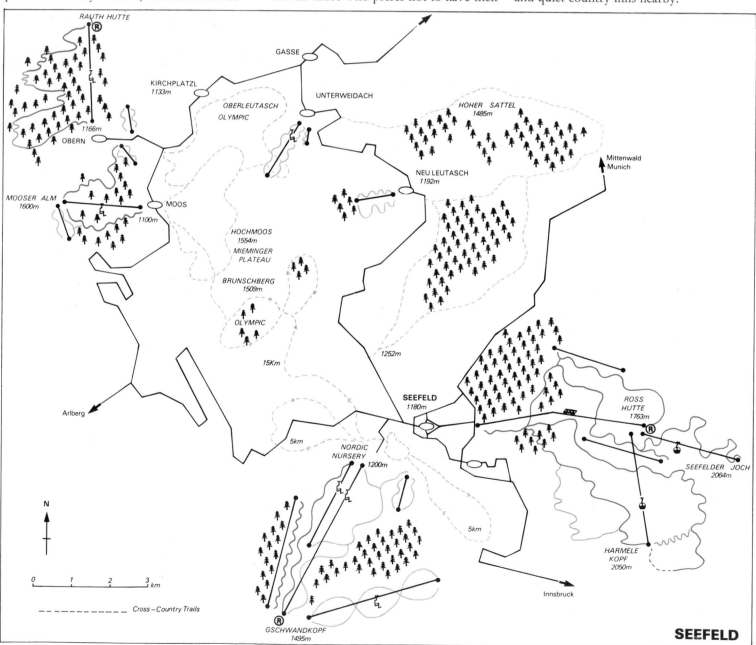

SEEFELD

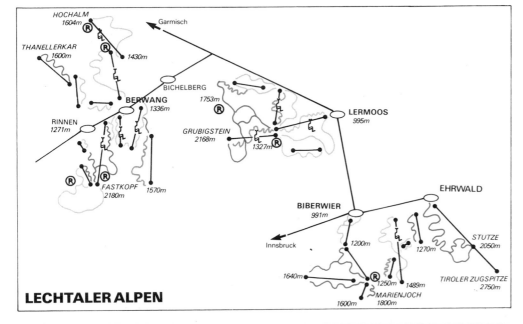

LECHTALER ALPEN

Seefeld is one of the few holiday places that has succeeded in keeping its character of a neat, country village and has almost banished cars.

THE LECHTALER ALPEN
Berwang/Lermoos/Biberwier/Ehrwald

This strange, ice-age relic should have succeeded in creating a more attractive image. The Moos, the geographic centre of the area, is a totally flat peat plain, suitable for Nordic skiing and Ehrwald is a very popular summer resort, but somehow something went badly wrong with the planning and hopes. Ehrwald, the start of the cableway to the German Zugspitze, provides only one run into Austria, and that is beyond most skiers, if only on account of the rather spectacular exit from the cable-car on mast 4. Ehrwald optimistically built three skilifts, but failed to observe that they served south-facing slopes. Biberwier did a bit better but it is such a poky, cold and unattractive roadside settlement and the skiing is so uninteresting that few except frost-bitten schoolchildren frequent it. Lermoos is more successful and with a minimum of lifts provides 1200 metres of downhill running and some very steep and testing runs. But again, for reasons indefinable, Lermoos is still not a very popular place.

Berwang, off to one side of the Moos, has done rather better and the village, which is perched on a high knoll, has a certain authenticity, despite the addition of many hotels. The skiing here is undistinguished and suffers from lift patchiness. The best fun is to be had on the Rastkopf but it is a little too difficult for the moderate novice and too easy for the expert. That it is a family resort for moderate skiers would be a fair verdict and not meant in any derogatory sense.

KITZBUEHEL

In the beginning there was 'Kitz' where the golden youth of the 1930s played and where in the late 1940s and early 1950s their sons and daughters tried to rediscover the glitter and glamour their parents knew. This reputation has now moved on to Megève, Courchevel and Val d'Isère but it has left behind a still-charming, medieval town, almost swamped by car traffic and suburban building, and a magnificent network of ski trails.

It was on the Hahnenkamm that the first ski circuit came into being which provided a lift network that permitted the skier to commute from area to area rather than go up and down the same slopes.

It is strange to compare this circuit of Ehrenbach Höhe, Steinberg Kogel and Giggling Höhe with the almost commonplace one of Courchevel or even the St Anton – Galzig – St Christoph roundabout. In 1948 a closed-circuit lift route was not only original but even considered a serious break with tradition and the diehards predicted the de-

finite end of serious Alpine skiing. Yet the concept was so obvious and simple that it is difficult to understand now why it took so long for the skilift innovators to realize the expansive potential of the so-called 'circus'.

The Hannenkamm bowl was also responsible for a further innovation. It divided the downhill skiers into those who preferred tracked and, even in those days, groomed trails and those who skied powder. It was normal to take one of two routes; up from Griesalm to Giggling Höhe, along the nar-

row ridge towards the Steinberg Kogel, down to Streitegg and back to Griesalm. The steep slopes between were left for the experts of untracked snow and the fall-line routes from either lift were often so badly cut up that they were abandoned and the gentle run towards the Pengelstein was the favoured alternative.

One way or another, Kitzbühel is a landmark in the history of recreational skiing and, with the Arlberg-Kandahar race, also set a new standard for downhill competitions. The old Streif course with its fearsome left-handed hairpin and nose-dive was the ultimate test for the downhill racer.

The skiing today in Kitzbühel extends from the Horn with its comfortable easy runs away from the crowds, through the complicated network of the Hahnenkamm and the irresistible temptation to ski the notorious Streif race course, over the Pengelstein and down to a roadside bus station, the Ski Rast, in Aschau, or from the Ehrenbachhöhe down to the new condominium settlement of Kirch-

berg. The same lift pass serves on the Bichlalm and brings the skier back along a delightful blue track right down into Kitzbühel, provided he survives the vilifications of a notorious farmer who, since 1948, has been trying, in vain, to stop skiers passing through his backyard near the end of this run.

Kitzbühel, like St Anton, should be in every serious skier's list of places to visit once. Despite the crowds and the cars and the prices, it will always be a very special resort with visitors from all over the world.

MAYRHOFEN AND THE TUXERTAL

Mayrhofen is a legend, a classic Tirolean market settlement, full of picturesque old hotels which, in turn, are well equipped with every conceivable form of après-ski entertainment. There are many visitors who go to ski in Mayrhofen year after year and have yet to succeed in doing more than two consecutive day's skiing. Here you can enjoy all the amenities of a real Tirol village holiday, with a village band, jodelling, costume, country dancing, rock and Country-and-Western, wine by the gallon – and even a little gentle skiing.

The skiing is moderate to mediocre; a bus goes to the start of either the Filzen Alm cable-car or the more ambitious Penken car. The Filzen Alm is purely for novices and it is here that the ski school operates. The Penken offers rather more, in a limited way, and there is only one run that deserves mention, the Schwendau scratch. It is not always open and

you will need a taxi home from there too. Recently the essential connection into the Finkenberg lift system has extended the skiing a little.

Finkenberg and its near neighbour Lanersbach are the jokers in the valley skiing pack. In Finkenberg you can enjoy all the best of the skiing in Mayrhofen but live at half the price and twice the peace. There is even a night-time bus to bring you back from Mayrhofen's après-ski life.

Now Lanersbach is a very different proposition. If you are awake early enough you will see the local farmers plodding the steep hillside behind the hotels, milk-churn on back, to milk the cows high above the village. Primitive hoists will be hauling up hay and lowering down the morning's milking, and on the slopes of the Eggalm it is not uncommon to have your happy slaloming interrupted by a string of cattle moving out to a different byre or by finding the signposted trail cuts across the backyard of a farmer busy

sawing his winter fuel while his wife is scalding the milk pails.

There are no discotheques or dance halls, but, while guests sit lazily replete in the larch-pannelled rooms of either of the two main hotels, there will be the music of a Zillertal harp and the voice of the hostess, dressed, as becomes a hostess, in her best valley costume. This is the real Tirol, the real Zillertal and none of that imported *Tratsch* from Bavaria.

A few miles up the valley is Hintertux, the start of the Tuxer glacier lift complex, a gondola and a small network of chair and T-bar lifts that land the skier up at 3000 metres with some delightful glacier skiing. The run down from the Sommerberg Alm to the gondola start is not very advisable except for skiers experienced at negotiating small waterfalls, log-jams, boulders and icy woodpaths.

I can think of little that would be more enjoyable than living in Lanersbach and skiing on the Tuxerferner in March – it would not be big skiing nor serve for after-dinner

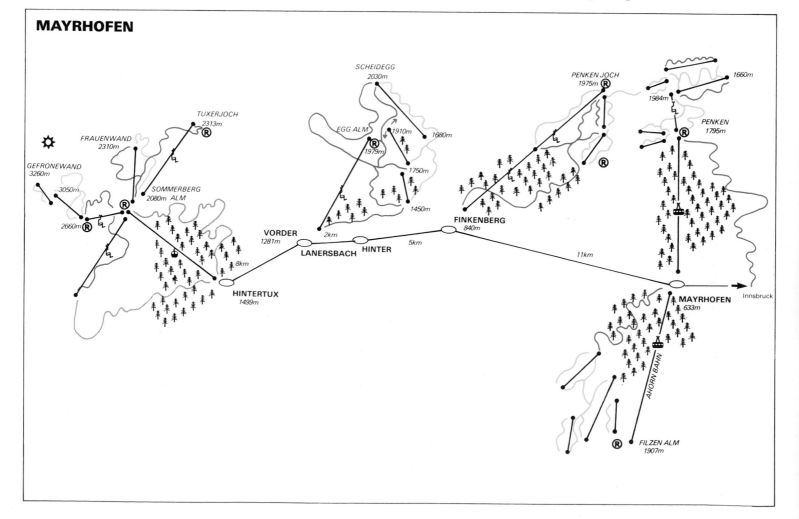

MAYRHOFEN

tales but it is infinitely more memorable than staggering home at four in the morning from the deafening confinement in a Mayrhofen discotheque.

THE WILDSCHONAU
Alpbach

The Wildschönau lies to one side of the main Munich–Innsbruck road. It is a National Park area and development is severely limited. The population was wiped out by plague in medieval times and this left it a place of legends with a strong sense of being 'different'. The plague seems to have affected the ski resorts as well for Niederau, Auffach and Alpbach (not strictly in the Wildschönau but always grouped with it) are an anomaly among the hundreds of small Austrian resorts.

Niederau has nothing to recommend it in the way of village ambience. It does have some very tough skiing best suited to those who like steep, icy gullies where the trails can be 'bashed' all day long, with endlessly repeated turns at the same places. The reward for such hard skiing is a very unsophisticated and uninhibited night-life. There are those who would ski nowhere else and there are those to whom Niederau skiing is anathema.

Auffach is something of a mystery. It seems to have been started with dreams of rivalling the French third generation resorts, but plans came to a halt before they reached the completion of stage one. There is really only one basic run and it is questionable whether that is worth the journey.

Alpbach is unique. It is everyone's dream of a Tirolean village, each building an architectural gem. It offers the theoretically perfect ski holiday where the whole tiny village and its visitors make one gigantic party. For serious skiers it is a constant source of irritation to have to take public transport five kilometres down a very steep road to reach the lift station and wait for the same transport in order to go home. Once there the skiing is limited to two basic routes with a few alternatives over a height difference of about 1200 metres. It is a classical example of the enigmatic nature of the popularity of ski resorts for Alpbach is full year after year and most of the guests have been going there for many years.

Reith, a few kilometres down the valley from Alpbach, can hardly be called a ski resort, though it does serve to an increasing degree as a dormitory area for Alpbach. The slopes are straightforward and most enjoyable for any category of skier if he is not too proud to be seen enjoying himself on simple open runs. At weekends it can be very crowded with day visitors from the nearby towns of Wörgl and Brixlegg.

Wildschönau, literally translated, means "the wild, beautiful grazing". The name is no exaggeration for this curious bowl, completely cut off from the valley below it by a ring of rocky outcrop, is an area of quite outstanding natural beauty.

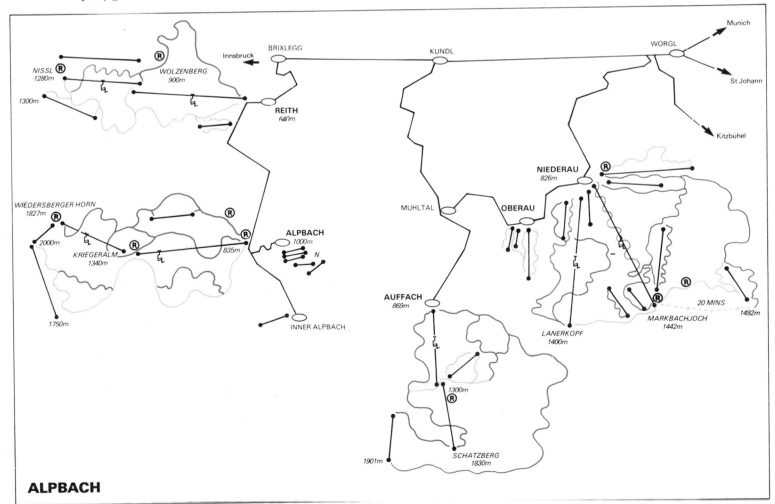

ALPBACH

EAST TIROL

The East Tirol lies like an island between the Dolomites of the South Tirol in Italy and the Venediger and Gross Glockner ranges in the north. This geographic isolation, despite the new Felbertauern Toll Tunnel has cut the area off from the great tourist boom. Vacationers are a spoilt and conservative crowd who demand large lift complexes and well-known resort names, and they will find neither here. This is a big mistake for there are some villages well worth visiting in these valleys.

Lienz, the capital of the Ost-Tirol is a market town, and is a comfortable place to live if you have transport. It also has two rather odd ski areas, the Zettersfeld – all nursery slopes and a fantastic view – and the Hochstein, which has no view and some difficult tree-lined skiing.

Kals, at the end of a very minor road, lies in the shadow of the Gross Glockner, Austria's highest mountain. There are two villages – Kals, the seventeenth-century parish and Kals Grossdorf, the medieval clan headquarters where the farmhouses grew with the clan. The village of Kals Grossdorf is a museum piece and is still a very active farming area. It

has the start of two chairlifts which lead to the Kalser Höhe, from where there is a snaking black run called the Figol. The combination of the village and this run make Kals Grossdorf a place to remember long after more sophisticated resorts have begun to fade. The Mattreier Tauernhaus is a project that never really took off. What is left is a tiny inn where ski mountaineers start off for tours in the Venediger range, and a chairlift slides disconsolately up to another tiny inn and a T-bar in the middle of nowhere which goes up another 200 metres. On weekdays any skier up here may well be the only customer for these lifts.

St Jakob in Defereggental could have become a second Zürs if the great Obersee development project had not been successful, for it would have been the natural staging post for the toll road that was to lead to the Austrian third generation resort. As it is, a mile or so below the village a chairlift and two T-bars hoist skiers up to two great empty grazing hills where the term trail is completely out of place, which makes for some very entertaining skiing on a fine day and a misery of disorientation if the clouds come down unexpectedly.

SÖLL/GOING/ELLMAU/ SCHEFFAU/HOPFGARTEN/ BRIXEN IN THALE/ WESTENDORF

This is a strange collection of villages and settlements which are loosely interconnected and which all, technically, belong to the Kitzbüheler Alpen. With a little less parish politics and a little more sensible co-operation they could, in fact, form one gigantic ski circuit. As it is, only Scheffau, Reith and Söll make any pretence at providing a joint lift pass and making skiing in the direction Söll to Scheffau possible.

The two most popular villages, Söll and Westendorf, require little comment. Both provide the customary facilities which visitors to the Tirol expect. Both have disadvantages. From a skier's point of view Söll probably offers a better variety and a greater spread of difficulty than any of the others. The Salvenmoos nursery area is very sunny and well organized for teaching; the Hohe Salve can tantalize the new moderates with the steep gully slopes that lead down to the Kraft Alm; and for those who like ski journeying, a simple series of lifts and blue runs take them down to Scheffau where a taxi will bring them back to Söll. The steep scratchy run down to Hopfgarten is best left to the young hopeful Killys and Moser-Proells of the village.

Going, Ellmau and Scheffau are nothing more than roadside settlements which offer very little for the serious skier, though from all three it is possible to go over to Brixen and from there by public transport across to Westendorf or down the valley to Kitzbühel.

ST JOHANN I. TIROL

St Johann claims to have 80 skilifts within ten minutes' drive of the main square of the town. Why it should have to lay claim to the lifts of Kitzbühel, definitely more than ten minutes away, is a puzzle, since this pleasant market town has some very adequate skiing of its own on the back of the Kitzbüheler Horn.

This side the mountain is called the Harschbichl and the two main runs from the summit are a perfect example of the folly of decrying a mountain's skiing because it is not festooned with black runs. The long fluent trail from the 1600 metre summit ambles its way down past a welcome inn at Pointen to finish through the trees close to the funicular departure station on the edge of the town. An enterprising restaurateur set up an open-air sausage grill there and the appetizing scent wafts up through the trees long before the trail ends.

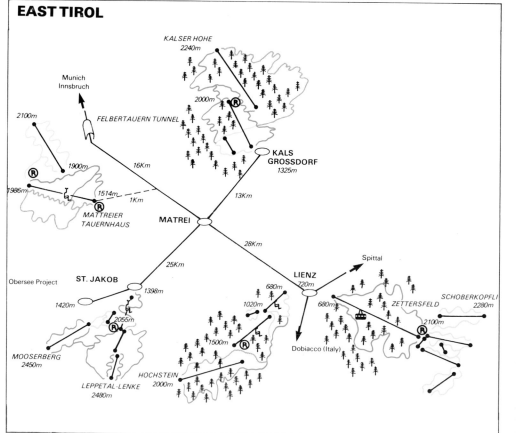

This is fast, fluent skiing which, done non-stop, will test most skiers' legs. The alternative, towards Penzing, is less exhilarating.

FIEBERBRUNN

Fieberbrunn is the cause of some amazement for those who know it. From the railway station at Rosenegg to the settlement of Walchau is at least five kilometres. The Neue Post Hotel is at least 100 years older than the official Alte Post, and it is said that it has the best Mexican food in Austria. There are likely to be more British school children in the village than there are local inhabitants. It is also the only place I have seen where in the centre of the very simple nursery slopes there are a hundred yards of truly black trail and this causes untold grief to all beginners.

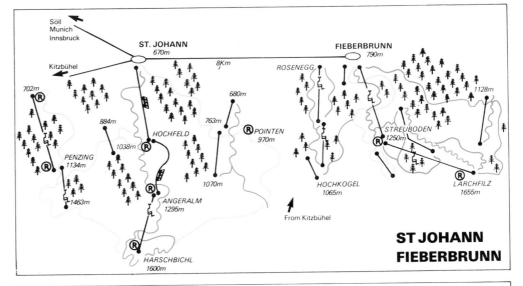

ST JOHANN
FIEBERBRUNN

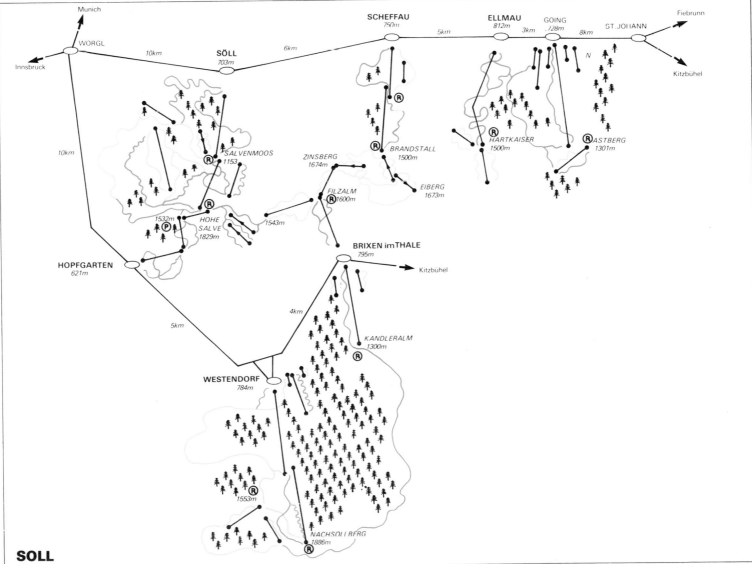

SOLL

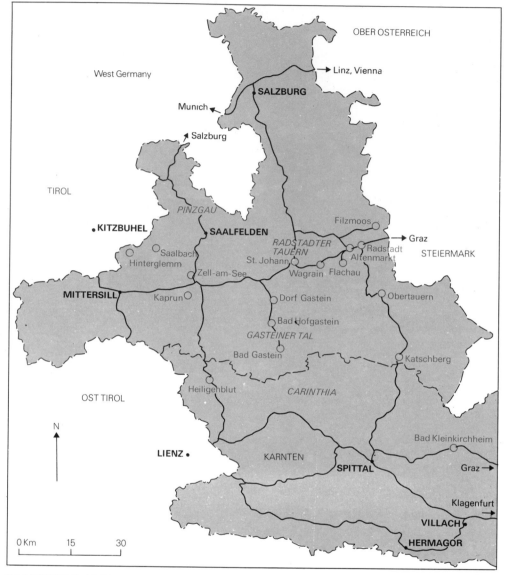

SALZBURG AND CARINTHIA

The Province of Salzburg is popularly associated with Mozart, *The Sound of Music*, and summer lake-side holidays. Skiers are discovering that there is a great deal more for them than this tourist image presents. The Gasteiner Tal is a magnificent ski area and the circuit on the Obertauern is more than just a rival to Kitzbühel for it is the only wholly planned ski resort in Austria. But Salzburg, apart from being a famous tourist area and a burgeoning ski destination, is essentially agricultural with great herds of cattle in the valleys and an extensive forestry industry and associated manufacture.

Carinthia, at least to the Austrians, spells holiday country. Mountains, lakes, forests and a share in the Gross Glockener, the highest mountain in Austria, combine with the still-remembered days when this was an independent kingdom (distant as this is) to make this one of the pleasanter areas for ski holidays. There is nothing great or startling about the few developed centres and Carinthia favours the ski mountaineer and the cross country wanderer more than the downhill-only specialist. Access for foreign visitors is awkward and long unless you are prepared to drive from Munich or Salzburg. This factor is likely to delay the development of this province.

Cross-country skiing in Bad Kleinkirchheim is a popular recreation for visitors to the area.

EUROPA SPORT REGION PINZGAU
Zell-am-See/Saalbach/
Hinterglemm/Kaprun

Finding themselves equidistant from Munich, Vienna, Zürich and Venice and planning a joint lift pass, these villages decided to group themselves under the name Sportregion Europa and they provide some formidable skiing.

Zell-am-See is the least inviting. It is a dead town in winter, and the curious dome-shaped mountain, the Schmittenhöhe, seems most menacing and should any unfamiliar skier

find himself on this bald summit in bad weather, he will have considerable difficulty in finding his way back to Zell. Twice, in thick fog, I have finished in Schuttdorf instead of Zell, having turned right rather than left at the half-way stage. Beware of the two black runs that sidle off to the left just after the Breiteckalm – both have disastrously shallow beginnings preceding very difficult country indeed.

Saalbach must be listed as one of the three or four most attractive ski villages in Austria. Wedged into a steep gorge, it is piled,

building upon building, along the one street which should, by now, be free of cars. Each building has all the exterior and interior characteristics of the eighteenth-century style of country inns and offices. Strangely it is all modern and only one wall of the old post inn and the church are original.

The main skiing is on and around the Schattberg with the long Jausern trail taking pride of place. Sadly, the long line of interlinked lifts on the Kohlmais Kopf are all south-facing and rarely have skiable snow for more than a day or two. Saalbach is linked

with Hinterglemm over the Schattberg, but only one way. A recalcitrant farmer and his family have refused permission for the building of one small lift on their land despite all the processes of law and persuasion. Consequently the ski journey from Hinterglemm to Saalbach is still difficult, and likely to remain so for the foreseeable future.

Hinterglemm, literally the 'back of the valley', is an untidy stretch of holiday homes and hotels that is a sad contrast to Saalbach, although the skiing here is much more extensive. It is not surprising that many skiers take

the simple long traverse down from the Schattberg to link into the lifts of the Zehner and Zwölfer before taking the bus home to their picturesque Saalbach.

Kaprun and the Kitzsteinhorn are, in fact, much better known than most people realize, for it is on the glaciers of the Kitzsteinhorn, now served by a funicular travelling in a tunnel, that most of the ski fashion pictures are taken in July and August and the Austrian ski manufacturers lay on week-long demonstration sessions of their new wares. Kaprun cannot lay claim to any beauty prizes nor, at

first sight, can its skiing. A little exploration might dispel this view, for Kaprun has a secret mountain hut hidden in the trees just below the Maiskogel, which is not signposted and where you can dream skier's dreams on the little balcony with the fabulous view of valleys and glaciers, before indulging in a little downhill madness for the next 800 metres of snowfield slopes past three more restaurants and two T-bars to Kaprun village.

The sport on the Kitsteinhorn is no different from all such summer skiing centres. The run home is best left to other skiers.

The village street of Wagrain winds steeply to the church where the lyricist of Silent Night *is buried.*

BAD KLEINKIRCHHEIM

This well-known summer cure centre, comprising a scattered collection of modest and not-so-modest hotels and sanatoria, has set out on a calculated investment programme to attract skiers who, either for themselves or for their friends, family or companions, are also interested in the cure, which in this case is particularly recommended for convalescence after serious illness, operations, or severe ski accidents. The quality of the skiing is very unlikely to produce a large number of the latter cases from its own trails.

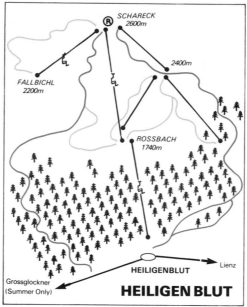

HEILIGEN BLUT

HEILIGENBLUT

Heiligenblut, at the foot of the Gross Glockner, used to be cut off in winter but it is now easily reached by automobile through the Felbertauern tunnel from Lienz. It is a small ski resort with very limited uplift that deserves listing in any Austrian selection for one single run from the summit of the Schareck at 2600 metres along the right-hand ridge and down into a treeless valley finishing 11 kilometres later and 1300 metres lower just outside the village of Heiligenblut.

Better known as a summer resort and the gateway to the Gross Glockner, Heiligenblut is an oasis of peace in winter and a most delightful, if restricted spring skiing centre.

THE RADSTADTER SEE-SAWS AND OBERTAUERN
Radstadt/Altenmarkt/Flachau/ Wagrain/Filzmoos

The mountains here are the frontier between the provinces of Salzburg and Carinthia. It is an area that once enjoyed considerable prosperity from the busy Imperial Military traffic into the Adriatic and, more recently, has once again prospered with the advent of the large Atomic ski factory and the development of some novel ski resorts.

The countryside and villages are characteristically Salzburgian and have a very different character to the typical Tirol village. They are widely spaced and almost majestic with their large farm houses and massive barns. Most houses are crowned by a small belfry and bell which many people suppose to be for giving a fire alarm. This is not the case. They are known as the 'Fressglocke', the feeding bell, and are rung to call home the farm labourers from distant fields.

The Altenmarkt/Radstadt See-saw crosses the Hoch Bifang providing, by means of only four lifts, a total there-and-back height difference of 1800 metres. The skiing is simple and open.

The Wagrain/Flachau See-saw is much more complicated and extensive, crossing over the Griesenkar with a whole collection of secondary lifts but providing about the same amount of height difference as the Altenmarkt route. The ground is very broken, forming a series of large knolls and shallow gullies.

Accommodation in Radstadt, Altenmarkt and Flachau is conventional countryside inn style, though Flachau is in some turmoil because a motorway now cuts right through the original village.

Wagrain on the other hand is very special. It has achieved fame through being the adoptive home of Austria's great skiing star Annemarie Moser-Proell and her sponsor, the Atomic ski factory, whose owner and founder, Mr Rohrmoser, was the former wheelwright of Wagrain. Wagrain, perched on high on a fortress-like promontory, is a very beautiful and imposing village.

High, wild and treeless, Obertauern is a created resort for skiers only. What is offered is a ski-drome which will take any competent skier, legs, time and weather permitting, a distance of 25 kilometres with 4000 metres of height over a variety of trails, from exciting gully skiing on the Hundskogel to fast, open, ego-building swooping on the Zehnerkar.

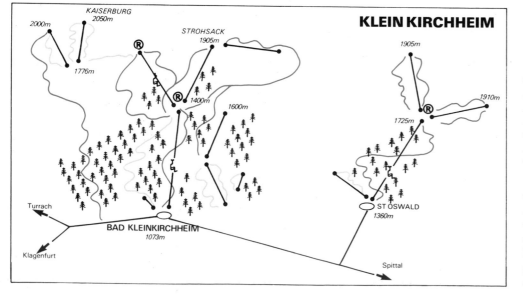

KLEIN KIRCHHEIM

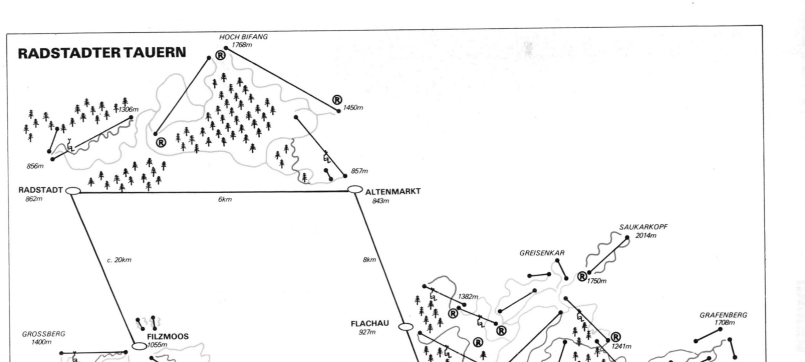

RADSTADTER TAUERN

HOCH BIFANG
1768m

1450m

1306m

856m

RADSTADT
862m

ALTENMARKT
843m

6km

857m

c. 20km

8km

SAUKARKOPF
2014m

GREISENKAR

1750m

1382m

FLACHAU
927m

GROSSBERG
1400m

FILZMOOS
1055m

1241m

GRAFENBERG
1708m

1290m

WAGRAIN
896m

ROSSBRAND
1600m

8km

Each main point on the circuit has a short up-and-down trail with slightly more difficult skiing and the standard route also allows a tiring performer to circumvent any difficult patches. There is only one objection to the very fine ski area and that is its exposure to wind and bad weather and the skiing can become difficult once visibility deteriorates.

Filzmoos, by any normal standards would not figure in a list of selected ski resorts. But it is the kind of place only to be found in Austria and only there could it succeed. It is a tiny village on a very minor road which in summer leads to the Dachstein cable-car and Ramsau. The skiing will not detain even a very nervous moderate for more than a morning and you can practically throw a stone from one end of the village to the other. But it has an incomparable atmosphere and a feeling of unity. After a first evening in the village the first-time visitor will know everyone and everyone will know him. The ski schooling is on an equally friendly and intimate basis and there are not a few novices who, about to give up the sport for more leisurely activities, have been brought back into the fold of ardent skiers by the school's care and attention.

Summer skiing on the Dachstein, once the cable-way has opened, brings a big change to this village.

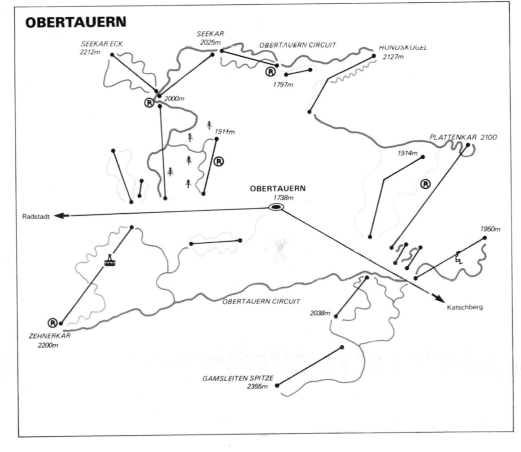

OBERTAUERN

SEEKAR ECK
2212m

SEEKAR
2025m

OBERTAUERN CIRCUIT

HUNDSKOGEL
2127m

1797m

2000m

1911m

PLATTENKAR 2100

1914m

OBERTAUERN
1738m

Radstadt

1950m

ZEHNERKAR
2200m

OBERTAUERN CIRCUIT

2038m

Katschberg

GAMSLEITEN SPITZE
2355m

BAD GASTEIN/BAD HOF GASTEIN/ DORF GASTEIN/SPORT GASTEIN

The Gastein Valley, running almost due north to south from the old Innsbruck-to-Salzburg road, was first popularized by the Emperor Franz Joseph I.

Today there are three fine resorts, Bad Gastein, Hof Gastein and Dorf Gastein, with a fourth, the so-called Sport Gastein, on the Nassfeld above Bad Gastein still in the very early and much delayed development stage.

Bad Gastein, buried in the steep cliff face at the end of the valley, is one of the most pretentious of all ski stations. It has hideous baroque, pseudo-baronial architecture clashing with modern, concrete, utility buildings on the upper slopes of the centre. The skiing is either on the Stubnerkogel, or on the Graukogel where a series of spider-web trails have been cut out of the forest.

Hof Gastein, a few kilometres down the valley, is built on a more open plan with well-spaced, large hotels and open public park areas. The skiing starts on the far side of the main road, a long walk or, preferably, a short bus ride from the town centre. It is based on the Schlossalm and is very extensive indeed.

A cable-car lifts skiers from the end station of the funicular to a point at 2050 metres. Below, from near the middle of the bowl, a chairlift rises to 2300 metres and provides, quite apart from its own wonderfully open red trail and truly magnificent run home to the bottom of the funicular, a clear 1500 metres of fast, open, downhill running. There are tentative plans for linking this enormous skiing bowl with the Stubnerkogel slopes which would provide a skiing area the equivalent of the Arlberg.

Dorf Gastein is the lowest village of the valley and the oldest with visible remains dating from the Roman occupation. It is the least fashionable but, perversely, the most sought-after residential area of the valley. The skiing is excellent with a succession of lifts rising from just outside the village to the Fulseck at 2030 metres and linking with a further series from the Gross Arl Valley.

Sport Gastein, still only a lift station and a part-time refreshment stall, was meant to provide high-Alpine, year-round skiing for the Gastein valley. It is five kilometres from Bad Gastein on the toll road that leads to the radium caves. At present two lifts, a chair and a T-bar, rise from the Nassfeld at 1580 metres to the Kreuzkogel at 2686 metres with a series of long moderate trails that cover the area between Nassfeld and the Weissenbach Tal.

KREUZKOGEL 2686

SCHARECK 3122

SPORT GASTEIN

SCHIDECK 2150

1580

STUBENER KOGEL 2231

HOHE SCHARTE 2300

JUNGER ALM 1810

1794

2079

2101

1094

SCHLOSS ALM
1930

2050

2075

1703

1540

840

HOF GASTEIN 858

France

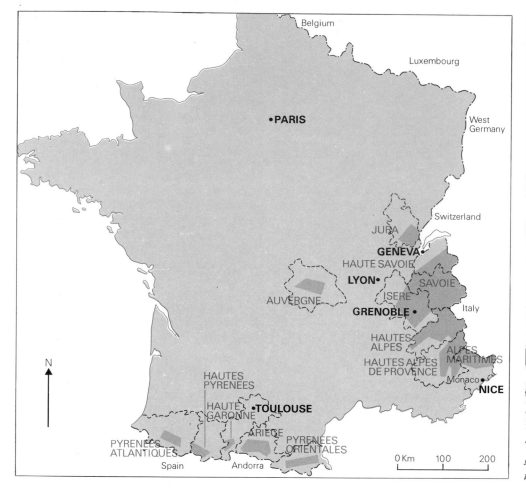

The skier looks down on Avoriaz whether he is skiing locally or coming over from Champery in the Valais, Switzerland.

France emerged as one of the great skiing countries during the 1950s. The renaissance of French competitive skiing, and the resurgence of national pride and enterprise under the De Gaulle banner resulted in a sudden growth of the industry. High and accessible mountains, and a well developed transport network contributed to this expansion.

Uninhibited by either tradition or existing resorts, the master builder of the French ski industry, Michel Michaud, achieved his aims in only ten years. Unlike any previous resort development, the architecture and trail planning were subservient to obtaining the greatest mileage of well-made trails with a minimum of mechanical uplift. The accommodation was designed to cater for the specific needs of the skier.

The prototype centre, Courchevel, on the edge of the Vanoise National Park, was immediately successful. By the middle of the 1960s, the idea had spread

from the shore of Lake Geneva, through the Haute Savoie and the Savoie, down the Dauphiné and the Hautes Alpes to the Côte d'Azur, barely 50 miles from the Mediterranean.

To serve the skiing population of south-western France, from Lyon to Bordeaux, the traditional summer resorts of the French Pyrenees looked again at their mountain pastures. They wove a network of lifts which provide pleasing local skiing and attract increasing numbers of foreign visitors.

For a newcomer to the French style of resort, three things will leave a lasting impression. The architecture is innovative and controversial. It has attempted to introduce into the conventional mountain village scene the spirit of modern skiing, which is instant access to slopes, covered walkways to shops and places of entertainment, and the use of many forms of condominium accommodation. The architecture in some centres has been brilliantly

successful, some has been extremely controversial, but all is imposing.

The second impression is that of trail organization. The combination of Poma drag-lift, chair and gondola transport has enabled the trail planners to provide a virtually wait-free ascent, even on the busiest days, to well-made and signposted trails. Standards of difficulty have been maintained and there are few icy, wooded paths, dangerous and difficult traverses or irritating climbs.

Lastly, it has been possible to link two, three, four or even five centres into one vast ski-trail network. In this way, resorts have been extended to offer downhill runs of 30 or more miles, and make the best use of snow and weather conditions.

With over one hundred resorts, varying from small villages in the Jura to huge complexes like The Three Valleys, France has become a most desirable destination for all competent and ardent skiers.

THE HAUTE SAVOIE

The ski area of the Haute Savoie, which might more logically be called the Northern Savoie, is the group of mountains lying between Lake Geneva and the northern flank of the valley of Chamonix. Pre-Alpine in character it encompasses a list of minor resorts. Because of their attractively wooded character and lack of overpowering glacier mountains, they have become known as family holiday places. Only Avoriaz has achieved fame because of its highly unconventional and successful architecture. One other, Flaine, is the first created resort to have been planned for families with children.

Since 1976, La Chapelle d'Abondance, Châtel, Morzine-Avoriaz and Les Gets, resorts lying very close to the Swiss frontier, have formed themselves into a loose grouping with their Swiss neighbours. They form an area now called Porte du Soleil with a common lift pass that is valid for the 152 lifts. However the only direct connection is from Champéry in Switzerland to Avoriaz in France. As the area is principally of interest to day-skiers from Geneva this is not a great disadvantage.

The Avoriaz architecture is the most unusual and the most successful of the third generation resorts.

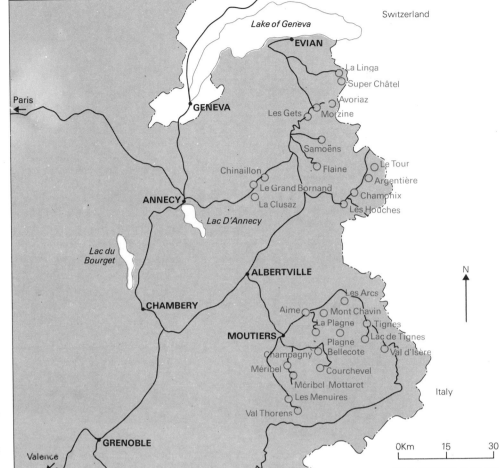

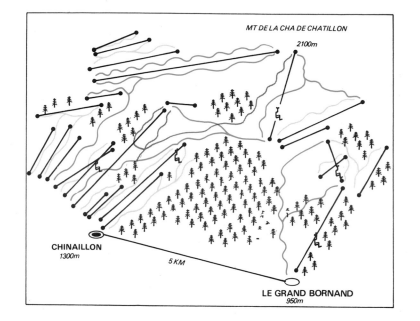

CHINAILLON
1300m

5 KM

LE GRAND BORNAND
950m

MT DE LA CHA DE CHATILLON
2100m

LE GRAND BORNAND/
CHINAILLON *Haute Savoie*

The old farming village of Le Grand Bornand has, mercifully, been spared the rigours of development and, although it is linked with the purpose-built settlement of Le Chinaillon three miles higher up the valley, it has retained its traditional agricultural character. Chinaillon, on the other hand, is a holiday village development with a long parallel line of lifts serving virtually tree-less slopes for novice and moderate skiers. Although there are three black trails, there are long, trouble-free runs with 800 metres of trail height, and country that is so open that even a hint of trouble can be circumvented. The return home to the old village on skis is easy but the morning start requires a number of carefully planned zig-zags. The relative proximity of this ski area to the inhabitants of the Geneva district has made Bornand a very popular weekend destination.

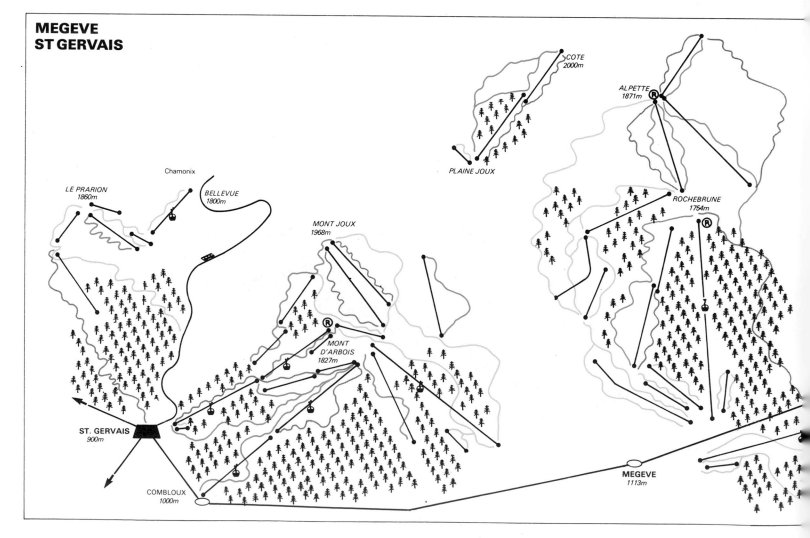

MEGEVE
ST GERVAIS

LE PRARION
1860m

Chamonix

BELLEVUE
1800m

MONT JOUX
1968m

COTE
2000m

ALPETTE
1871m

PLAINE JOUX

ROCHEBRUNE
1754m

MONT
D'ARBOIS
1827m

ST. GERVAIS
900m

COMBLOUX
1000m

MEGEVE
1113m

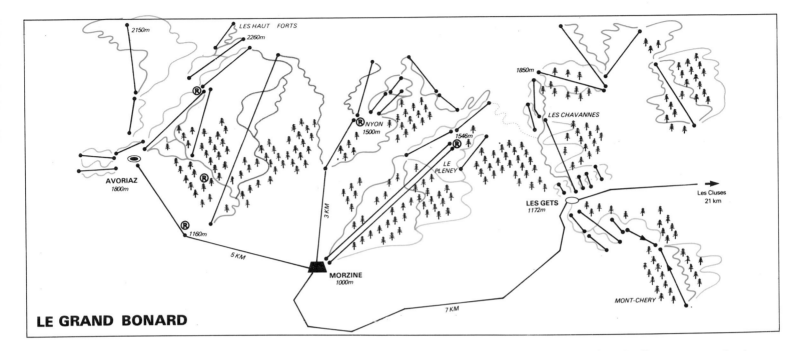

LE GRAND BONARD

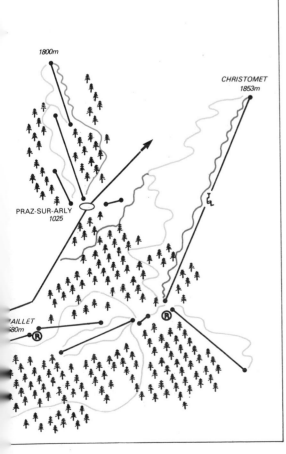

MORZINE *Haute Savoie*
Avoriaz/Les Gets

The pleasant little township of Morzine is the geographical centre for this group of three resorts. It grew as a centre for children's holiday homes, together with its near neighbour, Les Gets, which is an uninteresting roadside collection of vacation residences. Food and accommodation in Morzine is excellent and this is common where the French place their children into well-regulated confinement, thus liberating themselves for more adult pleasures on more difficult ski slopes.

The skiing in both Morzine and Les Gets is gentle and well organized. In theory it is possible to move freely from Les Gets to Morzine on skis but in practice this is only feasible from the Morzine side, over the Pleney to Les Chavannes.

For the more adventurous, a steep landmark a few miles outside Morzine, the Rocher de Nyon, provides some difficult, and often icy, runs. It can be reached either from Le Pleney or by bus from Morzine.

Avoriaz, perched dizzily above the headwall of the valley of the Joue Verte is spectacular. It looks like a beehive built into the cliff-face in a series of angles and terraces, which blend completely into the scenery, and provide no clue to the very large, modern, living complex which lies on the Alpine shelf invisible from below. Approach is only by cable-car, which is reached by ski-bus from Morzine. The skiing is open, simple and uncrowded with direct communication to Champéry in Switzerland. For the expert skier there is one trail which must be classed as a collector's piece — the extremely difficult, steep and exposed run from the shoulder below the Hautsforts to the valley bottom. The trail is rarely well made, and should not be undertaken lightly. In the manner of such trails, you emerge from the endlessly steep couloir into more congenial forested ground to find the most charming refreshment hut. This is now slightly spoiled by the rattle of a lift which goes back to the more civilized snowfields of Avoriaz.

MEGEVE *Haute Savoie*

Megève provides very different entertainment to that in Chamonix. The two valley sides have short runs for all categories of skier, and a direct link with St Gervais. The much enlarged village is classed as one of the three most fashionable winter-sports resorts of the world, vying with Gstaad and St Moritz for supremacy in the guest lists. Like St Moritz, these distinguished visitors live here for the skiing that can be found on their doorstep as well as for the fashionable night-life and discreet mountain chalets which house them. Megève is, however, very aware of the transitory nature of fashion and is currently making strenuous efforts to dispel the popular idea of Megève being only fashion and no skiing. The skiing may well not be as majestic as Les Deux Alpes but is not insignificant.

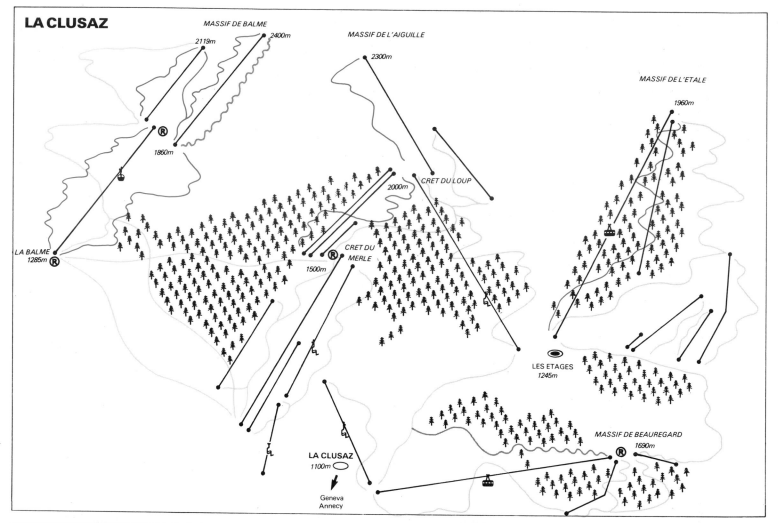

LA CLUSAZ

MASSIF DE BALME

2119m   2400m

MASSIF DE L'AIGUILLE

2300m

MASSIF DE L'ETALE

1960m

1860m

CRET DU LOUP

2000m

CRET DU MERLE

1500m

LA BALME
1285m

LES ETAGES
1245m

MASSIF DE BEAUREGARD
1690m

LA CLUSAZ
1100m

Geneva
Annecy

SUPER CHATEL/LA LINGA
Haute Savoie

These two curious, small resorts are five kilometres from La Chapelle d'Abondance, on the French-Swiss border. It is possible to slip over the frontier to Morzine and back again with ease. Mostly concerned with week-end visitors and cross-country enthusiasts, they provide the familiar mix of very easy trails through moderately wooded country and one hard, narrow and icy black trail to excite the local champions and future Olympic aces.

LA CLUSAZ *Haute Savoie*

La Clusaz, an old Savoyard mountain farming village, and its new satellite, the purpose-built Les Etages, form a pleasant, four-mountain resort for moderate and novice skiers. The trails are loosely linked by the Massif de

The little-used north-facing slopes above Flaine's residential area offer a route over the Samoëns.

Beauregard (1690 metres). This is essentially a family holiday place and one which is equally attractive in summer and winter. It is close to both Geneva and Annecy and consequently attracts heavy weekend crowds.

FLAINE/SAMOËNS *Haute Savoie*

Flaine is a purpose-designed resort intended for comfortable family skiing with a strong emphasis on facilities for younger children. In addition it is the only resort in Europe with a FIS 'A' Giant Slalom course, which is fully covered by sno-makers and consequently can guarantee adequate snow cover.

The central concourse forms a gentle snow slope where the lowest age-groups can play in complete safety. They are separated from adult skiers and yet can be watched from the terraces by their elders.

The architecture is well suited to the location and has avoided excessive concrete claustrophobia while retaining the features of the covered shopping arcades and easy, dry-shod access to all areas. The accommodation is equally divided between hotels and apartments.

Samoëns lies at the end of the neighbouring valley. It is a small chain of three villages, Morillon, Vercland and Samoëns, which are linked by a bus. The skiing is very limited and the area is better suited to leisurely summer vacations with a multitude of walks and scrambles over pleasantly forested hills. The ski route from Flaine is moderately difficult to difficult and can be excessively cold.

The area around Samoëns offers delightful summer walks as well as exciting winter skiing.

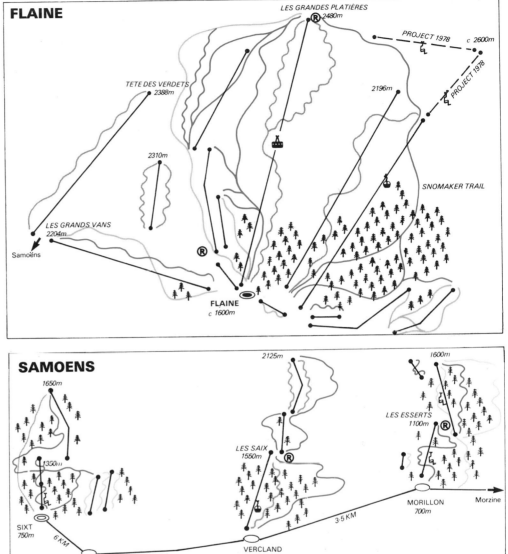

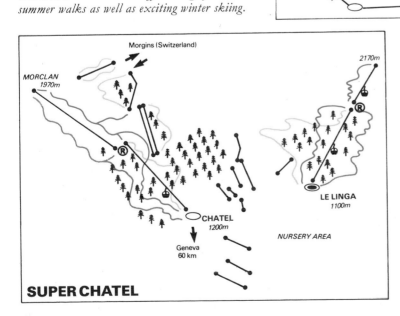

CHAMONIX *Haute Savoie*
Le Tour/Argentière/Chamonix/Les Houches/St Gervais/Megève

These resorts, taken individually, do not offer great skiing. They are, however, linked by one pass for the whole of the Mont Blanc area, and this greatly increases the facilities. Two high, Alpine trails have given these villages world renown: the dramatic Vallée Blanche run from just below the summit of the Aiguille du Midi to Chamonix, and the extremely testing glacier route from Les Grands Montets to the gondola station at Lognan above Argentière. The sight-seer and the skier can take a cable-car from the Aiguille du Midi across the Vallée Blanche to the Pointe Heilbronner on the Italian frontier. A difficult and long run takes the skier to Courmayeur or back into the Vallée Blanche. This journey alone would be worth a visit to the area for the competent skier, while the sight-seer can enjoy again the breathtaking view across the valley on his return in the cable-car.

The villages are loosely linked by rail and road, and, using the little town of St Gervais as a base, it is possible to find a large and difficult skiing area, which makes this traditional and fashionable area extremely attractive.

Chamonix town has little skiing beyond the rather frightening upper section of the Brévent to Plan Praz. Le Tour, at the Swiss end of the valley, is simple, single-slope sliding. Les Houches, joined by skilift over the Prarion to St Gervais, would not occupy even a moderate skier for more than a few days, and the runs into St Gervais are, except in perfect snow conditions, typically pre-Alpine, scratch trails.

It would, however, be very wrong to dismiss Chamonix as insignificant in terms of modern downhill skiing. It is, first and foremost, a base from which a great diversity of skiing is possible and the closely linked transport systems, both bus and rail, makes this practicable. For the serious ski mountaineer it provides the services, guides and facilities which make this minority sport simple. There are ample training routes for the town dweller to acclimatize himself for the long and arduous days on the Haute Route which customarily start or finish here.

Chamonix is not a modern ski-drome, but a traditional, slightly old-fashioned, vacation town which can provide anything and everything from expensive nightclubs to the simplest dormitory accommodation.

154

GARE HELBRONNER 3466

AIGUILLE VERTE 4121

GLACIER DU GEANT

LES GRANDS MONTETS 3295

LE CHAVANNE

CROIX DE LOGNAN 1965

REF DE LOGNAN

BALME 2150

CHARAMILLON 1950

LE TOUR 1462

MONT BLANC 4807

AIG DU MIDI 3842

LE BREVENT 2525

ST GERVAIS

BELLEVUE 1800

COL DE VOZA 1653

LE PRARION 1966

PLAN DE L'AIGUILLE

LES HOUCHES 1008

PLAN PRAZ 2000

MONTENVERS 1909

L'INDEX 2450

CHAMONIX MONT BLANC 1035

LA FLEGERE 1877

LA TRAPPE 1750

ARGENTIERE

THE VANOISE RESORTS *Savoie*
The Vanoise ski resorts lie in a great semi-circle around the 12,000 foot peaks of the Vanoise National Park. Each resort is like a tentacle probing into the forbidding glaciers and mountains that make this area one of great scenic beauty for a holiday of any kind.

Although most skiers prefer to travel to these resorts from Geneva airport by rented automobile or coach, they are most easily reached by direct rail connection from the Channel ports and Paris. In winter, special train coaches terminate at Bourg-St-Maurice.

The resorts are loosely linked. It is possible to move on skis from Val d'Isère, through Tignes and Champagny to La Plagne and Les Arcs. To facilitate the interchange, one lift pass is valid in all these resorts. Skiing throughout the area is on high, long trails. It is moderately difficult and very satisfying.

All the centres, with the exception of the little hamlet of La Rosière on the Little St Bernard Pass and Champagny, are created. They offer a diversity of architecture varying from the massive to the stark and simple. The skiing season extends from early in December through to mid-summer, with the preferred months being late February to mid-April.

From La Rosière, with a minimum of climbing, the skier can go into Italy to the hamlet of La Thuile, a few miles south of Courmayeur. The reverse journey is easier as no climbing is involved and it is less strenuous.

LA PLAGNE *Savoie*
Mont Chavin/Plagne Village/Plagne-Bellecôte/Aime-La-Plagne
The La Plagne complex, an entirely new centre, must be one of the most unusual and controversial resorts. The area is immense, and lies almost entirely above the tree-line in open Alpine pasture. Designed for the average recreational skier, it takes even an experienced skier a while to understand the entire trail complex.

Dominating the mountainside is the bulk of the Aime-La-Plagne condominium complex, which is also called 'Aime 2000'. The cable-car that links it to the centre of La Plagne is probably the only red-plush-lined vehicle of this nature. It runs all night, and departs and arrives within the building complexes. Equally surprising is the gondola which rises to the Grande Rochette. It has been well designed by an architect.

Summer skiing is now possible on the upper slopes of the Bellecôte and direct links with Champagny and Les Arcs make this skiing area one of the largest in the world.

LES ARCS *Savoie*
The complex of residential areas which make up Les Arcs – Arc Pierre Blanche, Arc Chantel, Arc 2000 and Nancroix – is the creation of Robert Blanc, the son of a local mountain farmer. Planned as a recreational centre, with no thought of gaining fame for its race courses, Les Arcs is now one of the most interesting resorts in the world.

The ski fields located to the right of Arc Chantel are designated as 'Ski Total'. No trails are marked out and, though there are a few signposts, the ground has been left in its natural state, with trees, rocks, boulders, and gullies. There is a piece of natural forest for those who like tree slaloming, and close by is a special area reserved for free-style skiing. The central area, served by a minimum of lifts, is open fields, 'go-anywhere' country. Beyond the long ridge that separates Arc Pierre Blanche and Arc 2000 lies the area of 'wild skiing' (*Ski Sauvage*) where, apart from one lift system which rises to 3000 metres, there are no other lifts. From the top of the lift the skier is free to climb to the entry of a series of gullies where he can learn, at his own risk, the pleasures of skiing the impossible.

Although most runs are confined to a drop of about 600 metres, careful use of the lifts can produce a series of circuits lasting all day and easily topping 10,000 metres of vertical height difference.

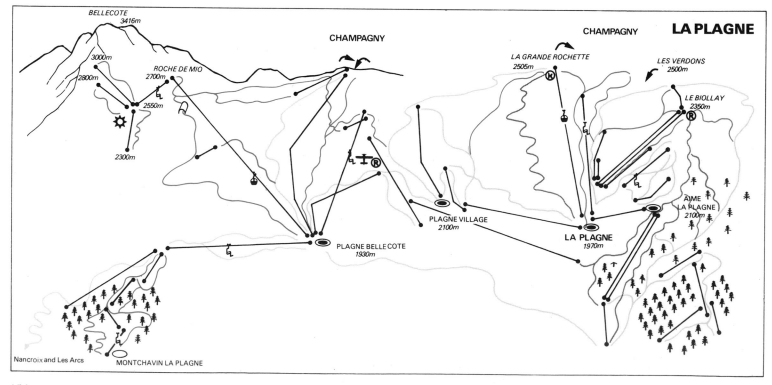

This huge building, Aime 2000, has become the landmark of La Plagne.

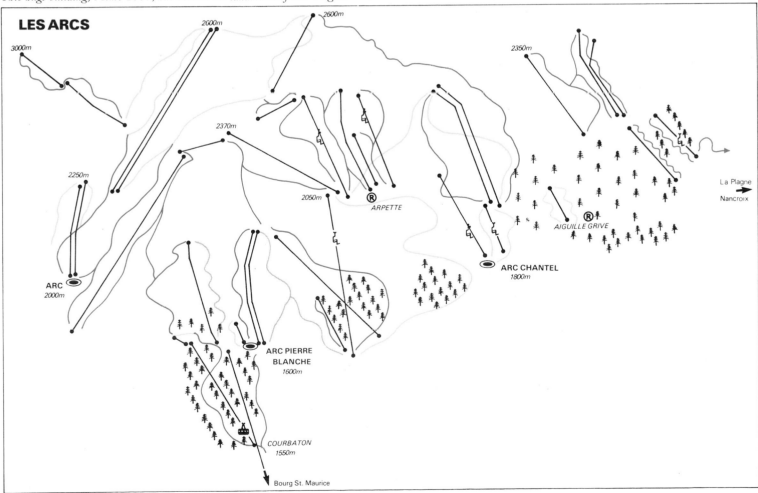

LES ARCS

3000m

2600m

2600m

2350m

2370m

2250m

2050m

Ⓡ *ARPETTE*

Ⓡ *AIGUILLE GRIVE*

La Plagne

Nancroix

ARC
2000m

ARC CHANTEL
1800m

ARC PIERRE
BLANCHE
1600m

COURBATON
1550m

Bourg St. Maurice

AIGUILLE PERS 3387m

3000m

2870m

GLACIER DE PISSAILLAS

L'OUILLETTE 3080m

2700m

TUNNEL

2730m

ROCHER DU CHARVET 2856m

LE MANCHET

BELLEVARDE 2850m ®

PARC A MOUTONS ®

TÊTE DE
SOLAISE
2550m

LE FORNET 1927m

VAL D'ISERE 1850m

VAL D'ISERE LA DAILLE

VAL D'ISERE/TIGNES/LAC DE TIGNES *Savoie*

These three resorts service six distinct ski areas. However, Tignes village and its neighbour, Tignes-Les-Boisse, are not lift linked into the very extensive snow fields of the two principle resorts, Val d'Isère and Lac de Tignes, which is commonly called Tignes.

Val d'Isère grew from a tiny roadside hamlet, at the foot of the Col d'Iséran, into one of the great resorts of the world on the strength of two ski areas, the Tête de Solaise and Bellevarde. The return to the village is still a difficult and often scratchy business, but the skifields above both these cable-car destinations are open, Alpine pasture, well above the tree-line, and few skiers return to the village before the end of the day. The two areas are linked only in one direction, from Bellevarde to Solaise. Most people opting for Solaise do so with the intention of using the vast, open areas of the newly opened Iséran and Glacier de Pissailles trails, many of which lie high enough for year-round skiing.

The Bellevarde forms a complete ski area in itself. It is approached either directly from Val d'Isère or from the new satellite, La Daille, and is closely linked with the Tovière area of Lac de Tignes.

Trails to Tignes also come down the open-

LA GRANDE MOTTE 3656m

POINT DE LA SANA 3437m

3600m

3500m

COTE 3016m

3029m

2800m

ROCHER DE LA PETITE BALME

COL DU PALET 2653m

LA PLAGNE

COL DE FRESSE 2578m

TOVIERE 2708m

POINTE DU CHARDONNE 2869m

CLARET

LAC DU CHARDONNET

LAC DE TIGNES 2100m

LA GRANDE TOURNE 2604

TIGNES

TIGNES LES BOISSES 1850m

MLYNN.78

but-steep slopes of the Chardonnet, or from the glacier lifts of the Grande Motte, which climb up to 3600 metres and are open throughout the year.

The entire area has high, Alpine trails and the novice or even the moderate skier will find most of them too difficult and too long for real enjoyment. These are mountains for the expert. Even the so-called easy trails can become testing with altitude and weather changes. The highest areas, Col d'Iséran and Grande Motte, are the easiest but the return to base inevitably leads to steep, long and testing trails which cannot always be circumvented by hitching a lift on a downhill chairlift.

A visit in late March or April is recommended for greatest enjoyment. The height is then no longer directly related to extreme cold, although the longer days demand early starts, and returns should be made before the snow has a surface of slush.

The Col d'Iséran/Aiguille de Pers area is not generally open before late April and has been developed for late spring and summer skiing.

Accommodation in the resorts is evenly divided between hotel and self-service apartments, though Lac de Tignes, an entirely created centre, has a greater number of apartments.

159

THE SOUTHERN ALPS

The area loosely called the southern French Alps runs along the Italian frontier from just north of Briançon to the Mediterranean coast at Nice. It is subdivided into the Hautes Alpes, the Alps of Provence and the Alps Maritimes. Lower in altitude than the peaks of the mountain chain which leaves France and follows the Italian/Swiss border, and beginning to reflect the Mediterranean climate with a higher timber-line, denser forestation and heavily eroded southern faces, this area still has the height and climate to provide excellent skiing on the northern faces of the mountains from January until April.

A group of minor resorts have developed as a result of the increased interest in skiing in France, and in order to provide both summer and winter use of the amenities. They lie off the main tourist routes, but are easily accessible from Grenoble, Toulouse, the Côte d'Azur and Marseille.

Although the resorts, without exception, are purpose-built, they do not, with the exception of Isola 2000 and Pra-Loup, exhibit the customary ski service station exclusivity of their more northern competitors. They, like the Pyrenean resorts, are French family vacation areas where the emphasis is more on general recreation.

The wild and beautiful mountain region known as the Dauphiné might have remained a mountaineer's mecca, with the climbing problems of the Meije its principle attraction, had it not been the site of the 1968 winter Olympics. Out of this event grew three great skiing centres, Chamrousse, Les Deux Alpes and Les Alpes d'Huez. The renewed interest in Nordic skiing has also introduced many visitors to the exceptionally picturesque, Alpine cross-country trails around Villard-de-Lans and the marathon distances of the Vercors traverses.

With year-round skiing guaranteed on the high glaciers and the easy access from Grenoble, this is an area that will steadily rise in popularity.

Les Alpes d'Huez is an example of all that is best in modern French ski resort planning. It has a magnificent balcony location.

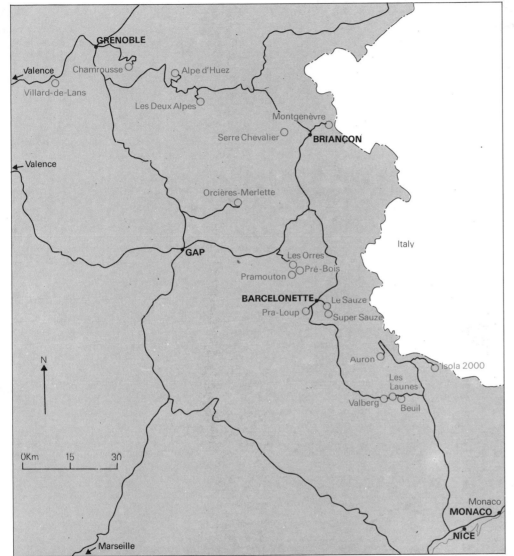

Just because it is labelled a Nordic centre does not mean that Villard-de-Lans (below left) is flat and dull. It is in the heart of Vercors, wild, rugged and exciting. The modern cross-country skier (above) spends part of his training on downhill equipment.

VILLARD-DE-LANS *Dauphiné*

For the skier with catholic tastes and a liking for mixing cross-country relaxation with some rigorous downhill skiing, Villard-de-Lans is an ideal ski resort. There is a 35 or 50 kilometre loipe (the Traverée du Vercors) and a very testing forest trail from the end of the Arolle ski lift down to the Le Clot centre. An alternative test is the Giant Slalom courses that snake through the trees from Côte 2000 down to the Les Pouteils centre, 900 metres of hard skiing below.

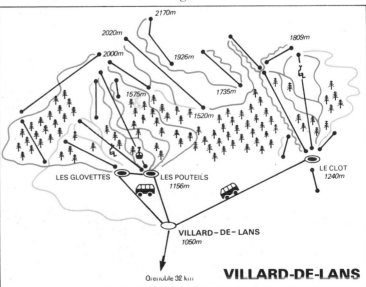

THE THREE VALLEYS *Savoie*
Courchevel/Meribel/Meribel-Mottaret/Les Menuires/Val Thorens

'The most extensive ski area in the world' is how the French people describe The Three Valleys in the Savoie. Nine separate residential clusters in neighbouring valleys form one ski super-centre, and the area has a total of 125 assorted skilifts and about 185 miles of marked trail.

The building of the area's original centre, Courchevel 1850, in 1947, was the most significant development in modern, recreational skiing. Courchevel was designed to cater specifically for the skier, and traditional aspects of earlier winter-sports resorts were abandoned.

There are now five distinct centres. In descending order of altitude they are Courchevel 1850, Courchevel 1650, known as Moriond, Courchevel 1550, Courchevel 1300, better known as Le Praz, and the local administrative village, St Bon. With the exception of St Bon, all the centres are linked by both road and skilift, and it is possible, wherever you stay, to put on your skis at your front door and move, by lift, into any area in the valley.

Accommodation is predominantly in apartment and condominium blocks. Each Courchevel centre is self-contained and well provided with shops and restaurants.

Meribel differs from the other centres in The Three Valleys in that all buildings have been constructed of wood and are limited in height. Smaller and more spread out than Courchevel, it has retained the attractive atmosphere and scale of a picturesque mountain village.

There is less skiing in the immediate Meribel area than in the other Three Valley centres, and the standard of runs is slightly

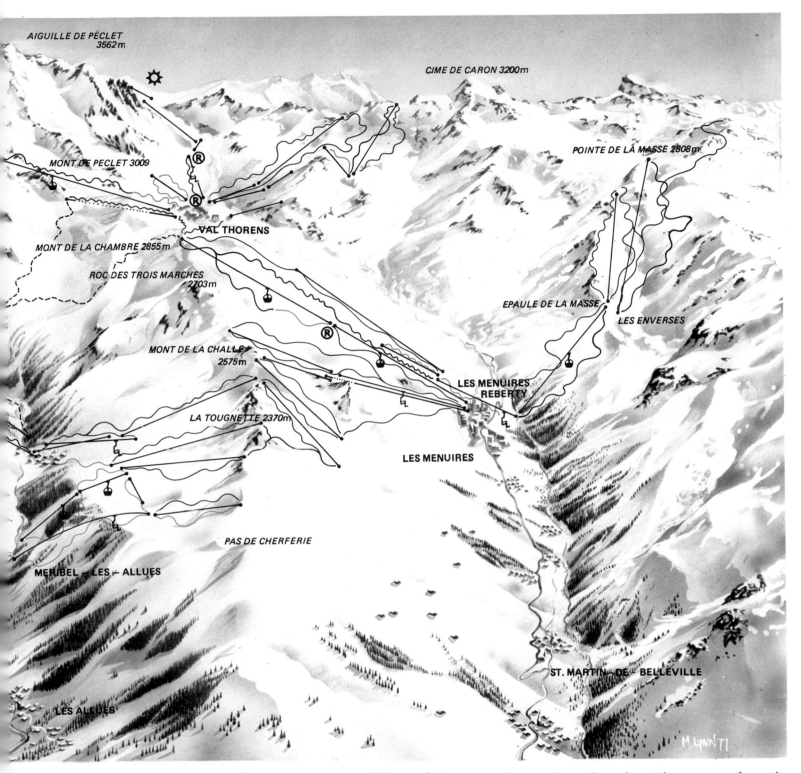

Labels on map:
AIGUILLE DE PECLET 3562 m
CIME DE CARON 3200m
MONT DE PECLET 3009
POINTE DE LA MASSE 2808m
VAL THORENS
MONT DE LA CHAMBRE 2855 m
ROC DES TROIS MARCHES 2703m
EPAULE DE LA MASSE
LES ENVERSES
MONT DE LA CHALLE 2575m
LES MENUIRES REBERTY
LA TOUGNETTE 2370m
LES MENUIRES
PAS DE CHERFERIE
MERIBEL – LES – ALLUES
ST. MARTIN – DE – BELLEVILLE
LES ALLUES
M. LYNN 77

lower. However, it lies in the heart of the region and direct lifts connect the skier with the Courchevel and Menuires area.

Meribel Mottaret is a new, small centre, with limited accommodation but extremely pleasant skiing. The direct descent from the Saulire at 2708 metres to Mottaret at 1735 metres is the longest and most difficult run in The Three Valleys.

Les Menuires presents a very startling contrast to the carefully planned intercommunications of Courchevel or the near-traditional atmosphere of Meribel. Modern, uncompromising hotel and apartment blocks form an amphitheatre facing a very large nursery and children's area.

Les Menuires does have some challenging skiing on the opposite side of its valley. Three lifts rise to the Pointe de la Masse at 1807 metres, leading to exciting, steep-slope, powder skiing.

Val Thorens was the last of The Three Valley resorts to be completed and it is the most interesting. The centre was built above the tree-line, at 2300 metres, and is surrounded by the highest peaks and glaciers of the Vanoise National Park. It provides the very best of high Alpine skiing which con-

tinues throughout the summer from the Peclet lifts.

The skiing is very open and simple, and provides unlimited variety. With the exception of one run from the Mount du Peclet (3009 metres), every lift provides a comfortable blue trail home. The expert skier will find innumerable difficult variants, and an abundance of steep runs.

From above Val Thorens a testing, unprepared, Alpine trail, over 1200 metres long, leads back to Meribel. The same trail can be joined from the summit of the Mont de la Chambre, above Les Menuires.

CHAMROUSSE *Dauphiné*

This resort is two linked centres, Roche Beranger and Recoin, situated only 30 miles from Grenoble. The area was developed for the downhill races of the 1968 Olympic Games. Chamrousse is well supplied with a great diversity of trails from simplest blue to the fearsome collection of downhill race tracks.

As other resorts have discovered, however, the ideal site for competitive skiing is not necessarily equally ideal as a vacation resort and it is probably on this account that the much more dramatic centres of Alpes d'Huez and Les Deux Alpes figure more prominently in tour operators' brochures. This is a little unfair to this smaller resort, for on week days, when the trails are empty, the skiing is extremely entertaining. Because it lies below the timberline, even bad weather does not bring the resort to a grinding halt.

ALPES D'HUEZ *Dauphiné*

Magnificent is a mild description of the skiing in Alpes d'Huez. It is an example of all the best that modern French planning can pro-

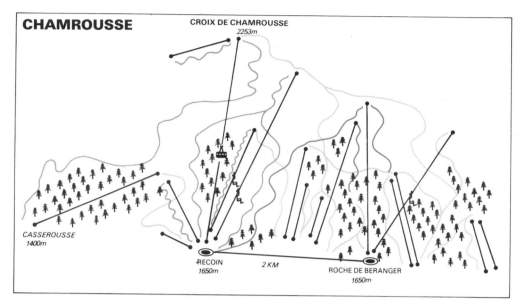

vide, whether you are a novice or a devotee of difficult high-Alpine trails such as that which comes down from the 3350 metre Pic Blanc or the run from the top of the gondola.

A-frame chalets below Alpes d'Huez village.

The Tunnel trail starts innocuously over the Glacier de Sarenne but then dives claustrophobically into a long, narrow, tunnel. Even that is poor preparation for the exit into the seemingly bottomless couloir that drops with frightening suddenness and does not let

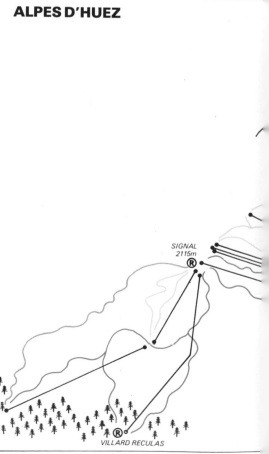

up for another 500 metres of height difference. The same glacier starts the 16 kilometre long run down to the Gorges de Sarennes and on to the chairlift that connects the main village with the Signal de l'Homme, and from there to the tiny hamlet of Auris and some fir-tree slaloming.

Skiers have a lot to thank the Grenoble 1968 Olympic games for.

LES DEUX ALPES *Dauphiné*

With steep, difficult and continually testing runs, this Olympic resort is a constant challenge to every expert skier. The trails are almost uniformly black or severe red, and the height drops from 3170 metres to the village at 1650 metres. Despite dream skiing in fresh powder, the runs can be punishing over worn and icy moguls. It is a relief to know that the lift pass is also valid in Alpes d'Huez and there is a daily, free bus going there and back again.

This is the kind of resort French skiers call '*sportif*' which is a roundabout way of saying the skiing is paramount and living is where you can find it.

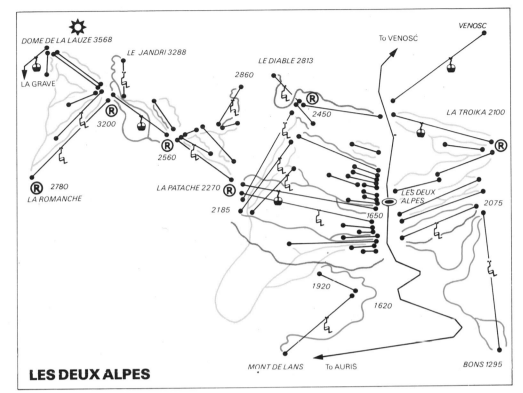

LES DEUX ALPES

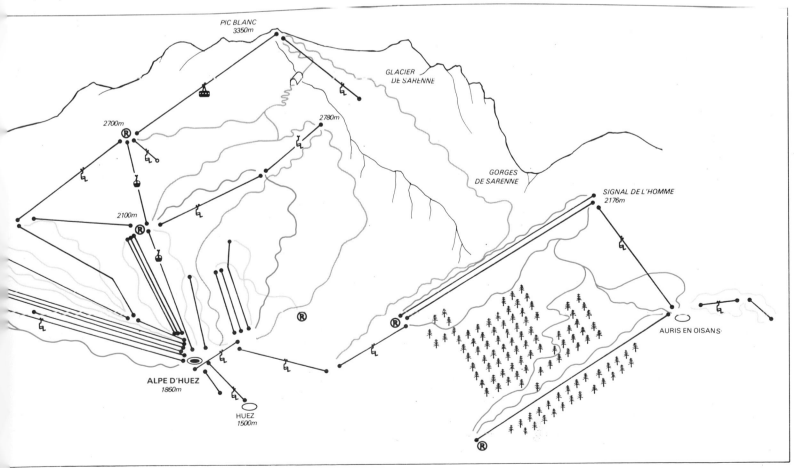

PRA-LOUP
La Foux d'Allos *Hautes Alpes*

Not very long ago, it appeared as if these two neighbouring centres were going to die quietly of neglect. However a simple lift link through a little-visited Alpine pasturage, Les Agneliers, has made them the finest holiday centre for moderate and family skiers in the southern Alps.

Ski-travelling has an irresistible attraction for the moderate skier and for the younger age groups. Here are two resorts where they

Honoré Bonnet, mastermind of many French ski team successes, had a great deal of influence on the development of Pra-Loup.

can indulge in this pastime with safety and considerable skiing pleasure.

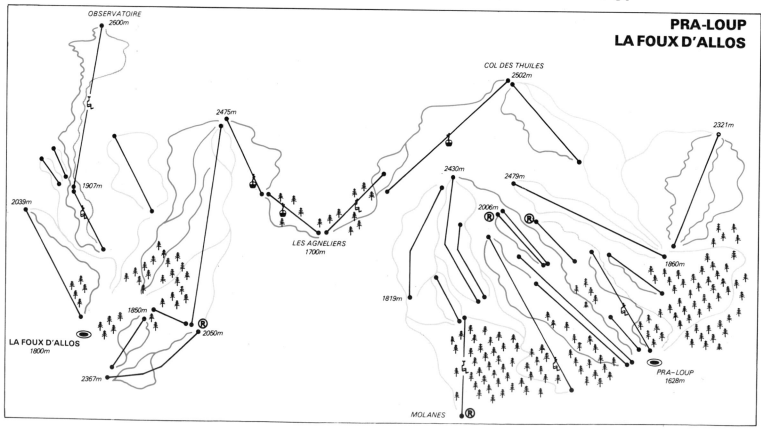

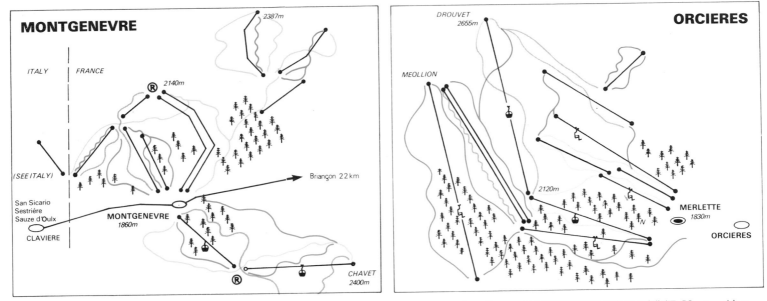

MONTGENEVRE Hautes Alpes

Seen in isolation as a small and limited resort lying almost astride the French-Italian frontier, Montgenèvre has little to recommend it as a vacation centre. But linked as it now is with Clavière and San Sicario in Italy it becomes a most attractive French resort where the best of both countries can be enjoyed, each nationality preferring the pleasures offered by the other.

SERRE CHEVALIER Hautes Alpes

Serre Chevalier takes its name from the dominant peak which rises, wooded and gently sloping, from the valley where four old villages, Chantemerle, Villeneuve, Les Bez and Monetier Les Bains provide accommodation. For those who prefer a more contemporary vacation, a new small complex just outside Villeneuve provides all the customary facilities.

The three areas are not formally linked though a single skipass serves all the lifts, and from December to March a bus shuttles between the villages.

Briançon is only six kilometres away, and so this area is likely to be very crowded at weekends and during holidays.

ORCIERES/MERLETTE Hautes Alpes

Orcière/Merlette may be a small resort, but it is typical of a long list of such places between Grenoble and Nice which have seduced many French families to skiing and encouraged them to spend summer and winter vacations in their own apartments in one resort.

Pleasant, easy skiing in clearings through the dense forest; a good, high peak for views and open skifields; an excellent nursery area; and an old village for old comforts and customs combine with the most modern apartments and full service facilities.

Weekend flats and second homes are a characteristic of resorts close to large towns. Serre Chevalier is no exception.

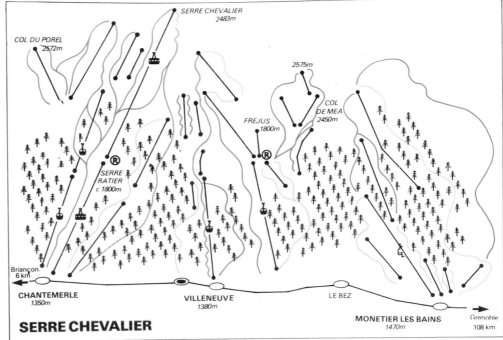

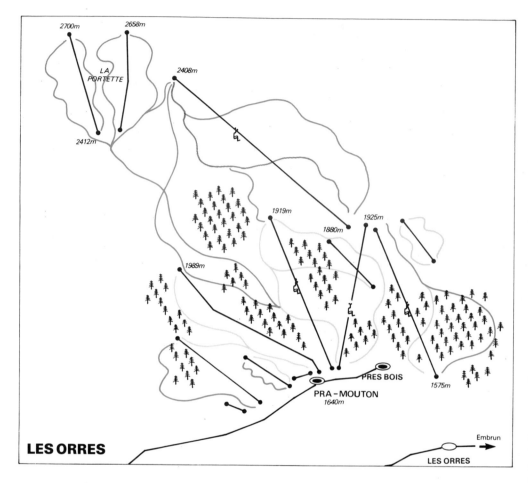

LES ORRES

LES ORRES *Hautes Alpes*
Pramouton/Pré-Bois

Les Orres is another example of the familiar French family vacation resort based on an old village. Pramouton and Pré-Bois are two created centres. The names alone, the Sheep Meadow and Woodside, suggest the kind of countryside this is. Heavily forested hills lead up to a respectable height of close to 2700 metres. There is open grazing meadow above the timberline and wide clearings through the timber down which funnel some good trails, almost all easy or at worst moderate, with just one a little more testing down a 600 metre drop from a small peak. Do not be deceived by the apparently small skiing – the best drop is a full 1100 metres of moderate skiing.

AURON *Côte d'Azur*

Where Isola is modern, compact, high and comparatively treeless, Auron is happily scattered, a judicious mix of old and new, with a surprisingly wide skiing area on three lift-linked mountains. Maximum drops are around 800 metres but the skiing can be difficult. The steep gullies from the top of the Cluot Dauphin cable-car should satisfy any expert. Like all good French family resorts, many of the runs are pleasant woody slides that circumvent the more difficult routes and make sure that all members of a family of mixed skills can start and finish at the same place while not overtaxing their abilities.

There is often an implied criticism in the term 'family' resort. It should never be applied in this sense to France where the term family concerns the living and eating rather than the facility of the skiing.

LE SAUZE *Hautes Alpes de Provence*
Super Sauze

A small two-level summer and winter vacation resort, Le Sauze has big expansion plans which will lift the skiing considerably. The projected gondola rises to 2450 metres and opens up some delightful easy trails through wide forest clearings, which are particularly suitable for family skiing. Otherwise, the runs will not occupy the more experienced for more than a day or so. This is a skiing holiday village and not a ski-drome.

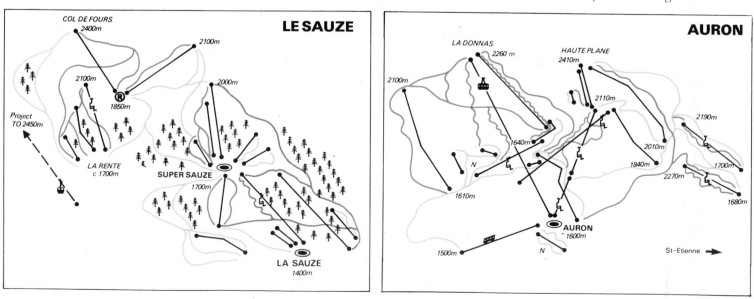

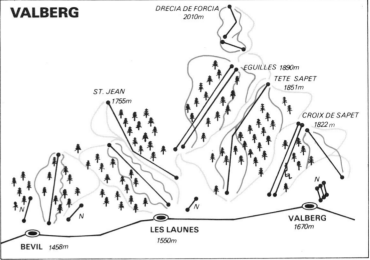

Even simple skiing has its problems and bumps, if taken too fast, leave the skier airborne.

VALBERG *Côte d'Azur*
Beuil/Les Launes
The construction of a few well-placed Poma draglifts produced some pleasant, simple skiing in Valberg. This added the winter-sports season to an already established summer vacation area, through which many tourists have passed on the scenic drive in coaches or cars from Nice to Grasse, through the ravines of Cians and Daluis.

ISOLA 2000 *Côte d'Azur*
Isola 2000, named after the village 7 kilometres lower down the valley, is renowned for being the only European ski resort owned and financed by a British development company, Bernard Sunley Investment Trust. This fact has had a great deal of influence on the character of the resort.

Created largely for the vacation visitor rather than the weekender, only 80 kilometres from Nice Airport, with a guaranteed snow cover and virtually tree-less skiing Isola has become a very popular resort for the mod-

erate and novice skier. It vies with Flaine as being one of the best Alpine centres for children, for the trails are nowhere frightening or hazardous.

If there should be a criticism of the skiing it is that many trails are short (around 300 metres drop) and the skier has to travel a little way away from the centre to find the best long runs.

The trail from the Sistron at 2610 metres leads down to a lonely little hut at 1800 metres where a lift eventually returns its passengers to their residences.

This view of Isola 2000 tells the whole story: Modern ski transport, moderate mountains and modern though inoffensive architectural style.

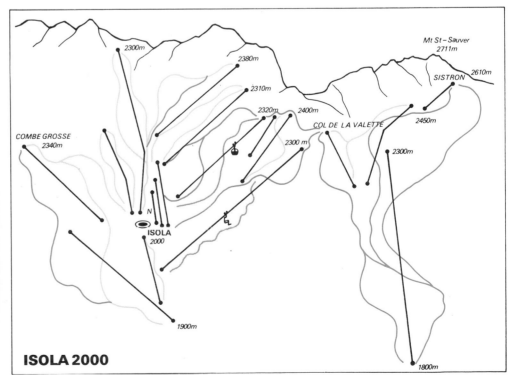

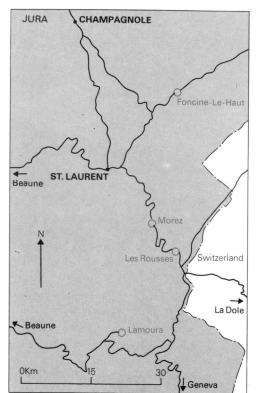

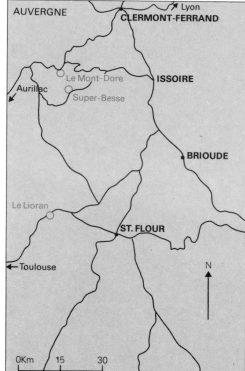

JURA/AUVERGNE

It would be very wrong to discuss French ski areas without some mention, however brief, of two of the oldest ski regions in France. Although completely overshadowed by the great specialist resorts in the high Alps, neither Jura nor Auvergne should be dismissed too lightly.

Curiously, the Jura skiing is better known to Swiss skiers living near Geneva, La Chaux-de-Fonds and Neuchâtel than it is to the French of Beaune and Annecy. The new interest in cross-country skiing should bring this area back into focus. During January and February, it is possible to wander along the gently rolling crests of this range of hills, from farmhouse to country inn, and enjoy a freedom that is rarely found in the more fashionable, downhill ski resorts.

The Auvergne, on the other hand, has

Deep winter in the Jura is as snowfilled and scenically rewarding as in the high Alps.

for many years been a skiing area for the Parisians who flock to the Mont-Dore which is conveniently accessible from the capital. It is enjoying a revival and is rapidly becoming the prime centre in France for cross-country skiing and, in particular, for farmhouse holidays that are reminiscent of the kind of enjoyment that was only to be found in Norway. Super-Besse is the latest of the ski centres to be developed. With Le Lioran and Mont-Dore, it forms a trio of ski bases from which to explore the dramatic countryside of long-extinct volcanoes and deep gorges which, in winter, are even more impressive than the more familiar, summer views.

Uphill telemarks in deep powder are very safe.

LE LIORAN/PRAIRIE DES SAGNES
Auvergne

Le Lioran and its third generation satellite Prairie des Sagnes are probably the nearest any ski centre can come to being a children-only development, taking children to mean any age from nursery to 18. There are 1200 dormitory beds, 300 special infant beds and associated nursery facilities out of a total capacity of 3500. It is also the only French location where you can take your car on the train, put on your skis in the station yard, slide a few metres and embark on the first of 19 lifts and a cableway.

The skiing for this part of the country is impressive. From a top elevation of 1805 metres to the Lioran station at 1235 metres, there are 40 trails of which 12 are black, 10 are red and the rest, that is to say virtually half, are easy and very easy blue trails.

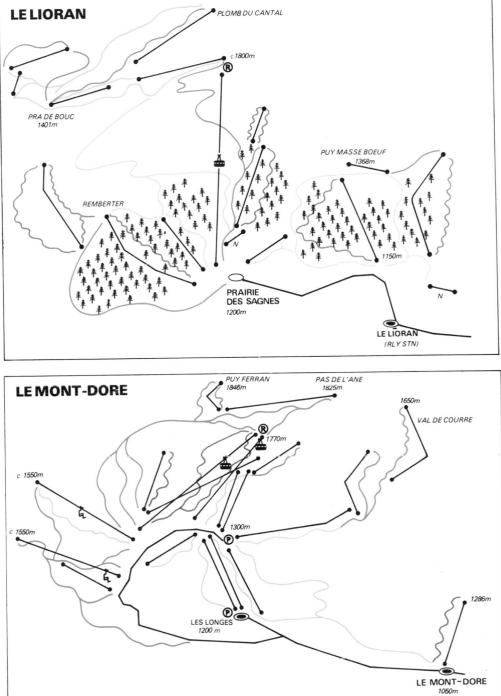

LE MONT-DORE *Auvergne*

Mont-Dore is the oldest and best known of all the Auvergne ski centres. It has a long history as a spa and holiday area and was extremely popular because of the easy access from Paris. It was totally eclipsed by the growth of the third generation ski centres in the Savoie and Haute Savoie but has taken on a completely new lease of life with the unexpected popularity of cross-country skiing. A combination of scenic beauty, an over-abundance of snow and 2500 beds has once again put it high in the popularity league. The downhill potential is not very great though with a top elevation of 1846 metres and a drop of 800 metres of easy-to-moderate skiing and 18 lifts, it can hold its own with any comparable pre-Alpine ski centre.

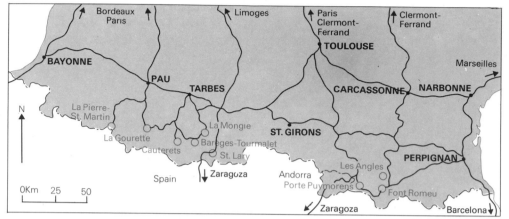

THE FRENCH PYRENEES

Almost unknown as a skiing area outside south-western France, the northern flanks of the Pyrenean chain is, surprisingly, the birthplace of French skiing. Stretching from the Atlantic to the Mediterranean, the area was explored and described by Prosper Auriol in 1901 and, although Chamonix quickly became the internationally known French winter sports centre, it was in the wild and beautiful mountains of Gascony and the Languedoc that serious recreational skiing was practised, and mules and sealskins were used as upward forms of transport. Since then a chain of 14 fully equipped and modern resorts have served the holiday and weekend needs of skiers from as far away as Paris.

That the international skiing world has not discovered, or alternatively, has ignored the great potential of this mountain range is largely due to the unavoidable problems of access. There is only one railway line which crosses the mountains and only four roads are open all winter. Access is either by air to Tarbes, the airport serving Lourdes, or Toulouse. From there an adequate public transport service leads eventually to any of the resorts. However the majority of the visitors arrive by automobile hired at the airport or directly from their homes.

Because of the absence of foreign tourists, the resorts cater specifically for French demands and there are no concessions to foreign habit. As a result, with a few notable exceptions, the accommodation is full board for large families or, in the smaller centres, is more limited for the requirements of the

day-visitor or the Saturday night guest.

The skiing is good, not too demanding and not what in international terms can be described as 'big'. But despite these possible limitations, the scenery is so superb, the country so wild and almost untamed and many of the trails so very exciting that any skier of whatever standard can be happily occupied for at least a couple of days. It is the kind of skiing country where it is best to have a central base and to explore the resorts in the neighbourhood.

Cross-country skiing is well catered

prepared circuits. Anyone interested in Alpine day-touring will also find an almost unlimited area of untouched mountainside and adequate maps and advice. Many of the guides know the mountains intimately through their summer activities of hunting and as wardens of the large National Park.

The snow cover is adequate and as most of the skiing is above the timberline the season lasts well into March. Although it is very dangerous to generalize on weather patterns, it would seem that the Pyrenees tend to have good snow cover in years when the Alps are suffering snow-drought and the converse is equally true. As in the Spanish Pyrenees, December and even January can be difficult months for skiers and the best conditions prevail in February and March.

Tuition and equipment hire is equal to and in many cases better than that found in the larger and more fashionable ski centres of France. Specific short-ski tuition is unusual.

La Mongie, once the most primitive of the resorts in the French Pyrenees, is now the most modern.

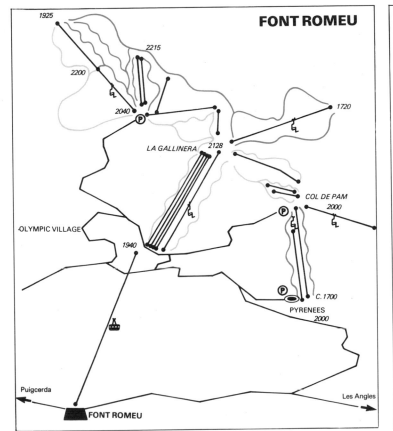

FONT ROMEU

1925
2215
2200
2040
2128
1720
LA GALLINERA
COL DE PAM
2000
OLYMPIC VILLAGE
1940
C.1700
PYRENEES
2000
Puigcerda
FONT ROMEU
Les Angles

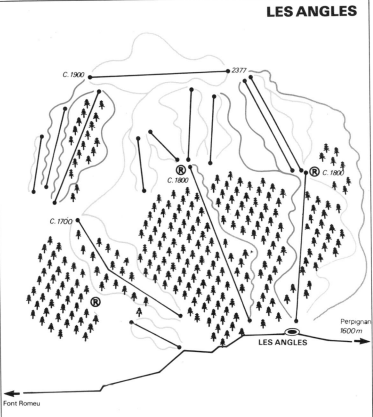

LES ANGLES

C.1900
2377
C.1800
C.1800
C.1700
Perpignan
1600m
LES ANGLES
Font Romeu

FONT ROMEU/LES ANGLES
Pyrenées Orientales

Font Romeu is better known for its solar furnace and research station, and as a gambling centre for tourists, but not as a centre for a skiing holiday. Designed specifically for winter-sports training for the Grenoble Olympic games, complete with a pre-Olympic village, it must be the most intensively mechanized small ski area in the world. The site covers a number of low hills, mostly treeless, which provide many slopes for slalom training and general ski conditioning. There is also a full set of Olympic cross-country circuits.

Les Angles is only 18 kilometres away and is a modern resort, well mechanized for the short-stay skier, with a great variety of runs. There is a very pleasant beginners' area on the open and treeless heights above the daylodge at about 1800 metres. Two black runs scratch their way through the trees and provide a variety to the standard red and blue trails and the drop of about 750 metres is just sufficient to test leg muscles.

This is the kind of snow and standard of style that a visitor to Font Romeu can find.

173

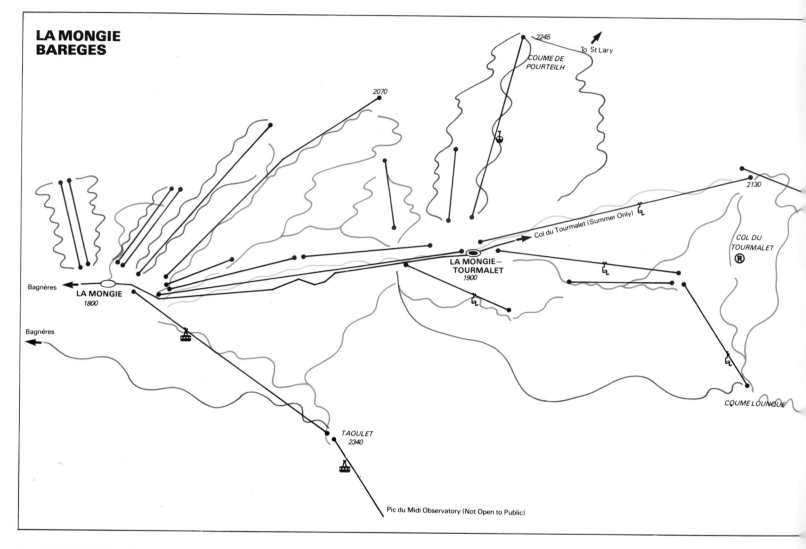

LA MONGIE/LA MONGIE-
TOURMALET/BAREGES *Hautes Pyrénées*
La Mongie is an expert's resort. Located on
the bare and inhospitable Col Tourmalet and
dominated by the space-age silhouette of the
Observatory of the Pic du Midi, La Mongie,
together with its modern satellite, La
Mongie-Tourmalet, has the most extensive
and challenging skiing in the Pyrenees –
providing snow conditions and weather are
favourable. In bad weather the area can
become a veritable trap with almost all slopes
in danger of avalanche.

Dominating the skiing in terms of difficulty
for the enthusiastic vacationer is the steep and
narrow descent from the Coume de Pourteilh,
from where, in time, it will be possible to ski
into the St Lary area. The Col Tourmalet runs
are uncomplicated but the long slide down to
Super Barèges (at present little more than a lift
station and a hay hut) and onwards to the low-
lying and heavily forested Barèges is a journey

to challenge even the Parsenn for length and
variety. Snow permitting, the return is fully
lifted.

Barèges provides a well-mechanized, low-
level, short run resort, though the black trail
from Ayre at 2050 metres down to the village
of Barèges can be a nightmare of ruts and ice if
conditions are not good.

LES CAUTERETS *Hautes Pyrénées*
The skiing in this area is based on the old spa
town of Cauterets and takes place in the great
snow bowl of the Cirque du Lys, which is
reached by a two-stage cable-car. It is safe,
open and ideal for children, but more extensive than the maps might show. The area
could have been specially planned with family
holidays in mind, for once in the bowl there is
virtually no escape and children can be
watched from the restaurant.

The large cross-country area at the Pont
d'Espagne has both prepared closed loipes

and long natural trails through the beautiful
countryside of the National Park with its
abundant wildlife. The town of Cauterets
itself is a delightful and beautifully preserved
example of Second Empire architecture.

PORTE PUYMORENS *Pyrénées Orientales*
This unassuming roadside village at the top of
the Puymorens pass is typical of many small
French resorts designed for day or weekend
visitors who prefer the seclusion and relative
cheapness of the modern accommodation on
the Pass to the more elaborate comforts of
Font Romeu. The skiing is easy, offering little
more than simple and shallow turn-and-
traverse trails. There is a doubtful black run in
the centre and an easy red back to the
residential area. The nursery and novice area
is above the treeline at the Lac d'Estagnol
(2030 metres) where it has a full day of
sunshine and is well sheltered from the
occasional Pyrenean winds.

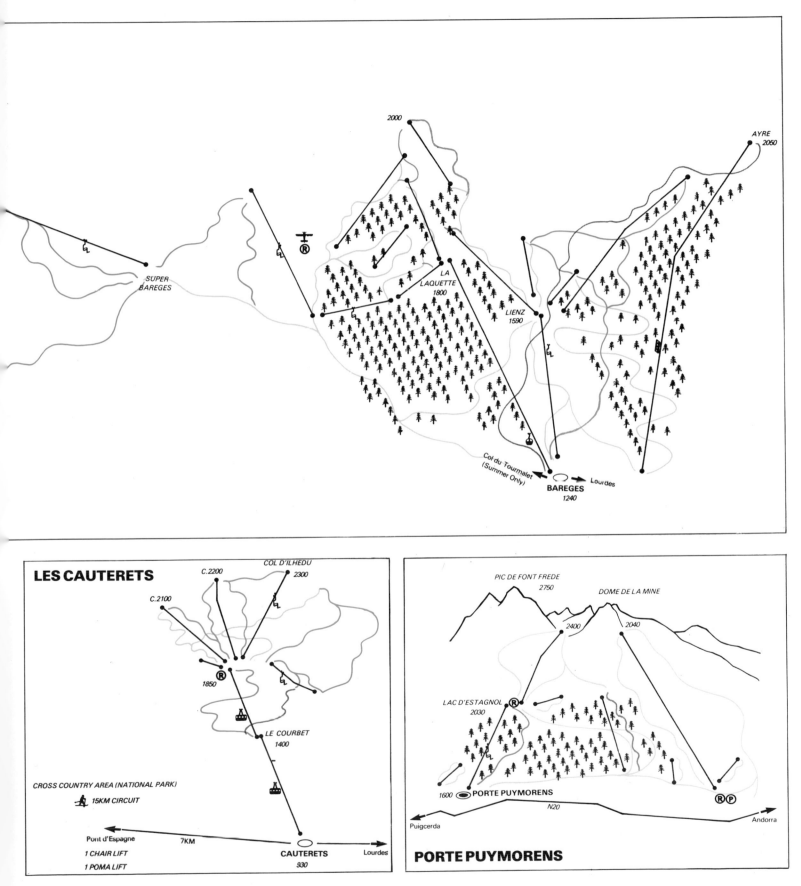

2000

AYRE
2050

SUPER
BAREGES

LA
LAQUETTE
1800

LIENZ
1590

Col du Tourmalet
(Summer Only)

Lourdes

BAREGES
1240

LES CAUTERETS

COL D'ILHEDU

C.2200

2300

C.2100

®
1850

LE COURBET
1400

CROSS COUNTRY AREA (NATIONAL PARK)

15KM CIRCUIT

Pont d'Espagne
7KM

1 CHAIR LIFT

1 POMA LIFT

CAUTERETS
930

Lourdes

PIC DE FONT FREDE
2750

DOME DE LA MINE

2400

2040

LAC D'ESTAGNOL
2030
®

1600 PORTE PUYMORENS

®P

Puigcerda

N20

Andorra

PORTE PUYMORENS

175

SAINT LARY *Hautes Pyrenées*
Do not despair at the first sight of St Lary.
The village is unspectacular and even after
having gone up to the modern constructions
of the Pla d'Adet and consulted the trail map
you will still be confused and possibly
disheartened.

In practice, starting from Pla d'Adet, lifting up to the Sommet de Soome, skiing down
to Espiaube, lifting on to La Tourette and
then exploring the wide open slopes towards
point 2025 and skiing all the way back, taking
in La Soumaye, the skier can cover the best
part of 20 kilometres horizontal and 5000
metres of vertical skiing. Most of it is for
those of a moderate standard though the
lower parts of the slopes invisible from La
Tourette will be much easier. In due course St
Lary will be connected to La Mongie.

What confuses in this ski area is the fact
that, without showing a survey map, it is
impossible to portray the true topography.
Espiaube lies in the centre of two mountain
masses. Crossing from this area to point 2025
(apparently nameless but also referred to as
the end of the 'Ours' (Wolf) trail either over
La Tourette or the Col 2290, the trail drops
behind the line of mountains to the left of
Espiaube.

St Lary is also unusual in the fact that it has
constructed this entire ski complex out of
village funds, without outside financial help.
This was made possible by money received
from the construction of the Cap de Long
hydroelectric project which left the valley rich
but unemployed.

LA GOURETTE *Pyrenées Atlantique*
This recently completed ski resort is typical of
the kind of surprise that awaits the visitor to
the Pyrenees and confounds the skeptics who
are inclined to dismiss the area as being
'uninteresting'.

Dominated by the spectacular mass of the
Pene Medaa which bisects the area, La Gourette not only caters for the moderate-to-good
skier but also provides all-year-round skiing
in a sheltered, north-facing bowl below the
Pene Blanque. The non-stop run to the village
has almost exactly 1000 metres in height
difference and for those who delight in really
difficult skiing the 500 metres drop from the
same starting point to the central lift meeting
point is enough to test all their techniques and
the cross-country area is very extensive.

The open ground skiing of La Gourette.

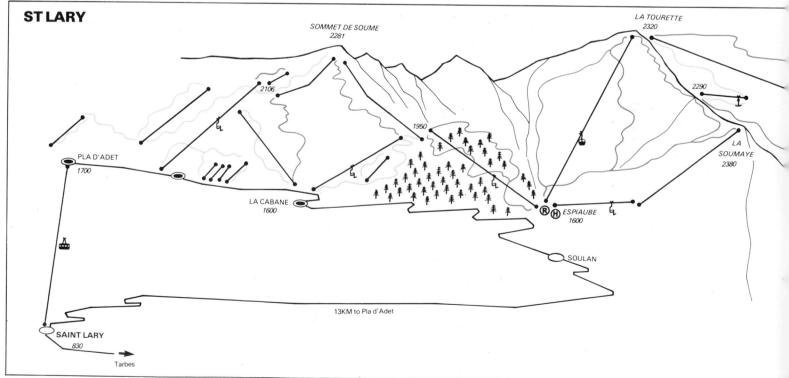

LA GOURETTE

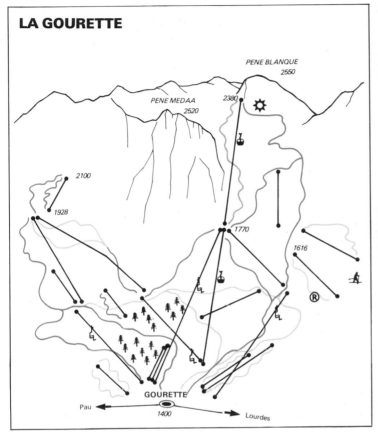

PENE BLANQUE
2550

PENE MEDAA
2520

2380

2100

1928

1770

1616

GOURETTE

Pau ← 1400 → Lourdes

LA PIERRE ST MARTIN
Pyrenées Atlantique

This limited ski resort, the most westerly of the Pyrenean ski centres, is typical of the small French family resort, catering for the moderate and novice skier in near-idyllic surroundings. High enough at 1650 metres to be

The village concourse of La Gourette may look modern but the atmosphere is that of a traditional ski village.

sure of good snow conditions, well-forested to make for picturesque walks and rambles, the ski area extends on to a large 'go-anywhere' upland which is most enjoyable.

LA PIERRE ST MARTIN

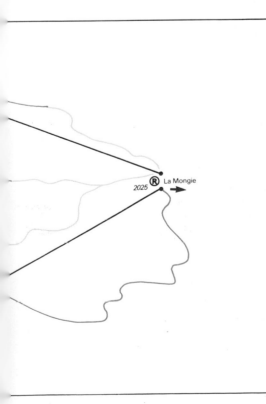

La Mongie

2025

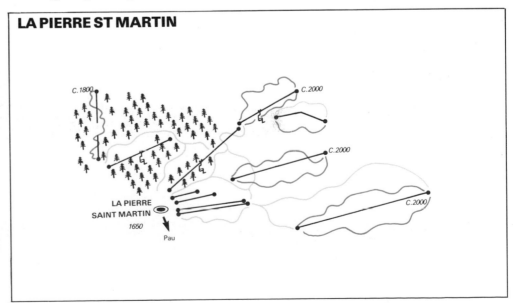

C.1800

C.2000

C.2000

C.2000

LA PIERRE SAINT MARTIN

1650

Pau

Spain

Spanish mountains have always been overshadowed by the Alps for the sport they have to offer. However, one million Spanish skiers have found, in the Pyrenées and the Sierra Nevada, 17 different resorts, lift rises of up to 3400 metres, and a season which begins in November and lasts until June.

Some of these resorts are little more than a ski tow and some primitive accommodation, and several could not be rated above minor holiday villages if judged on an international scale. Navacerrada, only 20 miles (32 kilometres) outside Madrid on the road towards Segovia, is dominated by some extremely ugly club hostels and a mountain the shape of a pudding basin surmounted by a television mast. It is the kind of centre which would not attract the serious skier and, despite its many lifts, it is either too crowded, too windy or too limited for more than a day's visit from the city. Others, such as Puerto de los Cotos in the Guadarrama range, or Puerto de Pajares in the Cantabrian mountains, are based on club huts and offer light relaxation for serious mountaineers rather than holiday facilities for downhill enthusiasts.

Spain is left with an exciting list of major resorts once these minor places have been eliminated. With the exception of the Sierra Nevada centre, Sol Y Nieve in the south, they are all located in the deeply ravined line of the Spanish Pyrenees and its extension along the Atlantic coast in what is known as the Picos de Europas, inland from Santander.

Although, theoretically, the ski season extends the full length of the winter and into late spring, the snow is likely to come late and the early winter months have a reputation for being windy. Long-term records suggest that Spanish snow-cover is most ample when the Alps have a poor snow season and vice versa. This is explained by the fact that, again in very general terms, the Spanish mountains receive their snow from the south-west, whereas the Alps depend upon cold air from the north and north-east meeting up with the warm moist air rising northwards from the Mediterranean basin.

The standard of skiing and the instruction are good and could be called

a judicious mixture of Austrian and French styles. Rented equipment is poor and, although Rossignol have a Spanish ski factory, the cost of new equipment is high. Living and entertainment prices as well as lift passes. are, by Alpine standards, inexpensive but inflation is rapidly eroding this differential.

Access to the Pyrenean resorts is either from Barcelona, Zaragoza or Bilbao. The Sierra Nevada is most easily reached from Granada although Malaga airport is more often used as it also serves a number of fashionable summer and winter holiday resorts on the Mediterranean coast.

Skiing equipment (left) is readily available in Spain and all the best makes can be found. Pyrenean villages (right) are old, huddled and picturesque with few amenities for tourists.

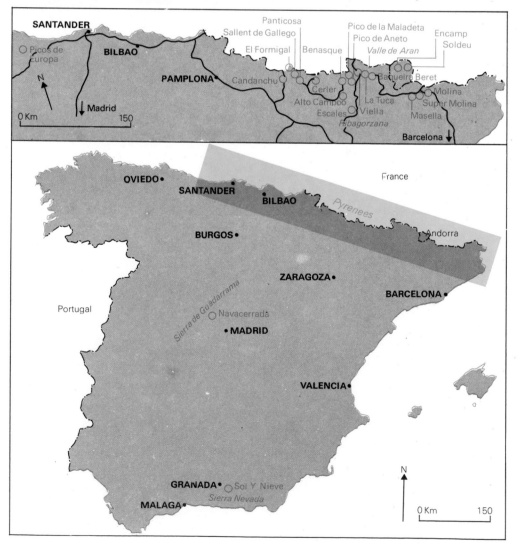

As in so many mountain areas, hydro-electric engineering produces dams, which make hitherto inaccessible mountain valleys a tourist attraction.

LA MOLINA/SUPER MOLINA/ MASELLA

Anyone looking at the trail map of these three resorts could be excused for being impressed with the apparent diversity and size of the skiing offered. Unfortunately, rivalry and obstinacy have made of this oldest of Spanish ski areas a completely disorganized, disjointed mess.

The Molina complex, based on a dreary railway station on the Barcelona – Puigcerda – France railway link, consists in essence of a rather crude dormitory area, La Molina, in the valley, and a modern, scattered and unplanned resort known as Super Molina. These two are linked by a chairlift. However, from the top station there is still a very long walk either into the very simple skiing of Super Molina or the completely independent and poorly planned lifts of the Comells on the Barcelona road. In theory this should produce some entertaining skiing which would take a good skier back to the vicinity of the station. However, snow cover here is so poor and the trails so uncompromisingly difficult, icy and narrow that they are rarely used and cannot be relied upon to be operational.

The pride of Super Molina is the two-stage gondola which leads to the highest point, the Tossa d'Alp, at 2535 metres. The start is a tortuous, ten-minute car ride from the centre of Super Molina and the skiing here is not linked with that of the Comells. The skiing is long and interesting, particularly the only partly prepared black-to-red trail, but any carless skier is faced with a long and tiring walk home.

For Molina skiing three separate lift passes are currently required and an automobile is almost essential.

Masella shares the Tossa d'Alp with Molina but is a very different kind of resort. At present it consists of no more than a single large low hotel, tucked into the forest. It has a multitude of trails which wind through the dense trees and a cunningly planned set of lifts, the work of a Basque/American/Swiss called Ted Armengol. Unfortunately, so far, no amount of argument has persuaded the Molina Tossa d'Alp lift company to agree to a joint lift pass with Masella, a move which would make the Tossa d'Alp skiing extremely attractive.

This area suffers from one further disadvantage. It is only two and a half hours from Barcelona and on a fine weekend the crowds can become quite impossible. Fortunately Masella is saved from the worst of this and the great masses surge around the Comells area where the easy trails and the open ground manage to swallow most of the skiing hordes, which the Tossa d'Alp cannot do.

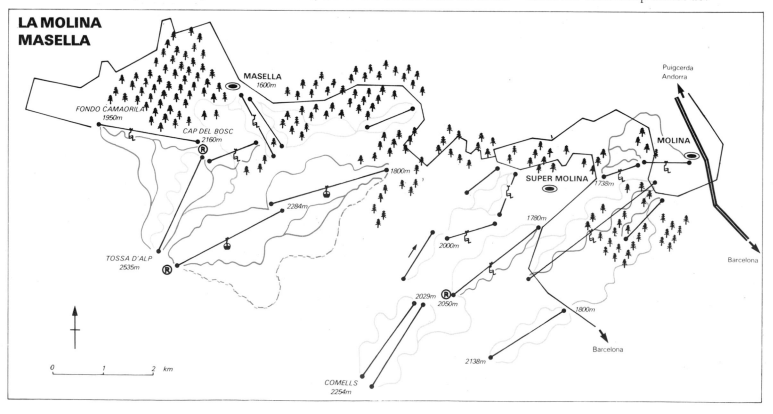

LA MOLINA
MASELLA

MASELLA 1600m

FONDO CAMAORILA 1950m

CAP DEL BOSC 2160m

1800m

2284m

TOSSA D'ALP 2535m

2000m

2029m

2050m

2138m

COMELLS 2254m

SUPER MOLINA 1738m

1780m

MOLINA

1800m

Puigcerda Andorra

Barcelona

Barcelona

0   1   2 km

ANDORRA
Soldeu/Pas de la Casa

Andorra is more readily associated with duty-free liquor than with skiing, though a quick look at the map shows that, like the Spanish Pyrenean resorts, it is well placed to provide ski slopes. This it does in three places: Arinsa, a tiny settlement with only one ski lift at the end of the Orat Negre river, Soldeu and Pas de la Casa on the Envalira to Toulouse road.

Of these Soldeu is the better known and more acceptable. It is a tiny roadside village offering limited accommodation, although its neighbour, Encamp, a suburb of Andorra-La-Vella has more hotels. After a dizzying walk across a narrow iron bridge from Soldeu, a chair lift goes up to a very pleasant mountain inn and a small collection of lifts. The skiing is distinctly limited and simple, much of it through clearings in the dense forest with one open, moderately steep run from the local summit, which is nameless, and

a steep and very scratchy black trail from the inn down to the bottom chairlift station.

Pas de la Casa, on the northern side of the Envalira Pass, is a huddle of modern hotels on the very edge of the French frontier. It suffers from being on the route of smoke-belching lorries carrying their sealed loads of duty-free merchandise to the emporiums of Andorra-La-Vella. It is a cold, high, cheerless place with some very long and cold lifts which rise to the Col Blanc at 2800 metres. From there it is possible to go down to Grau Roig, through sparse trees and open meadows and spend the rest of the day, in the sun, away from the crowds, exploring the innumerable alternative routes that provide a complete spectrum of difficulties from simple blue to steep, unremitting black.

One day, a cable-car will be built linking Grau Roig with the Soldeu skiing, but it may take a long time for the complicated feudal laws governing such undertakings would

appear, for the moment, to be insoluble.

A small compensation for this missing link is a rather remarkable restaurant, about half-way between Grau Roig on the Envalira road, called *The Snail and Quail*. Cross-country skiers are more likely to find it than the downhill enthusiasts, and having found it, it is unlikely that skiing will be of further interest that day, for a diet of snails, quails and red wine is not good for a keen sportsman.

Despite the considerable potential for future development particularly in the Arinsa area, skiing inevitably takes second place to the basic tourist attraction of duty-free shopping. Awkward access for foreign skiers does not contribute to the popularity of the otherwise uninteresting two or three resorts and the unmanageable crowds that flock up from Barcelona at weekends further detract from the ambience of the area. The ski-mountaineer and touring skier should not, however, be deterred from these lovely mountains.

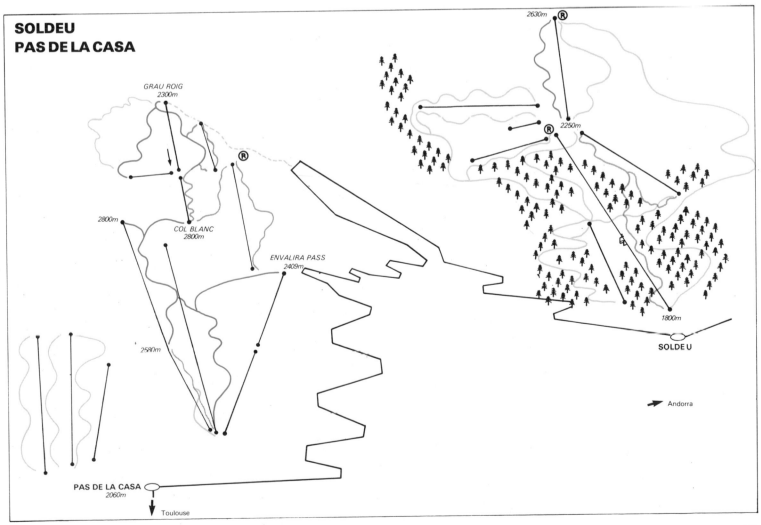

SOLDEU
PAS DE LA CASA

GRAU ROIG
2300m

2630m Ⓡ

2250m Ⓡ

2800m

COL BLANC
2800m

ENVALIRA PASS
2409m

2580m

1800m

SOLDEU

Andorra

PAS DE LA CASA
2060m

Toulouse

BAQUEIRA/BERET

Twelve kilometres from Viella on the summer road leading over the Bonaigua Pass, Luis Arias designed and built Spain's finest ski resort. The hotels and apartment blocks are unobtrusive, luxurious and deliberately limited and lie a short bus journey from the entrance to the ski area. The lifts rise to a maximum height of 2470 metres providing a drop of just over 900 metres over open, virtually treeless slopes. Although there is an excellent, fenced, nursery slope this is an area for moderate and advanced skiers with a great variety of skiing equal to that of any resort in the Alps, with the exception of one or two of the truly big centres.

The organization of Baqueira is superb and this centre is the only one in Europe to provide ski hostesses who introduce the newcomer to the entire skiing area – an idea copied from Vail, Colorado with which this resort is twinned.

One particular run deserves special mention. The Esconacrares dives down a near-vertical couloir very shortly below the sum-

VISTA BERET 2100

BERET 1800

mit of the Cap de Baqueira, and emerges in a picturesque, boulder-strewn valley where the trail slaloms between sparse pines, the valley floor and the boulders to finish at Orri, 700 metres lower. This is a connoisseur's trail of extreme difficulty and links up with a number of other trails leading into this valley, all of which come into the black category. Two lifts go back towards Cap de Baqueira and another opens up a whole new area above the flat plain of Beret. In due course a further lift complex will be constructed in this area to double the present number of trails.

The longest and most consistently difficult trail, though only black for a short distance, is the long route around the Cap de Baqueira known as the De Manaud trail which finishes on the pass road about 500 metres away from the car park.

Uncrowded and beautifully run with an immense future potential Baqueira must rank among the leading ski resorts of Europe.

All the standard runs at Baqueira meet up at the top of the first-section lifts.

CAP DE BAQUEIRA

Spain

2500

2300

® 2200

ORRI 1850

SLALOM STADIUM

Ⓝ

® 1800

®

1750

® BAQUEIRA 1500

Wind is the constant enemy in Formigal and a chairlift can be a very cold vehicle. However spring and hot sun comes early to the Pyrenees.

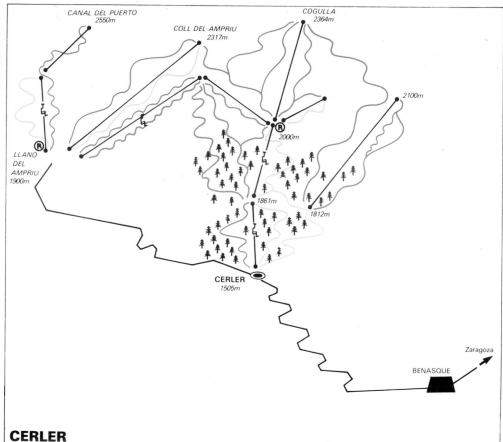

CERLER

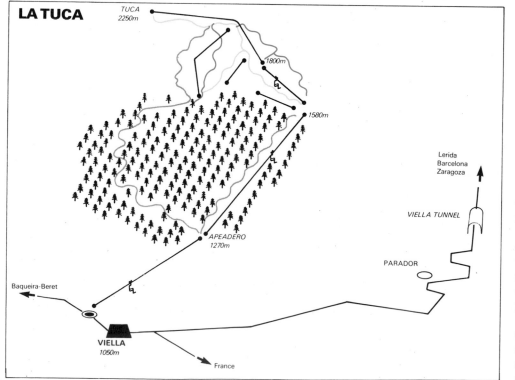

LA TUCA

LA TUCA

The Valle d'Aran, of which Viella is the capital, is a political anomaly for it lies on the north side of the Pyrenees in what, logically, should have been France. It is linked to Spain by means of the road tunnel which runs under the main mountain chain and into the wild valley of the Ribagorzana.

Viella is of little interest except as a shopping and money-changing centre. The new apartment and hotel settlement of La Tüca lies on the western outskirts of the town. The skiing area served by this modern village lies hidden from view on the north-facing slopes of the mountain known as Tüca. The resort is still suffering teething troubles and will never overcome the disadvantage of the long flat area between the hotels and the slopes. This is at present bridged by the first stage of the chairlift, which is an unavoidable journey for all skiers.

Immediately after a good fall of snow, the slopes served by the highest lift to La Tüca summit are rated as excellent powder snow slopes. The wind does, however, soon produce difficult crust.

CERLER

Cerler in the Aragonese Pyrenees lies at the end of a private road which winds steeply up from the medieval town of Benasque. The crude blocks of grey concrete that are being built, which form the created ski resort, are in stark contrast with the ancient stone buildings of the village of Cerler itself, only a few hundred yards behind the modern incursion. The old village is a protected site, and will fortunately not suffer the indignity of being modernized. Undoubtedly, in due course the tiny local inn will become a disco and already one or two outlying dwellings have modern decorations inside their thick stone walls. Apart from these the old and the new live side-by-side in silent animosity.

The skiing here is big, unexpectedly varied and invisible from the bottom lift station. The great white bowl that can be seen from point 2000 is still only a part of the total ski area which extends over and beyond the Ampriu ridge and down into a very sunny valley. It is in this valley that new nursery slopes are to be constructed. They will be reached from the hotels by mini-bus. The existing area has no nursery slopes. Two new lifts leading from the Llano del Ampriu to the Canal del Puerto will mechanize a further vast snow bowl and provide almost unlimited open skiing with no slope closed to the enterprising soft-snow skier.

There is very little entertainment in Cerler and for variety, either in food or music, a journey to Benasque must be made. It is an excursion not to be missed for this externally forbidding town, once entered, shows itself to be a virtually unspoiled example of medieval Spanish complexity and charm.

The scenery around Cerler is magnificent. The towering walls of the Maladetta and Arneto mountains, two of the highest in Spain, and the impressive extension of the Monte Perdido, make this a dramatic place to stay. Exploration into the trackless areas of the wild mountains and the deep-cut valleys reveals countless ancient mountain villages leading a meagre farming existence.

EL FORMIGAL

Only a few interesting hours of ski mountaineering from Candanchu but a long, four-hour drive away, is the tour-operator conceived resort of El Formigal. It is served by a pass road, open only in summer, from Sallent de Gallego to Pau. The village, which comprises one dull, straight street lined with hotels and bars, is inaccessible from the ski slopes which are across a river valley. However, the main lift takes care of transport both ways, collecting returning skiers on the far side of the river. The skiing is extensive with a variety of difficult runs, the longest of which from Pico Tres Hombres to the valley bottom provides a testing 800 metre, downhill drop. The delightfully sheltered, sunny, and extensive nursery slopes on the far side of the mountain restaurant are the hallmark of this resort. They provide an essential ingredient of the skiing in Formigal for the main slopes from the restaurant to the valley bottom can be extremely windy.

There are well-advanced plans for extending the skiing into the broad valley leading up from the nursery slopes towards the Izas mountains. When these plans mature, El Formigal will be one of the best ski areas in Spain. For those interested in mountaineering, this resort is, in theory at least, a very good centre with a great variety of high peaks suitable for ski ascents. However, the village is not in any way geared to such activity and guides would be very hard to find.

Whether by chance or design, Formigal skiing is a model for an instruction complex. The slopes progress steadily from the simplest novice slide through moderate open trails to severe, narrow, steep and mogulled expert ground.

The Spanish trails offer little scope for the downhill racer but Spain has consistently bred world-class slalomers such as Ochoa and Arias.

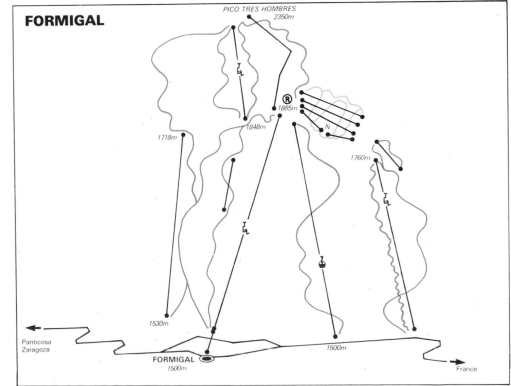

FORMIGAL

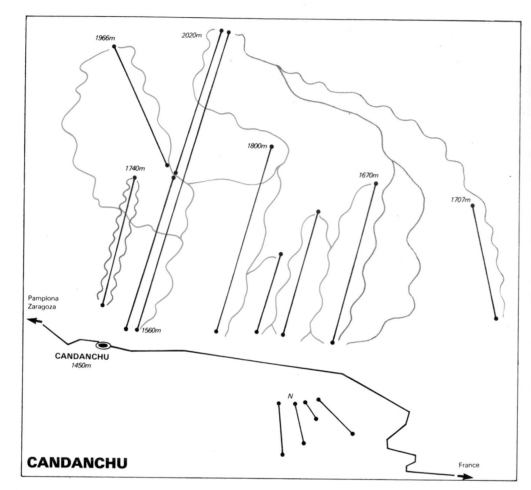

CANDANCHU

Panticosa in the Spanish Pyrenees is an inviting and attractive town. The skiing is on ground which is steep and limited and so many people stay in the village and commute to Formigal.

CANDANCHU

Candanchu is the most westerly of the Spanish Pyrenean resorts. It lies a few hundred yards from the French frontier on the main Huesca to Pau road. Dominated by the Aspe and Zapatillo mountains, it is an uninviting resort serving a wide slab of steep slopes mechanized by a line of parallel lifts. The nursery area on a south-facing slope is very sunny but, as a result, has very little snow. For experienced skiers, all of the routes are difficult to very difficult and provide a maximum of 600 metres downhill running. For those who delight in this kind of skiing, which the French call *sportive*, there is ample ground to practise tight turns with no distractions.

The headquarters of the Spanish Ski School is in Candanchu as well as the main army training base for Alpine troops. There has been considerable talk of developing a nearby area which would provide more interesting skiing, but as yet no progress has been made.

Ski mountaineers can cross from Candanchu to Formigal after a four-hour climb.

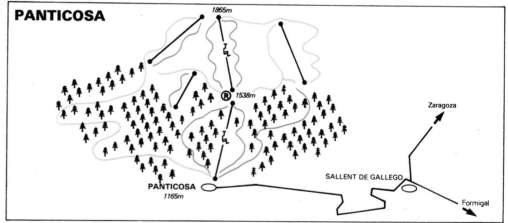

PANTICOSA

A few miles down a narrow country road from Sallent de Gallego is the old, farming and spa village of Panticosa. Very recently attempts have been made to turn this into a rival for El Formigal but the skiing ground is uninteresting and unsuitable. In contrast, the village is attractive and welcoming. Since the land is heavily forested, with no acceptable nursery area and rather abrupt, steep and limited slopes above the mountain restaurant, it is unlikely that very much more can be done to improve the skiing. In practice many of the visitors commute to El Formigal for their skiing and return in the late afternoon with delight to the comforts and rustic surroundings of Panticosa. It is strange that this is the only ski resort in Spain where the original village is used as the accommodation centre. This, alone, will ensure its continued popularity despite the drawbacks of the skiing which is only part of the Panticosa scene.

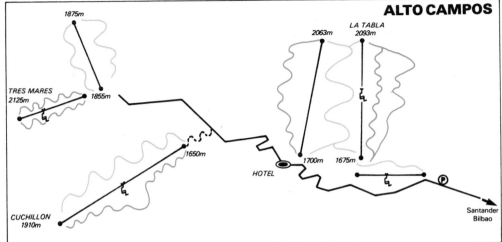

ALTO CAMPOS

There are moguls and moguls; these gentle waves are a pleasure rather than a purgatory.

SIERRA NEVADA
Sol Y Nieve

The most southerly ski resort in Spain – in fact the most southerly major resort in Europe – is dramatic, to say the least. To ski a 3400 metre mountain in powder snow in sight of the sea in a blazing hot sun is an exciting experience. To ski home to the ugly modern development called Sol Y Nieve is a serious disappointment for which there is no real excuse. However, living in the Parador *Sierra Nevada*, even though it is cut off from the discotheques of Sol Y Nieve from 6 pm until the following morning, compensates for all the ugliness of the modern 'village' far below. (The real name of Sol Y Nieve is Prado Llano – the sheep-grazing.)

The skiing is unique. It is moderately easy and very open so that the term 'trail' is really misplaced. The trails are long and incredibly sunny, so that even thoroughly toughened mountain faces can suffer immediate sunburn. There are few places, except perhaps on Parnassus in Greece, where you ski facing nothing except a bottomless blue haze from the distant plain.

Access to this remarkable skiing area is from Granada or Malaga airports, which also serve many summer resorts. Theoretically it is possible to bathe or water ski and glacier ski on the same day.

ALTO CAMPOO

Alto Campoo in the Picos de Europa range has developed principally for skiers living in Santander or Bilbao. It is a single hotel on a barren and desolate valley shelf providing some undistinguished skiing with a maximum height difference of about 300 metres. The resort deserves mention as an example of the enthusiasm of the Spaniards for the sport and the standard of accommodation and service that is the hallmark of Spanish skiing. The food in this isolated hotel is superb, the comfort is above average and the scenery to be enjoyed on a fine day from La Tabla or Cuchillon is magnificently wild. For the adventurous skier there are a number of Alpine touring routes starting here that would certainly repay a visit.

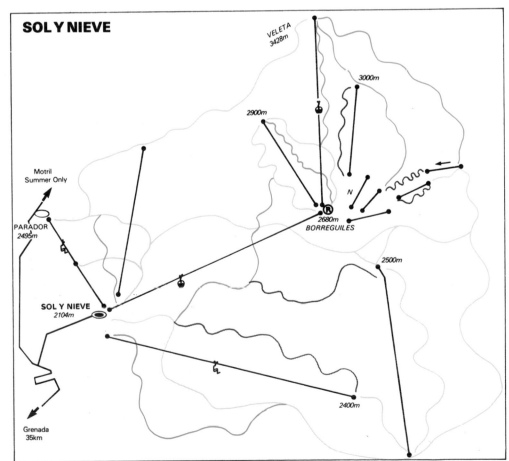

Italy

Skiing in Italy is a post-war development although centres such as Cortina d'Ampezzo and Sestrière were acknowledged resorts many years earlier. The late growth of the industry was due to problems of access from Switzerland, Austria, France, and Germany, the principal countries from which skiers travel, and in each case the routes passed through established ski areas. The few Italians who did ski preferred to spend their money in the fashionable resorts of the Alps and the majority of the inhabitants of northern Italy had neither time nor money for such frivolities. The big change began in the late 1940s and early 1950s when work and money came to the industrial areas of Turin, Milan, Bergamo, Brescia and Venice, and at the same time the habit of a fixed vacation time in winter was rapidly translated into a basic condition of employment.

Today Italy lists, officially, just under 400 resorts and this number is still growing. Many of these places are little more than a summer vacation mountain with transport pressed into the service of skiing. Eliminate these and there are still 50 or 60 major ski centres.

For the most part these resorts, except for the dozen or so that depend on foreign package-holiday tourists, are half empty mid-week. From Friday evening until Monday morning the population is virtually doubled with the arrival of weekend visitors. This can have the unfortunate result for the holiday-maker that many of the lifts are closed or only operating a very much reduced time-table during weekdays. Owing to the relative proximity of the ski areas to the main centres of population and the excellent road access, mainly by motorway, the weekend population can easily reach suffocation point. Day skiers flock in with their vehicles filled with old and young alike of whom only a small percentage will ski while the rest clutter the bottom of the ski trails with every snow vehicle ever invented. The inevitable lift queues are unruly, ill-tempered and badly organized. Car parking is inadequate and the geography of the countryside often makes out-of-town parking lots an impossibility.

Currently Italy is suffering a further complication as a result of its ever-

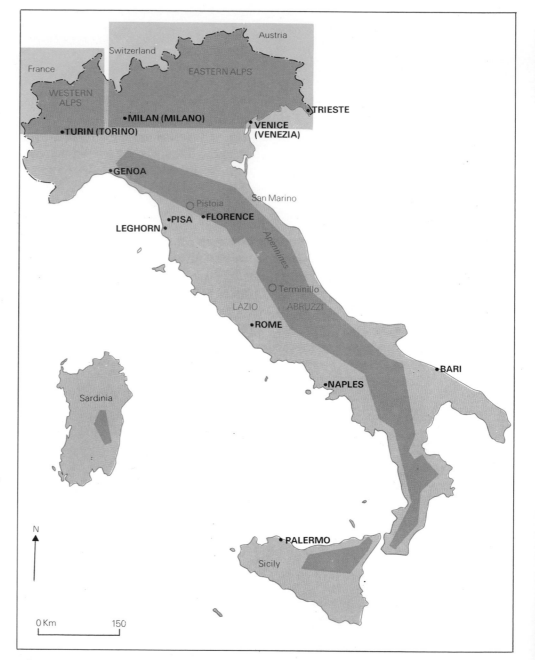

increasing popularity among the low-land nations as a ski vacation country. The number of available hotel beds is shrinking catastrophically owing to staff shortages while at the same time the number of self-catering apartments is growing even faster than the loss of hotel accommodation.

While this may seem a negative approach to vacation skiing in Italy, it should not be taken as advice not to try it. It is merely a warning. Weekends are very likely to be very crowded;

accommodation is not as readily available at short notice as in many other ski areas and provision shops are less international and more purely Italian than for example in Davos or even Les Menuires.

On the other hand, skiing in Italy has compensations which far outweigh any disadvantages. The trails can be magnificent with a scenic diversity and impressiveness that no other winter sports country can match. The season is long, lasting well into May and June.

The summits are very high, the trail standards excellent, prices moderate and the nightlife is enjoyable. Italian resorts are also expert at providing for moderate and novice skiers. There is hardly a major cable-car or chairlift summit which has not, as a first priority, a moderate or easy trail – in fact if any criticism could be levelled at skiing in Italy it is that, in general, the skiing is not difficult enough. But that is something which will, in all truth, worry only a very few people for there is nothing more pleasurable than skiing a trail well within your technical ability

THE WESTERN ALPS

A skier's northern Italy divides conveniently along a north-south line through Milan. The western side includes the lesser-known Alpine area of Piedmont which borders on France and the Valley of Aosta. The Autonomous Province of Aosta occupies the long valley that leads from just north of Turin – to the south face of the Mont Blanc tunnel. It was formerly part of the kingdom of Savoy and the language spoken is French, although all official communications are in Italian.

The strategic importance of this valley has attracted invaders and feudal lords from all over what is now Lombardy and Piedmont. The entire route from Pont St Martin to Courmayeur is lined with the ruins of forts which once guarded the valley. It was first occupied by the Salassians, then from 24 BC by the Romans until the Barbarian invasion, and subsequently by a variety of French dukedoms. Today, the motorways through the Great St Bernard and Mont Blanc tunnels bring the holiday makers who easily outnumber the 100,000 Val d'Aostan natives.

The valley is flanked by the Valais giants in the north, the Monte Rosa to the Grand Combin, the gigantic fortress walls of the Mont Blanc range to the north-west and the Gran Paradiso to the south-west. It is not surprising that the few resorts in the valley are a reflection of the size and grandeur of their mountains.

Only one resort has achieved international status, and that is Cervinia, formerly called Breuil. The rest remain to be discovered. Courmayeur is an

under perfect conditions in beautiful scenery.

The main ski areas border the southern face of the main Alpine chain along the Austrian, Swiss and French frontiers. They are administered by the provinces – a somewhat confusing situation in, for example, the Dolomites which are shared between the Alto Adige (South Tirol), Trentino, Belluno and Bergamo. In addition to these traditional areas, the spine of Italy, notably the Abbruzzi, lying to the east of Rome, is being developed.

It is also characteristic of Italian skiing

that the lift companies will, with a minimum of fuss and great panache, swing a cable-car to the highest available point. There are more ski summits above 3000 metres than anywhere else in Europe. They are also beginning to link resorts and, if the present tendency is anything to judge by, the great circuses such as The Three Valleys in France are facing very serious competition. Two examples of this expansion are the Via Lattea in the Piedmont, which links Montgenèvre in France with Sestrière, and the still unrivalled Sella Ronda in the Dolomites.

Cervinia shares an unfamiliar looking Matterhorn with Zermatt. This view is from the Lago Blu.

ancient climbing village now blossoming with a forest of new lifts. Pila, the ski mountain of the town of Aosta, was once served by a cableway from the centre of the town. Cogne is still totally undeveloped for wintersports. Valtournanche, high up the avalanche-prone valley that cuts between the Valpelline mountains, the Aya and Champoluc, tiny and delightful, are hardly known beyond Aosta and Turin.

Alagna, often wrongly classed as part of the Val d'Aosta, may one day achieve the hoped-for link with Gressoney, a mere two lifts to the west. It is as unknown to skiers as is Champoluc. Macugnaga, to the north of Alagna, can also conveniently be grouped with the Aosta ski resorts, though its valley is even more distant and on skis can only be reached from the Aosta centres by skilled mountaineers. This is

occasionally the final destination of the uncommon, lesser *haute route* which leads from the Val Ferret at Courmayeur, over the St Bernard and along the Swiss frontier of the Valpelline, past Cervinia and Champoluc crossing to Gressoney and on to Alagna, over the Pass of Turio into Macugnaga valley.

Piedmont, which extends from a mile or two west of Novara to the Hautes Alpes and Hautes Alpes de Provence on the French frontier, cannot compete in Alpine grandeur with Aosta or with the dramatic Dolomites but should not therefore be devalued. The mountains which encompass the main skiing areas centred around the frontier promontory of Bardonecchia and the Montgenèvre rise close to 3000 metres.

CERVINIA

Cervinia, once called Breuil, is an expensive and fashionable created centre. Even in the days of Edward Whymper, the English mountaineer who, in 1865, was the first man to climb the Matterhorn, it suffered from a sense of inferiority when compared to its famous Swiss neighbour, Zermatt. It has the misfortune of being below the less attractive face of the Matterhorn which overshadows the town's haphazard crowd of hotels, shops and restaurants.

Once the crowded terminals of the three-stage cableway are left behind the view improves, and the skier emerges into the blinding light and cold of the Plateau Rosa, which is also called the Testa Grigia. For all the drama of the cableway ascent, the customary routes down into Cervinia, which have intermediary lifts the entire way down, are tame and can be tackled safely even by the most timorous novice. Given reasonable snow conditions and fair visibility, none of the trails via the Theodul Pass to Plan Maison or even to the valley floor should present any problems other than length and speed. Nor need the Swiss Theodul lifts, which the joint lift pass includes, be any problem.

However, for those with good control and strong legs, the interminable Ventina trail that leads directly to Cervinia with no intermediary branches is a major undertaking. The frighteningly steep first section of the Furggen trail is best left to the real expert. Both these wings of the Cervinia skifields are the true reward for the queueing they entail.

The unmarked routes that lead to Valtournanche (the next village below Cervinia) or to Champoluc are quite the best skiing to be found here, but they should only be attempted with a guide.

Regular visitors have taken to living in one of the small pensions on the way down to Valtournanche and, by taking a car, bus or taxi to the first of the Lago Blu lifts, they zigzag comfortably to the terminal of the Plan Maison cable-cars. It is in this area that most of the skiing is done in December and January when the high lifts are not open.

Strangely, Cervinia has virtually abandoned any pretence of being a ski mountaineer's centre though there is an active summer climbing school. The Breithorn and the traverse to Castor and Pollux, the Lyskamm and the fabulous circumnavigation of the Monte Rosa group are all as easily started from Cervinia as Zermatt. It is presumably a case of supply and demand.

MONTE ROSA 4634

THEODULHORN 3468

MATTERHORN 4474

FURGGEN 34

LYSKAMM 4527

BREITHORN 4165

GOBBA DI ROLLIN 3906

KLEIN MATTERHORN 3883

KILOMETRO LANCIALTO

SWITZERLAND

THEODUL GLACIER

ITALY

THEODULPASS
Ⓡ
3328

PLATEAU ROSA 3480

CIME BIANCHE 2860

TO CHAMPOLUC

TO VALTOURNANCHE

Ⓡ PLAN MAISON

(2500)

2360

LAGO BLEU

2022

BREUIL – CERVINIA 2006

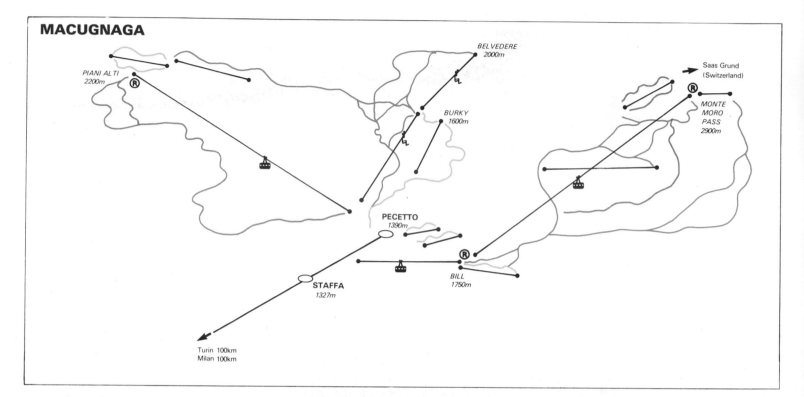

MACUGNAGA

PIANI ALTI
2200m

BELVEDERE
2000m

Ⓡ

Saas Grund
(Switzerland)

Ⓡ

MONTE
MORO
PASS
2900m

BURKY
1600m

PECETTO
1390m

STAFFA
1327m

BILL
1750m

Ⓡ

Turin 100km
Milan 100km

MACUGNAGA
Pecetto/Staffa

Almost equidistant from both Milan and Turin this picturesque valley end, which is always known simply as Macugnaga, comprises two small Alpine villages, Pecetto and Staffa, which are separated by a half-hour's walk. This is a fact which tour operators frequently fail to mention for the skiing is centred on Pecetto while beds seem always more plentiful in Staffa.

The scenery is magnificent, almost overwhelming, for the valley is closed by the near-vertical south face of the Monte Rosa which rises 3000 metres in one great ice-hung swoop from the very doorstep of Pecetto.

The skiing is in three unconnected areas. Burky and the Belvedere serve most novices while the moderate skiers prefer the longer and more taxing runs from the Monte Moro Pass, a bleak and windy crossing point into the Saas valley and Switzerland. It is possible from here to ski down into Saas Grund and enjoy a day's skiing in Saas Fee, though the return journey can prove to be very complicated if the road home is blocked by snow (which it often is). Skiers are rarely attuned to a steep four-hour trudge home.

On the Piani Alti side a cable-car has been out of operation for some years. When this is remedied it will add considerably to the facilities at Macugnaga.

PILA

Sixteen kilometres from Aosta, Pila is at the end of a steep and inordinately busy mountain road, where there has been created a vast building that serves as an underground garage, shopping, entertainment and restaurant area and dormitory for a thousand or so members of the Club Valtur, an organization for adults who like their creature comforts. It has a most pleasant ski area when visited on a quiet weekday. The weekends are like Coney Island on Washington's birthday.

The skiing is not particularly demanding, but with a minimum of lifts fanning out from Pila there are a variety of steep and not so steep, treeless trails that provide a very good day's sport.

The wise visitor will stay in Aosta and enjoy the unhurried pleasures of an evening stroll through the medieval alleys that house a multitude of shops, bars and restaurants, or visit the heavily restored Roman remains built by the Consul Terentius Varronius in honour of the Emperor Augustus to dignify this very important garrison town.

CHAMPOLUC

Champoluc in the Ayas side valley of Aosta is a tiny ski resort that attracts great loyalty from its visitors. The village is small with few modern amenities. The uplift is minimal – a gondola, a chairlift and a T-bar with the promise of three more lifts that will connect with the existing system. Despite this apparent paucity of lifts, the end result – a run from Sarezza at 2780 metres to the valley floor 1200 metres lower – is not only difficult and challenging but scenically tremendous. From Sarezza, it is possible to see the unfamiliar south faces of Lyskamm, Castor, Pollux and Breithorn, a tiny Matterhorn, the Mont Blanc and the entire panorama of the Vanoise, Dauphiné and Gran Paradiso. Nowhere else in the Alps has a view that includes so many high peaks

The dramatic crossing from Cervinia ends at St Jaques but this is only the first stage of the miniature haute route to Gressoney and on for another two valleys. The Gressoney stage starts from Sarezza and demands a short hour's climb which soon will be circumvented by a skilift. Scenically this route is breathtaking and Italian panache is not going to leave such an area undeveloped for long.

The summer hay barns and cow byres are the real Macugnaga though summer and winter tourism are beginning to take over from farming.

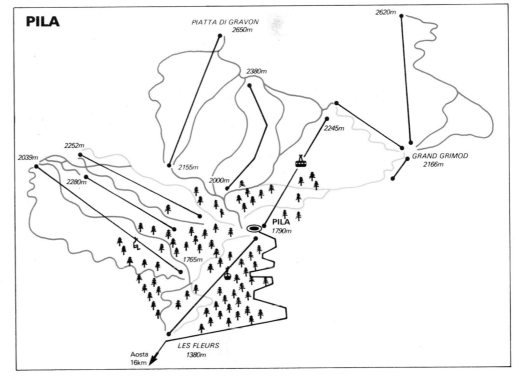

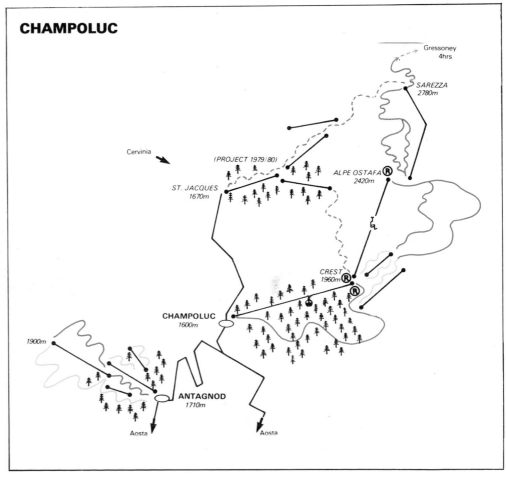

COURMAYEUR
Entrèves

Courmayeur, in the shadow of the great Brenva face of Mont Blanc, has always been a mountaineer's village and, despite the growth of modern hotels, has succeeded in keeping much of its old world charm.

The skiing has acquired a mixed reputation, largely on account of the unfortunate location of all the skifields on the far side of the valley for which transport is required both to and from the village. The transport is a gondola lift, and a gigantic cable-car to Checrouit. Once on the trails the variety of skiing is considerable, especially if snow and avalanches permit skiing on the newly developed Val Veni side.

The Alpe d'Arp route can hardly be called a trail for it is barely signposted. It starts from the top of the Arp cableway, dives down into a former glacier basin to a temperamental hoist which is not shown on any maps, and then drops down a seemingly endless valley to emerge at the lowest stopping point of the Checrouit gondola. It offers over 1300 metres of untracked downhill skiing and if the snow is not up to expectations the views are compensation.

No mention of Courmayeur would be complete without reference to the Pointe Heilbronner – Vallée Blanche traverse to Chamonix. It starts with the three-stage cable-car journey from Entrèves and usually finishes with a taxi ride home through the Mont Blanc tunnel. It is perfectly possible to do the return journey on skis, but it is not recommended as a form of relaxation. The run from the Pointe Heilbronner to Courmayeur is the blackest-of-black high-Alpine routes and, coming after a 4.30 am start and the long journey to Chamonix, it is a test of stamina, the reward for which is less the pleasure of skiing than the satisfaction of achievement. There is, however, one compensation on this route which only spring ski mountaineers can appreciate, and that is the first real rest and refreshment at the Pavillion, the lowest point normally skied on the Italian side. In fact, a day spent there in the spring with no thoughts of skiing is very satisfactory for, as Alpine balconies go, this one in particular is among the finest with magnificent scenery.

The south-west facing slopes of Courmayeur have no skiing whatever. It is a situation which is more than compensated for by the long hours of sun.

MONT BERRIO BLANC 3252

MONT FAURE 2967

CRESTA D'ARP 2755

TESTA D'ARP 2747

CRESTA YOULA 2624

2570

LAGO CHECROUIT 2256

COLLE CHECROUIT 860

2029

COURSA DZELEUNA 2080

PLAN DE CHECROUIT 1704

2030

ZEROTTA 1520

PRE DE PASCAL 1912

LASSY

VAL VENI

TO
PTE HEILBRONNER
MER DE GLACE
CHAMONIX

1293

ENTREVES 1306

LA PALUD 1400

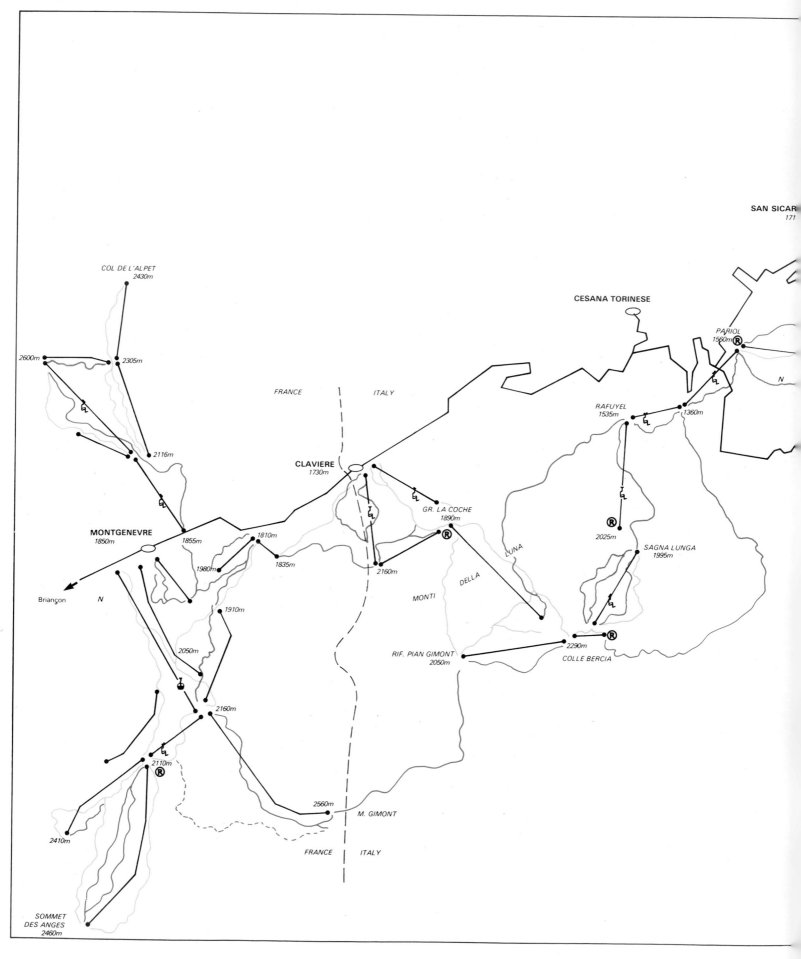

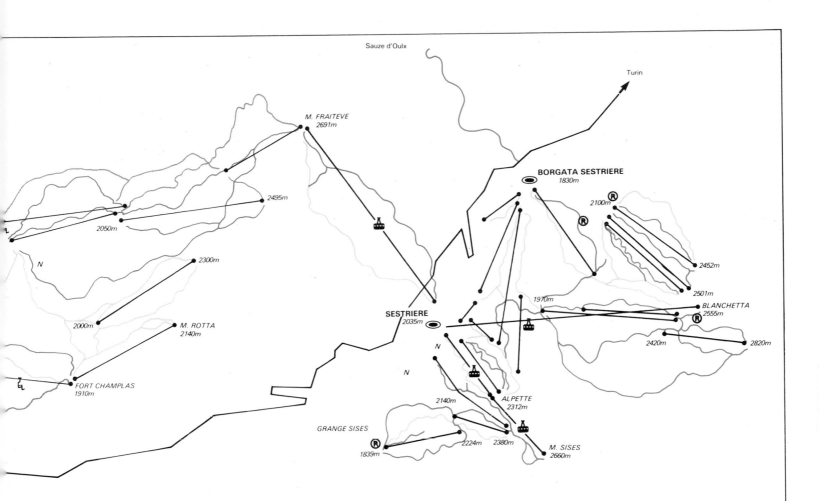

Sauze d'Oulx

Turin

M. FRAITEVE
2691m

2495m

2050m

2300m

N

2000m

M. ROTTA
2140m

FORT CHAMPLAS
1910m

BORGATA SESTRIERE
1830m

2100m Ⓡ

Ⓡ

2452m

2501m

1970m

BLANCHETTA
2555m

SESTRIERE
2035m

2420m

2820m

N

N

2140m

ALPETTE
2312m

GRANGE SISES

Ⓡ
1839m

2224m   2380m

M. SISES
2660m

SESTRIERE AND THE VIA LATTEA
Montgenèvre (France)/Clavière/San Sicario/Cesana Torinese

This is one of the finest multi-centre, long-distance ski routes. It is about as long as the Sella Ronda and considerably longer, there-and-back, than The Three Valleys. It is also better than the others in its neat completeness. Without fuss or complication, without interruption or irritation, it is possible to start quietly at either end at Sestrière or Montgenèvre, or anywhere in the middle, go all the way and home again or stop, turn round and pack in. Each section has its variations. The whole route can be skied on blue trails or on a good mixture of red and black. Restaurants are numerous and, as the altitude is not too high, even bad weather is no real complication.

There is one snag – there has to be for anything even approaching the perfect. There is, in the whole of this long trail network, very little accommodation. No more than 1500 hotel beds and about the same number of apartments are shared between five resorts.

Montgenèvre is detailed in the French section. Its near-neighbour Clavière is even more limited, and is a typical frontier village with that curious air of impermanence and scruffiness that is characteristic of all border places. You have to duck under customs barriers as you make your way from hotel to bar or restaurant, or even to go shopping in the general store that sells currency, drink, antiques and sports goods.

San Sicario is created – to be more exact is being created – and when completed will be the customary collection of some hotels and a large proportion of apartments.

Cesana Torinese might repay closer examination for, tiny though it is, it might hide the ideal little village inn which would solve all lodging problems.

Sestrière is suffering from being the world's very first created ski centre. Of the three tower hotels built in 1934 only one still stands and, except for the property taken over by the Club Méditerranée, there are only three other hotels. It is a windy place which accounts for the seeming excess of lifts. Each cableway has duplicate hoists for the many days when winds make cableway operation impossible. The skiing here is quite the most difficult on the Via Lattea. Many skiers of this trail network avoid Sestrière in case the Fraiteve cableway closes because of wind.

LA THUILE

Once an important staging post on the carriage route to France over the Little St Bernard Pass, La Thuile is now an almost forgotten farming village, with a small Bersaglieri training camp and three interesting ski lifts that rise up to Chaz-Dura, 1100 metres above the village. Here on almost any day the skiing can be a solitary occupation and the resulting fun far outweighs the possibly limited quantity of runs that can be done.

For the adventurous, a short climb on foot opens the way down to La Rosière, a tiny French ski resort above Bourg St Pierre, and from there to Les Arcs on the far side of the valley. The return is more troublesome unless a daring jeep-driver can be found who will chance the snow drifts on the French side of the pass. Since La Thuile is only twenty minutes drive from Courmayeur it certainly deserves a day's visit, if only for the superb view of Mont Blanc.

SAUZE D'OULX
Piedmont

The origin of the name is controversial, though there is no argument that Sauze means 'willow'. It lies next door to Sestrière and a popular day trip is over to Sestrière but it has not become part of the Via Lattea.

Sauze d'Oulx claims to have the longest hours of sunshine in winter of any resort in the entire Alps. It is the most popular place in the Italian Alps for British skiers, and has been for many years. The village is in the throws of development but it does have some very entertaining and extensive skiing and the standard required to enjoy this resort is just high enough to be a challenge to the moderate skier and easy enough for the novice to enjoy. It has a very good restaurant in Sportinia and some absolutely delightful through-the-trees, off-trail skiing on the Moncros. Unfortunately, Moncros is run by a rival lift company, and is not always open for business. From the top of the Fraiteve lift there is the most fearsome, unprepared black trail called the Rio Nero that ends miles from the resort at a point on a minor road called the Saw Mills, where it is possible to meet a pre-arranged taxi. The black run from Sportinia to Prarion has a fearsome gully for which there is no warning whatsoever. It tests the forward release on bindings and the shatter-proof qualities of ski goggles. This obstacle has been there for at least ten years.

It is a pity that town planning has not matched the excellence of the skiing.

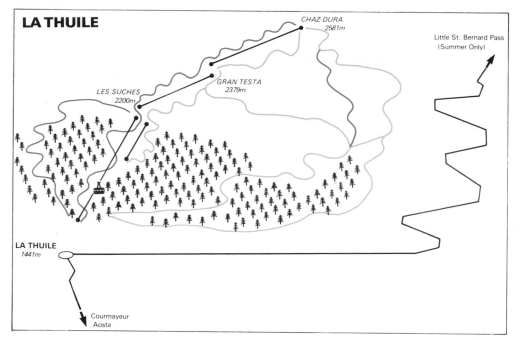

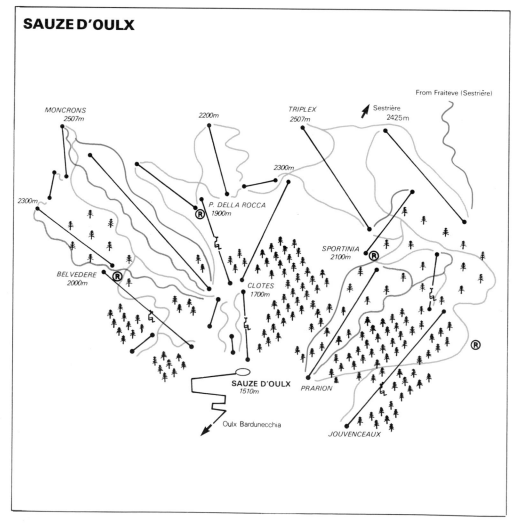

CENTRAL AND EASTERN ALPS

The central and eastern ski areas of Italy follow the frontiers of Yugoslavia, Austria and Switzerland and can be divided into the Friuli Venezia Giulia in the east, the Dolomites of the Alto Adige, Bolzano, Belluno, the Brenta and the central area of Sondrio.

The Friuli Venezia Giulia, this tragic and impoverished corner of Italy, has not yet figured in the lists of great winter sports areas. It is known as the victim of the long succession of flood and earthquake disasters to which the area has been subject.

However there are four resorts being developed which are worth a brief mention – Tarvisio, Zoncolan, Forni di Sopra and Sella Nevea. All except one are ancient mountain farming villages while Sella Nevea is a created centre with three modern hotel and apartment blocks of modest architectural proportions. The skiing is moderate and for the dedicated downhill skier will not be of great interest. However, the heavily forested valleys, the dramatic peaks and easily accessible cols and passes are an open invitation for the Alpine or Nordic tourer. For anyone wanting a restful, old-fashioned ski vacation, this is an area that can provide it.

The Dolomites has become the most popular of all the Italian ski areas. The skiing is good, extremely extensive and superbly organized.

The resorts are attractive and easily reached and the prices are very reasonable.

The province of Sondrio lies centrally below the southern face of the Swiss Alpine chain. The eastern limit is Bormio, the western limit Madesimo and the province capital Sondrio is almost exactly half-way. The resorts here have no great mountain to champion their public relations campaigns, nor do they have the doubtful advantage of fashion or notoriety. Livigno, Bormio, Santa Caterina Valfurva, Aprica, Chiesa and Caspoggio, and Madesimo are small, quite delightful (except perhaps for Livigno, but more of that later) and provide some very good skiing indeed.

Bormio's ski slopes come right into the town and the lowest are open, treeless meadows.

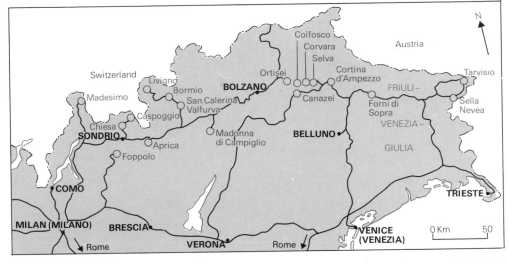

MADESIMO

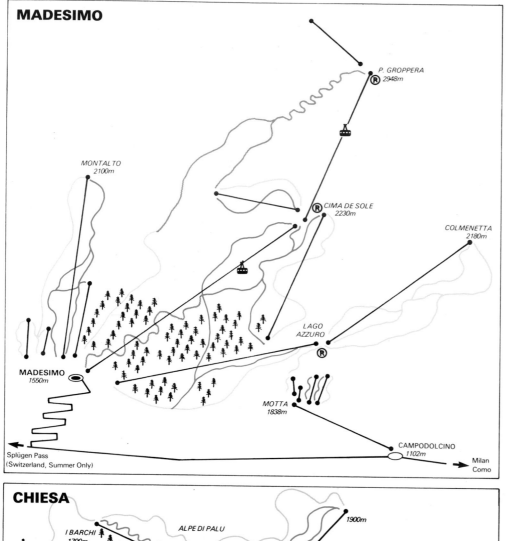

Splügen Pass
(Switzerland, Summer Only)

MADESIMO

Madesimo is a case of the accommodation parasite totally devouring its village host. Very little remains of the original buildings. It is a tight huddle of hotels and apartments and two, virtually separate, ski areas, one beside the other and it is very popular with the smart Milanese and Como residents. The Montalto area is dominated by ski teaching and children. There is a small drag lift there reserved entirely for small children and the skiing is easy to moderate with a drop of 550 metres.

The main area is on the Piz Groppera and it is from this summit that the fearsome and famous Cannelone run starts. The upper third of this severe black run is narrow, extremely steep and offers no resting place until it flattens out, relatively speaking, before either diverting over into the Montalto area or joining the short drag up to the Cima de Sole. The return to Madesimo from Cima de Sole has its own trap for it starts gently but once in the trees it bares its teeth and rewards your trust with a horrid sequence of very icy, steep, narrow woodpaths. An easier route is down to the Lago Azzuro and home on a gentle, blue plough-path.

Invisible from the village and rather confusingly shown on the official trail maps, the single lift behind P. Groppera mechanizes some really delightful, open slopes. It is a magnificent, quiet area to do some practice.

CHIESA/CASPOGGIO

Simple, awkward Chiesa and steep, wooded and scratchy Caspoggio would not, at first sight, commend themselves to anyone in search of the good ski life.

This, on my first approach up the long rustic valley of Malenco, was my initial reaction. But a day later, watching the carefree play of children on the sunny safe shelf of Palü, skiing the simple runs around Monte Motta and gazing across the valley at steep Caspoggio I fell in love with this very minor ski resort. Anyone with a family of small children would too, despite the inevitable cable-car journey from the old quarry village of Chiesa. The food in Chiesa and the local wine complete the attractions. For more serious exercise a short car ride to Caspoggio and a quick dash down the steep black trail that snakes through the trees from the Piazzo Cavalli will redress the balance of the too-simple trails of Alpe Palü.

There is little that can be done to extend the skiing of these two centres except possibly to make a proper trail down to Chiesa from Palü.

CHIESA

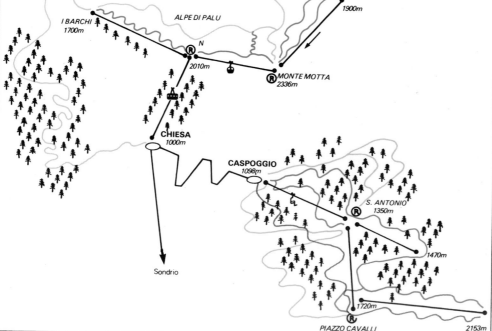

Sondrio

FOPPOLO

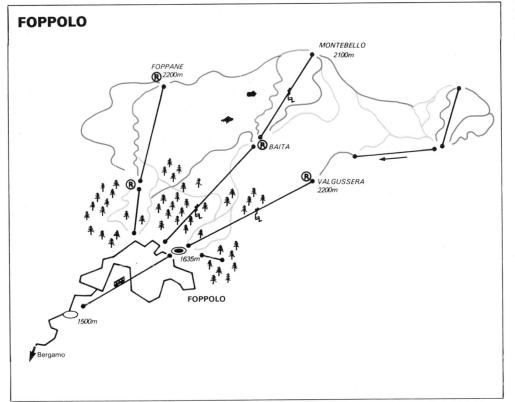

APRICA

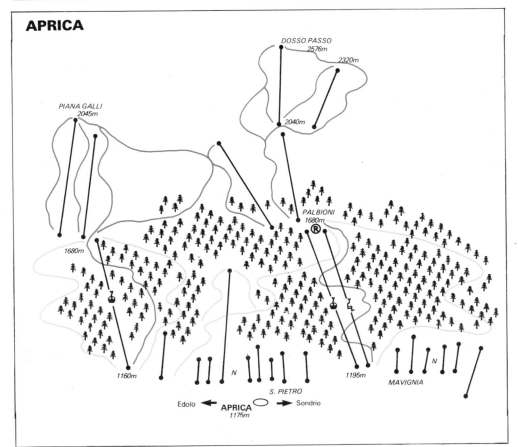

FOPPOLO

This resort began as a summer vacation area, and converted its facilities to double-up for skiers' use. There is an old village and a new development of villas and chalets which are connected by a funicular. The limits of the skiing prevent too great an expansion, although the Foppane and Monte Bello areas are a useful addition to Val Gussera.

Montebello in the background of the old village of Foppolo is an obvious ski mountain and it is to the credit of this small resort that such a distant slope has been brought into the ski area.

APRICA

Aprica is a typical day resort rather than a vacation village. A long, martial line of nursery lifts, some lifts rising to half way up the mountain and a final set of drags to the modest summits provide a respectable 1400 metres of downhill skiing, snow permitting. The appalling weekend crowding and the not very interesting skiing make this resort more a convenient day off from the office than a genuine ski holiday.

Aprica is the exception to the generally well-planned Italian ski resorts and probably represents a first attempt at providing ski facilities for the unexpected popularity of the sport among the industrial towns in the area. What it does provide – and this is something missing in most Italian resorts – is an area where the younger generation of Italian skiers can indulge in some fast amateur competitive skiing without getting too involved with the vacation skiers.

A number of attempts have been made to popularize Aprica with the tour operators who like the easy transfer route from Milan.

MARMOLADA 3342
2950
3270
2557
CHERZ 2082
PRALONGIA 2140
ARABBA 1617
CREP DE MONT 2200
ARMENTEROLA 1620
1700
SOREGA 2003
1900
2060
2000
SAN CASSIANO 1537
2077
CORVARA 1568
CORTINA
LAGAZOI 2778
SAN CROCE 2043
LA VILLA 1443
PEDRACES 1324

SELLA GROUP
GARDENA PASS
2300
DANTERCIPIES
SECEDA
2480
FURNES
2107

THE DOLOMITES

The area loosely referred to as the Dolomites by skiers covers that area of the Dolomite range known as the Alto Adige or South Tirol but also takes in Cortina d'Ampezzo which strictly speaking belongs to Belluno.

With the exception of Cortina d'Ampezzo, the spoken languages are German and Ladin, a Rhaeto-Roman language related to that spoken in parts of Switzerland and known as Romantsch. The problem of German-language education and administration is a delicate issue and one which the many German visitors appear to ignore, assuming that because the area has had German as its second language this is universally accepted.

Scenically the area is dramatic. It comes as something of a shock to find ski trails between the Gothic towers of pink rock, and lifts rising into narrow chasms between dolimitic columns at the base of which there are gentle grazing meadows and summer pathways.

For skiers the area has become well known because of the exceptionally long and inter-linked lifts known as the Sella Ronda, a single-pass area that takes in Ortisei (St Ulrich), Santa Caterina, Selva (Wolkenstein) Corvara, Colfosco, San Cassiano, and Canazei, all grouped loosely around the great mass of the Sella. These are all small villages that have adapted themselves cheerfully to the role of ski resorts. They are, with one exception, Selva/Wolkenstein, original villages such as it is rare to find today and the pleasure of being able to stroll, after skiing, through a village street with all the scents and sights of village life is a pleasure that many have forgotten or never known. Selva, the one exception, has suffered, like other Italian resorts, from a total lack of planning and a rash of ugly, unsuitable buildings that have made an already crowded little village very

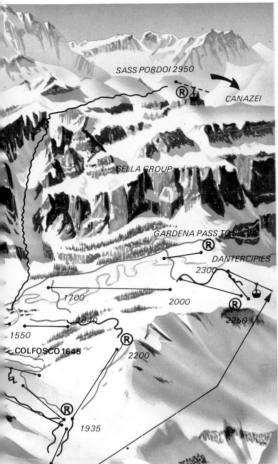

unattractive. On the other hand, Ortisei/St Ulrich, the capital of the valley, lying slightly outside the immediate ski-circuit, has retained all the charm of a mountain township.

The trails are frequently criticized as being too easy. This may well be the case, but there is a lift circuit that opens up at least 30 kilometres of downhill running which can take two whole days. Nor is the skiing in any way boring for it is easy enough to permit free movement but long enough and frequently tricky enough to keep the skier's attention fully focussed – a difficult task, at times, when the constantly changing views are so enchanting that you can spend as much time gazing as skiing.

For summer skiers and those who like altitude records, it is just possible, with a short walk, to skilift into the Marmolada massif where a cable-car and several lifts open up the glacier below Piz Serauta (3035 metres).

The Alpe di Siusi, (Seiseralm) above Ortisei is a geological curiosity, a National Park, and a superlative Nordic ski area.

Skiers in Santa Caterina can make full use of the extended skiing made available by the single lift pass covering the Sella Ronda area.

MADONNA DI CAMPIGLIO

The hotel town of Madonna di Campiglio, dramatically situated below the Brenta Dolomites, is a fair sample of the classic Italian resort, created for Italian families and little patronized by foreigners. With a total of approximately 15,000 beds, mostly in hotels and apartments in Madonna, but some in Pinzolo, Mezzana and '1300', it would be a catastrophe if all visitors were active skiers and proceeded at one and the same time to the departure points of the two main ski areas. However, the mass are mothers with small children who tend to restrict themselves to the gentle, trouble-free slopes around the Pradalgo or the nursery areas. Serious skiers make their way to the Groste where, crowds permitting, some long very fast skiing is possible, suitably seasoned with an occasional dash down from Monte Spinale. Palon, the location of the international FIS 'A' downhill and giant slalom courses, is, like so many of these competition areas, a disappointing and tame experience under normal conditions. On race days, it is very, very different.

Children dominate the scene in any Italian family resort such as Madonna di Campiglio.

Only ski instructors (right) would risk such an imminent collision in deep new powder snow.

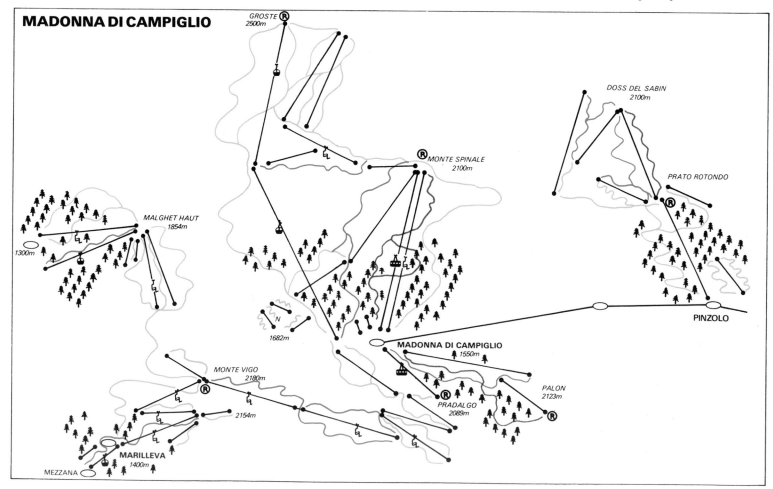

CORTINA D'AMPEZZO

The name means the Parish of Ampezzo and, even before it hosted the 1956 Olympics, it enjoyed a reputation for smartness and exclusivity that rivalled St Moritz. The reputation has stuck and has done this delightful centre a great deal of harm.

Cortina is a sizable town, with a number of luxury hotels. There is a most pleasant pedestrian precinct, a long list of restaurants where you can eat both cheaply and well, a few discotheques and some truly magnificent skiing.

The skiing is, geographically, most unfortunately distributed. With three main areas lying on opposite sides of the valley and town whose starting points are uncomfortably distant from the accommodation, transport is essential both outwards and homewards and skiers are reduced to their own transport or taxis. This is a situation which tends to take the glow off even the best skiing.

The standard is moderate to expert and the real expert will find a suitable variety of steep to very steep couloirs to show his daring and skill while the more timorous can find happy routes round all these ski nightmares.

Pocol, a very fashionable suburb of Cortina, deserves special mention, less for the day-long fashion shows than for the quite exceptionally excellent nursery slopes this area has provided. Here is a really big area where children can safely be left outside the hotels armed with lift passes. They can spend the day bombing the trails to their hearts' content and never get into any kind of geographical problem. The area is loosely linked with Pomedes, at least in a homeward direction, though it is not really practical to rise from Pocol into Pomedes and from there into the Tofana fields.

It is possible to ski from Cortina to Ortisei in a day by starting from the Falzarego Pass and using the Lagazuoi cable-car. There is a very long and truly magnificent high-Alpine run down into Armenterola and from there, zig-zagging for the rest of the day, through San Cassiano over La Brancia to Corvara and on over the Gardena Pass to Selva and Ortisei. The return journey can only be skilifted as far as Armenterola from where a jeep or a bus or even a taxi will be needed to complete the journey to the top of the Falzarego Pass.

The skiing on this pass is not very distinguished though in perfect conditions it is just possible to reach the outer limits of the Pocal area. It is surprising there is no lift link.

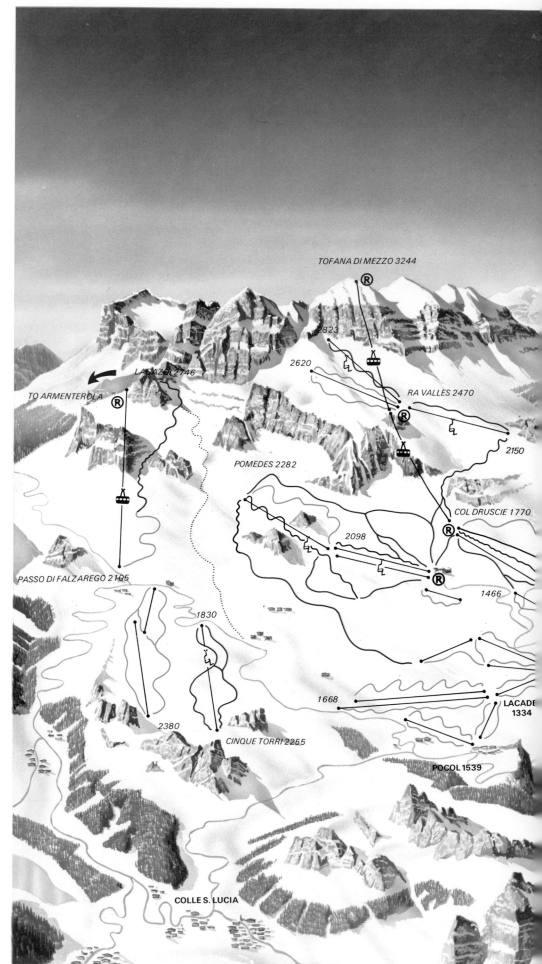

GRAN CRISTALLO 3216

STAUNIES 2930

COL DE VARDA 2200

SAN FORCA 2240

Ⓡ

1710

MISURINA 1756

1423

RIO GERE 1660

Ⓡ

2080

FALORIA 2120

TONDI 2340

CORTINA D'AMPEZZO
1224

AURONZO

S. VITO DI CADORE

G. Nicholson

LIVIGNO

Livigno is a duty-free valley between Bormio and the Engadin. It has had a complicated and chequered history having passed from the Counts of Bormio, who had owned it for a 100 years, to the Bishops of Grison in 1200. In 1600 it was bartered to the Habsburgs and in 1790 Napoleon gave it to the Dukedom of Lombardi. In 1876 it became Italian. However, because of a bureaucratic oversight all this time it still belonged legally to the Arch-Bishopric of Chur. Because the intervening mountains made the area difficult to administrate it was left to Italy to run this isolated little community. In return the people were granted relief from all duties and taxes in perpetuity.

Today Livigno is a thriving winter-sports resort enjoying a duty-free status – a situation which has contributed greatly to its popularity. It is reached either from Bormio in about two hours by automobile or from Zernez in the Engadin through a privately owned tunnel.

An ugly, elongated, haphazard collection of hotels and shops Livigno extends at least three miles through three parishes. The slopes on both sides of the valley are not connected and are run by two lift companies and two ski schools which are incapable of merging. It is a high, virtually treeless valley and is often referred to by its habituées as a kind of Tibet. Both the ski areas are moderate to easy and offer a maximum height difference of about 900 metres. The season is very long and has a very good weather record. The enthusiastic skier would enjoy Livigno, but there is little to test the skills of the experts.

The nursery slopes in Livigno are on the Blesaccio side and only a few minutes walk from the main centre of this long, straggly village.

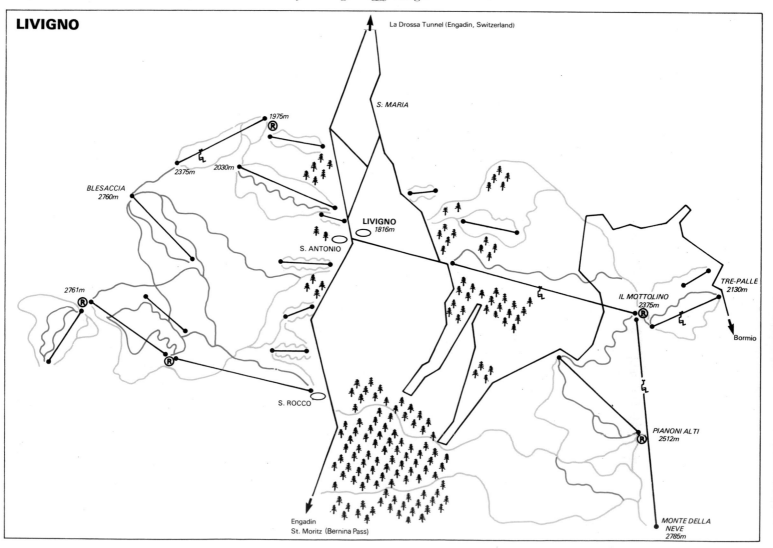

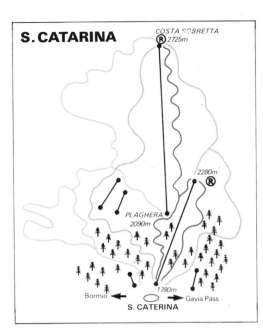

SANTA CATERINA VALFURVA

About 40 minutes from Bormio in an easterly direction is the little holiday village of Santa Caterina in the Furva valley. For those who feel that even a small town is not quite the right atmosphere for a vacation, this alternative is within commuting distance to the much bigger skiing of Bormio. There is a delightful blue trail down 1000 metres of easy mountain with two further moderate-to-difficult alternatives. The only drawback to Santa Caterina is the fact that variety is not one of its assets, but a visit to Bormio will redress the balance. It is interesting that Santa Caterina was a ski centre long before Bormio had joined the club; it has been a popular summer resort for even longer.

This is the view on the lower slopes between Ciuk and the town. The giant slalom course here is in regular use as is the downhill from Cimino.

BORMIO

With the heritage of a Roman Spa and a perfectly preserved 17th century town centre, cobbled streets, coaching inn, covered market with arcades and washing troughs, and a 3000 metre mountain growing on its doorstep, Bormio is approaching a skier's ideal. The only wonder is that it has taken so long for skiers to discover this.

One small negative qualification is that the accommodation is outside the old town and although it is very much closer to the cable-cars that swing up to the summit of the Vallacetta, the pleasures of an evening stroll through the old town are therefore further away.

The skiing is phenomenal. There is a gently ambling blue trail which will slide a near-novice from 3012 metres to the bottom of a skilift at 1600 metres from where, with a little planning, he can continue on down, via Ciuk to the floor of the valley at 1230 metres – a full 1800 metres of downhill skiing. For the more adventurous there is a not always very difficult trail from the summit to Bormio 2000. On the whole, this is a place for the moderate skier where his needs will be perfectly catered for. There is good accommodation at both Ciuk and Bormio 2000. Although guests are somewhat isolated at the higher location, a jeep service and a late-night cable-car return revellers home to Ciuk.

The spa aspect of Bormio is still very active and skiers can buy bargain price tickets for a regular muscle relaxation in the hot (and smelly) waters.

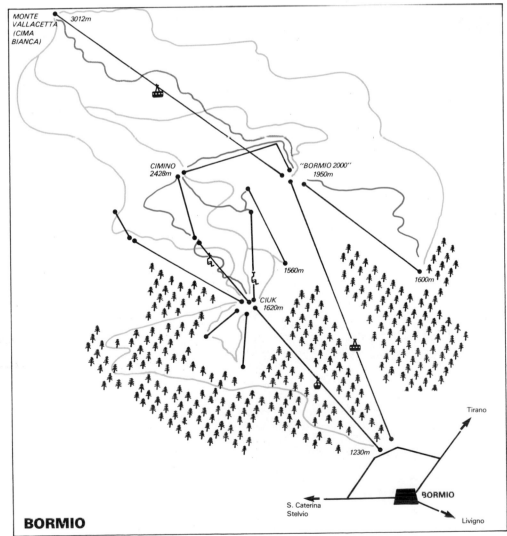

Club races are a feature of many of the smaller Appenine resorts. This is the start of a slalom.

TERMINILLO

Rome is not normally associated with skiing and the advertisements 'Why not ski from Rome?' seem a trifle optimistic. Since the roads into the Appenines have been improved ski resorts are springing up all the way into the Abbruzzi. Terminillo, the oldest and the best known of these resorts, is only 85 kilometres from Rome. It is low, heavily forested and very crowded on Sundays, but apart from these limitations it is an entertaining place.

ABBETONE

Abbetone in the Tuscan Appenines, roughly half-way between Pisa and Florence, has been a major ski centre for more than 30 years. It is a regular venue for World Cup races and provides a great variety of skiing which, if not very long, is difficult enough to please even the fittest enthusiast. The black run through narrow forest clearings from Foce di Campolino on a cold windy January day with a minimum of snow cover can be an icy nightmare. On a fine February afternoon when the sun has softened the scratch it can be a pleasure for a moderate or skilled skier.

Florence and skis make curious companions, but if you do intend to ski there or in any of the other little resorts (cross-country is more suitable in most of them than downhill) it would be advisable to take your own equipment. Ski hire in either Florence or Pisa – or even in Pistoia – can present difficulties. A combined cultural visit and skiing holiday in the area can be most rewarding.

THE APPENINES

The Appenines are the north-south watershed and run down the centre of Italy from Genoa to Catanzaro on the southern toe of the country. From Florence to Rome these mountains were regarded as wild, untamable and unapproachable. Roads and railways are virtually absent and a journey from one village to the next could take a day in a vehicle but a mere hour or two on foot. Until a decade or so ago this had maintained the undeveloped pattern of life in the Appenines since prehistoric days.

Tourism and the unabated growth of the urban centres of Florence and Rome have changed all this and slowly the Appenines and the Abruzzi are finding their true place in the Italian holiday scene. Skiing has been in the forefront of this development and, while little foreign attention has been drawn to the new – and some not so new – resorts, it has become very much part of winter recreation in central Italy.

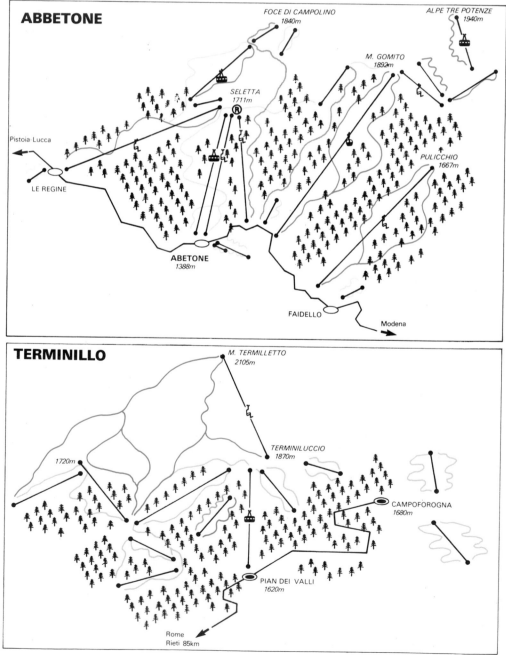

Scandinavia

Scandinavia, the legendary home of skiing, covers an area almost as big as the rest of Europe. It is a country of lakes, forests and, in the west and north, deep coastal indentations, the Fjords. There are few big mountains and those that do exist occupy the area at the extreme north of Sweden and the north-central area of Norway and are relatively inaccessible and far from major centres of population. The tree-line is low, often as low as 300 to 400 metres and the high country, rising to about 1200 to 1400 metres is bare except for scrubby birch and mountain ash. The winter season is long, lasting from October to late April.

The big towns have hundreds of kilo-metres of prepared ski tracks, many illuminated after dark and it is common to go for a brisk few kilometres after office hours.

Those skiers who do not go to the Alps for their skiing vacation move into the great unpopulated countryside to live for a week or a fortnight in a mountain hotel or hostel from where they set out for day-long excursions. Entire families go out together. Babies are pulled on a miniature *pulka* or sledge and grandmother goes too. They take huge rucksacks containing food, warm clothes, cooking utensils and, above all, a reindeer skin which is spread out under a convenient rock or tree while the more energetic members of the family exercise their ski legs over a few tens of kilometres. The older members and the children watch and play much as any family would in the summer on the beach.

During the week before and the week after Easter there is not a bed to be found in mountain hotels or huts for this is the fortnight when the big tours are carried out. Skiers often travel over hundreds of kilometres along sparsely marked trails that lead across the almost featureless uplands from hut to hut. This is also the season when the great herds of wild reindeer can be found streaming across these same uplands, the Ptarmigan is beginning to lose its white plumage and the snow hare acquires a black, stumpy tail. The skiers use maps

The summits of the lesser Jutenheim mountains (right) are not dramatic, but the views are limitless.

and compasses to find their route and volunteers man the Red Cross rescue huts that are dotted along the trails.

The equipment used is not the familiar ultra-light skis and shoes the Alpine skier uses when exercising on the loipes that fan out from every Alpine ski station. They are rugged *Fjellski* worn with light boots and cable bindings, for the trails are neither prepared nor cleared of minor obstructions.

For those unfamiliar with Scandinavian habits, the term mountain hotel *Fjellhotellet* or mountain hostel *Fjellstua* may give a wrong impression. These establishments are, in fact, extremely comfortable and often luxurious, and are located in single buildings on minor roads. There is rarely a village or township within tens of miles and a hotel will have its own tiny shop and can collect, within 24 hours, anything which is not in stock. Life in one of these isolated hotels is leisurely – a self-service breakfast from which many will also put together their picnic lunch, a hot, self-service lunch and a three-course served evening meal. Some gentle old-fashioned dancing, a not-too-serious game of bridge or some

conversation ends the evening. A single stranger soon finds himself part of a group of friends or a family and inevitably there will be one or two strong men looking for a companion to do one of the 30 or 40 kilometre trails.

Almost every one of these hotels will have some form of skilift – even if it is only a few feet of lift on an ancient rope tow. There are probably in the region of 1000 to 1500 such hotels dotted around the wild lands of Scandinavia.

Both Sweden and Norway do have a few Alpine-type resorts – Voss and Geilo in Norway and Åre in Sweden. They are not like Davos or Courchevel, but within the unavoidable geographic limitations they provide as good and as varied an example of Alpine skiing as any small resort in Austria or Italy. The ski instruction is based largely on the Austrian system; compact skis are still viewed with some suspicion.

Of the three main Scandinavian countries, Norway is the most developed and has the greatest number of ski hotels. Sweden, partly because of the geography and partly because of distance, is less well supplied, and Finland is only now beginning to provide the sort of basic accommodation and services recreational cross-country skiers have come to expect.

A distinction must be drawn in Norway between the west side, that is the Bergen skiing area and the east side of Oslo. The Bergen side, apart from the Hardanger Vidda, is much more mountainous and the trails are frequently up a mountain and down again. On the Oslo side, however, the trails are comparatively flat and pass through heavily forested country. An exception to this is the Jotunheim area which houses Norway's highest mountains, including Glittertinden 2470 metres and Galdhöpiggen 2469 metres. A luxury hotel, Eidsbugarden, is a very comfortable place for a base for these and a series of other 2000 metre mountains, which are best skied in mountaineering fashion. The Oslo or eastern side also has a neat cluster of true resorts in Lillehammer, though these cater largely for cross-country tourers rather than for Alpine skiers.

Oslo itself must be counted as a major ski resort, for on its doorstep, literally at the end of the tram line, there are some 1500 kilometres of marked and prepared trails as well as several dozen lifts which serve a number of limited downhill slopes. It is also the location of the famous Holmenkollen ski jump.

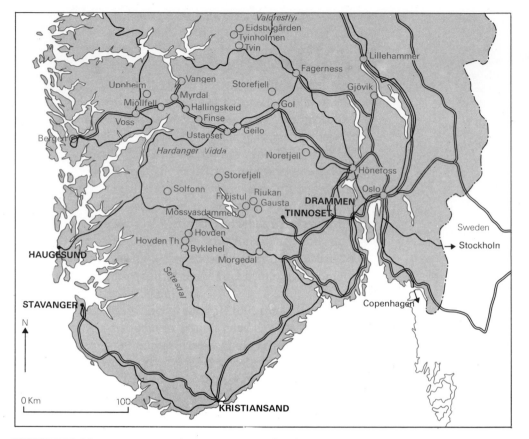

HOVDEN *Norway*

Hovden is a good example of modern luxury in the middle of otherwise completely empty countryside. It is a large, modern and comfortable hotel, and can also pride itself on a very interesting chairlift for downhill skiers. This lift has an exciting exit at the top – particularly for those equipped with cross-country skis. A considerable network of local trails can be extended indefinitely and for those for whom skiing is too active a sport, the two lakes close to the hotel can provide a first taste of a sedentary winter sport – pimpling, fishing through a hole in the ice.

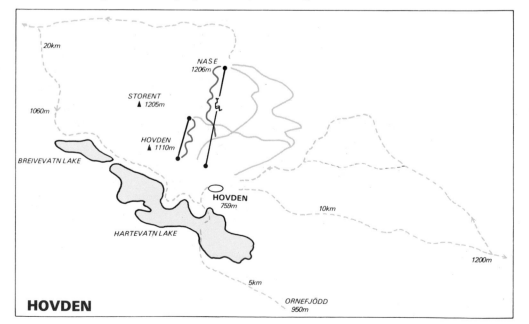

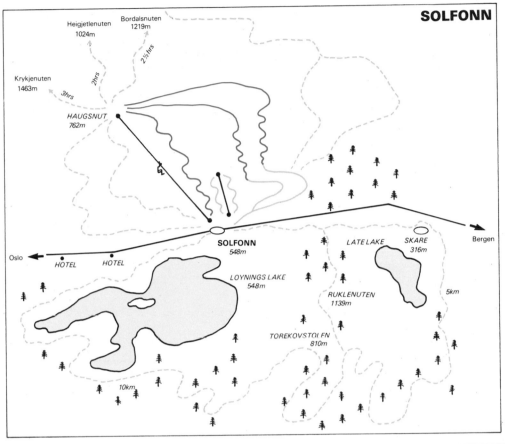

The trails winding through tall firs are characteristic of central and eastern Norway.

SOLFONN *Norway*

Solfonn, a tiny hotel and hostel settlement about two hours west of Geilo by train, is not as well known as it might be. With a single chairlift and a small tow it has some of the most difficult downhill skiing in Norway while, at the same time, it has also one of the most varied and interesting collections of cross-country trails. The available accommodation is very comfortable, though it is more suitable for a long weekend than a week-long stay.

RJUKAN *Norway*

Rjukan, on the eastern edge of Telemark, is now probably best known as the site of the raid on the Heavy Water Plant in 1942/43. The plant is still in existence and untouched since the day it was put out of action by Norwegian and British commandos. Rjukan is now an unremarkable single-industry township which has also succeeded in becoming an important skiing centre. From Rjukan town a short cable-car rises onto the Hardanger Vidda and serves as the southern gateway to this area. Slightly to the west, lying above the Møsvatn, is the mountain hotel Skinnarbu, one of the older, but nevertheless very comfortable small hotels that are the hallmark of Norwegian skiing. There are 150 kilometres of marked cross-country trails and there is a very pleasant selection of gently undulating walks in lightly wooded gullies

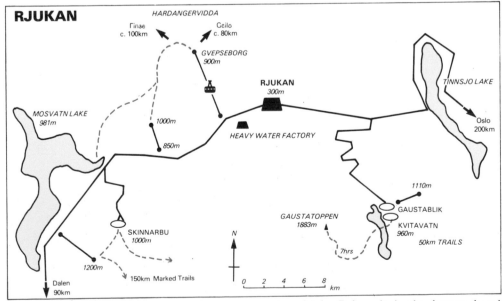

and over rounded hills that never rise more than 200 metres above the average level. The Mosvatn is a very popular pimpling area and the lake itself also provides long, completely flat loipes.

High above and to the east of Rjukan is the lonely and unmistakable landmark of the Gaustatoppen, a bald, rounded peak, 1883

metres high. Below it is the luxury hotel Gaustablik and a few metres away the Fjellstua Kvitavatn which serves as the headquarters for the British cross-country and Biathlon teams. A short T-bar provides uplift for basic downhill training and the Gaustablik is a constant temptation for those who want to test their fitness and endurance.

OSLO *Norway*

There are many cities in the world where it is perfectly feasible to go for a quick ski run after work in the early evening or during a luncheon break. Innsbruck and possibly Vancouver are two examples. But there is no city other than Oslo where skiing is part of city life and one of the greatest ski events takes place actually within the city. The silhouette of the Holmenkollen ski jump is part of the city skyline and beneath it is the Oslo ski museum. It is the only city in the world where, in the evening rush hour, there are as many people carrying skis as brief-cases queueing for the town trolley-cars and commuter trains and bound for any one of the dozen or so parks within and on the city boundaries where ski loipes are maintained and illuminated.

The Norwegian Society for the Promotion of Skiing maintains 2200 kilometres of marked, tracked and partially illuminated trails within the city boundaries. Their use is free but most Oslo skiers belong to the Society and the physical cost of maintenance falls on the city finance office.

In addition to these trails and the set of ski jump hills at Holmenkollen there are a number of steep slopes to the north-west of the city boundaries where Alpine skiing is practised and there is a variety of lifts.

The majority of these loipes and trails are located in public parks which are used in summer for recreation and athletics. For those skiers who are anxious to enjoy their skiing in organized surroundings, the customary area to be visited is the Nordmarka, a vast expanse of gently rolling hills and forested valleys with an almost total lack of habitation. It is an area stretching virtually to the downhill area of Norefjell, about 25 kilometres wide and 50 kilometres long, and it is laced with marked but not prepared trails and a limited number of huts.

Public transport is well organized for carrying the most awkward pieces of luggage such as skis. For very little money they can be sent off in special containers, a hundred pairs at a time, to virtually any destination in Norway. The local and commuter trains are equally well organized. Credit for most of this ski efficiency must go to the *Ski idrettens fremme*, the society for the promotion of skiing. Among their more notable contributions has been the organization of skiing for disabled and blind people.

For Norwegians there are two kinds of cross-country skiing. You can set off on a

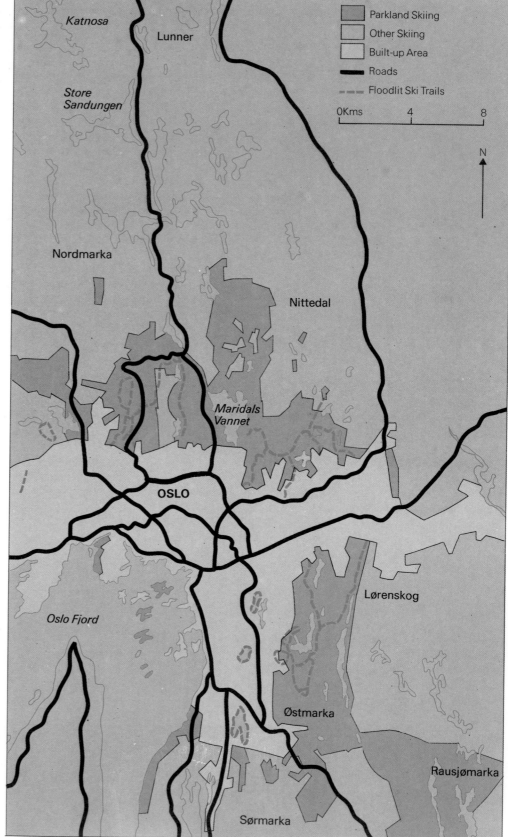

well-marked, often prepared trail such as the thousands of kilometres to be found around Oslo and Lillehammer and almost any other town in Norway, but the real touring is out on the trackless immensity of the unpopulated countryside. More surprising for skiers not familiar with this kind of skiing is the fact that it frequently divides quite sharply into a long, gently rising section and an even longer, continuously downhill run. It can be leg-wearying crust but not too infrequently it is Norwegian powder. Not without reason the Norwegian name for pwder snow is silky snow – coarse-grained, thin-layered snow that whispers at you as you whistle down a kilometre or so of undulating dream slopes that run down quietly to some tiny frozen lake before continuing for another kilometre.

This is country where you can meet with a herd of wild reindeer, a thousand or more that flow like a black river across the hills, unhurried and unchecked by any gradient. The leave a motorway of perfectly groomed trail behind them and that might be a thought for the fossil fuel ecologists.

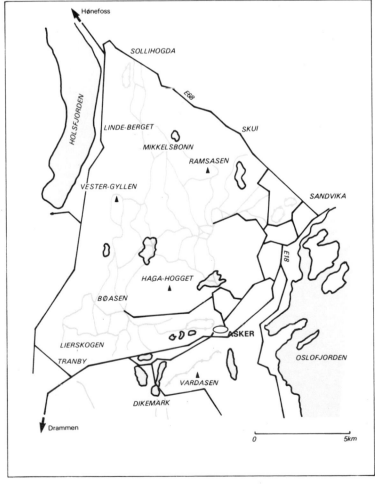

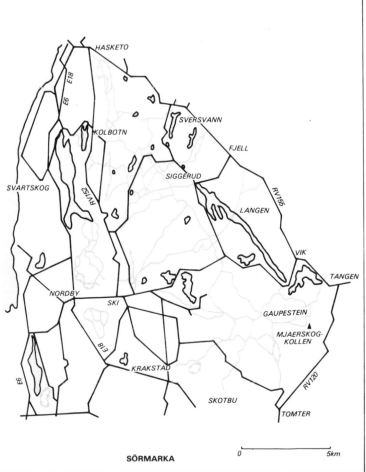

VOSS *Norway*

Voss, about two-and-a-half hours by train from Bergen, is Norway's senior downhill resort. An ugly town, completely rebuilt after being destroyed in 1944, serves as the dormitory area for the Hangur ski area. An inadequate cable-car is the main access route to the skiing which takes place out of sight of the town on wide, go-anywhere slopes between a hollow known as Trästøl and a rounded bump called Hangur. Although not difficult, the skiing is sufficiently varied to interest all except the committed downhill expert. The rather inadequate nursery area is around Hangur and the return home is either by cable-car or by taxi from Bavallen, which is not a very satisfactory end to a day. The route shown on the map as moderate should be avoided unless absolutely necessary for it consists of little more than a very uncomfortable trip down a wood path which has been rutted by the transport of logs. Ski touring from here is either very limited, to the left and above Hangur, or wind-blown and icy at the top of Lønahorgi, though the view is stupendous. On the far side of the lake there are routes along the long flattened crest of the Graasida.

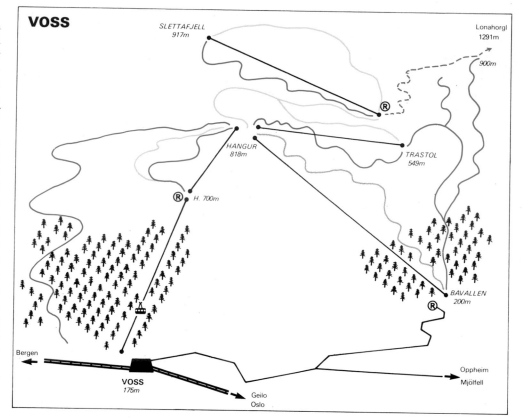

GEILO *Norway*

A further two hours from Voss, on the Bergen to Oslo railway, lies Geilo, a small industrial village which produces cutlery, and which has become a true ski resort. This is largely due to the enthusiasm and skill of Arne Palm who has run the ski school at Geilo for more than 20 years and is rapidly becoming a Norwegian Hannes Schneider. The skiing is undistinguished and very limited and for the experienced Nordic skier will serve as light relief for the more serious business of long day-trips either in the direction of Hallingskarvet or to the edge of the Hardanger Vidda of which Geilo is the northern limit. The view from the top of the Geilo chairlift is a glorious first experience of the strange 'top of the world' feeling that this part of Norway gives better than anywhere else.

For ski-touring *afficionados* Geilo is the starting point for some of the classic multi-day tours of western Norway to Rjukan or to Oppheim.

The rescue huts on the Vidda contain a sledge stretcher, emergency food, blankets and some fuel. They are maintained by volunteers.

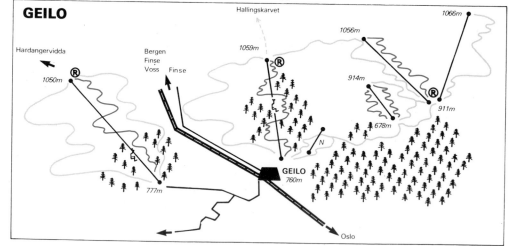

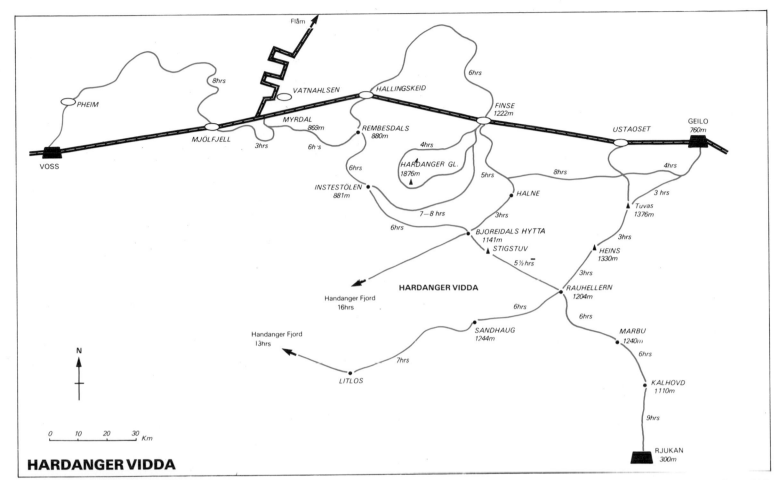

HARDANGER VIDDA

THE HARDANGER VIDDA *Norway*

The Hardanger Vidda (Vidda meaning Plain or empty) earned its name from the highest point within this island of emptiness, the glacier covered Hardanger mountain. The Vidda itself, the biggest arctic plain in Europe extends from near Geilo in the east to the Hardanger Fjord in the west – some 70 kilometres – and from Finse in the north to Rjukan in the south – about 90 kilometres. It is roughly circular, a jumbled plain of a thousand lakes and hundreds of hills which rise a few hundred metres above the general level of the plain, which in turn is about 1000 metres above sea level. A large number of sparsely marked trails which criss-cross the plain are divided up into three-to-six hour stages from one hut or shelter to the next. Many of these huts are manned during Easter week though food is generally not available and tourers are expected to carry their own.

The entire area is a national park and regular guided tours, with or without dog sleds, are organized in both Rjukan in the south and in Finse in the north.

Finse deserves brief mention. It was here

that the Scott Antarctic team trained in 1909 and it is also here that the film of that fateful expedition was made. Finse itself is nothing more than a rail stop at the highest point reached by the Bergen-Oslo railway but it can also claim to possess the loneliest luxury hotel in Europe. From Finse it is possible to reach Oppheim, just outside Voss, in three days, stopping at Hallingskeid and Mjölfjell. One of the more exciting downhill runs can be had from the summit of the Hardanger Jökull to the Hardanger Fjord where the run in spring starts in truly arctic conditions and finishes at sea level among the fruit blossom. It is considered an eight hour trip from Finse. The return is, however, difficult and can take another whole day.

Tours on the Hardanger Vidda should not be undertaken lightly. At any time during snow-cover conditions, the weather can turn what seemed like a pleasant day's stroll into a fearsome fight against truly polar conditions. Very accurate navigation is essential and experience of multi-day cross-country touring should be not acquired for a first time on this dangerous territory.

LILLEHAMMER *Norway*
Susjöen, Nordseter

Lillehammer, 195 kilometres north of Oslo, is a small industrial town and, though many people stay in the town itself for skiing vacations, the two tourist satellites are Susjöen and Nordseter, a few kilometres to the north. Both of these attractive colonies of hotels and hostels follow the customary pattern for all the Norwegian mountain hotels and are completely self-sustaining. Guests have no need to have recourse to Lillehammer for anything other than window shopping or the purchase of major items.

Although Susjöen and Nordseter have basic skilift facilities, the attraction here lies in the fascinating touring through deep forests which can be extended indefinitely in every direction. The classic 35 kilometre marathon, the Birkebeiner loipe, starts just outside Susjöen and follows the route supposed to have been taken by the infant King Haakon Haakonson in 1206 when he was rescued by dissidents supporting the King's succession.

The timber-line is much higher than in western Norway and the trees, instead of being stunted birch, ash and elder, are tall spruce and the trails wind through these stately trees. It is probably the most enjoyable area for touring in Norway with plentiful wildlife and well-spaced huts and shelters.

NOREFJELL *Norway*

Just over 120 kilometres north-west of Oslo, this long hogsback mountain has for very many years been one of the more important skiing centres based on Oslo. It was the site for the 1952 Winter Olympics (Alpine disciplines) and is now one of several youth training centres organized by the Norwegian Ski Federation. There are a number of hotels and hostels in the immediate skiing area, which follows the long ridge running high above the valley.

The Alpine skiing is limited to two ski tows opening up some easy slopes above the Norefjell dormitory area and a chairlift which rises from the valley floor to just below the centre. This chairlift provides the only really black run in Norway, a very steep 600 metre drop which is rarely well prepared because it is steep and winds mercilessly between narrow clearings in the forest. An alternative red route is not much more inviting.

You may be only a few hundred metres high under a lowering arctic sky but you feel that you are the last living people standing on the top of the world.

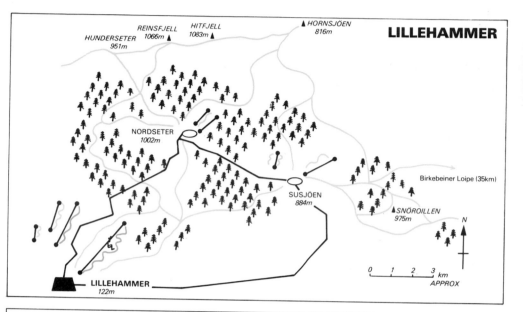

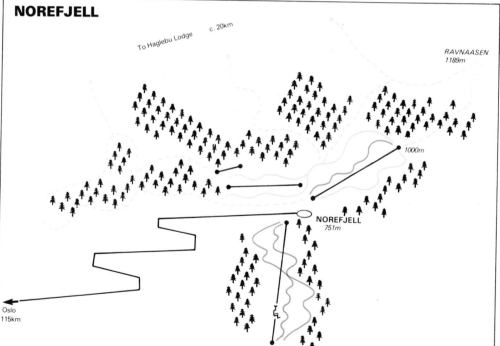

218

SWEDEN
Åre

Recent statistics show a greater number of lift installations in Sweden than in any other country in Europe. Any village with a hill erects a tow of some sort. There is not the large number of inns and hostels suitable for skiing vacations that is a feature of Norwegian skiing. This is due partly to the geography of the vast uninhabited regions of Sweden, and partly because of a deliberate policy to keep these areas untamed. In practice, if there is snow on the ground, Swedish people put on their skis and go out. There are hundreds of marked but unprepared trails and a considerable number of huts for skiers' use.

Åre, close to the Norwegian border and a very long way from both Stockholm and Göteberg, has achieved a degree of renown and has been the site for a number of international Alpine competitions. The skiing is almost uniformly difficult and the snow conditions, this far north in winter, can be troublesome. The 1000 metre descent from the bare, bitterly cold Åreskutan summit to Åre village is not a run to be undertaken lightly. The recent development of the neighbouring hamlet of Duved has more than doubled the ski domain and as an Alpine centre it has enjoyed popularity for very many years. The touring facilities are extensive on the western side of the small lake by which Åre is situated.

The Lapps are not habitual skiers although they will use their skis towards the end of winter.

FINLAND
Suommu

In Finland, as in Sweden or Norway, the skiing is where the snow lies. Having taken a train or automobile to any area it is possible to set off through the endless forests for as many miles as strength and good sense permit. There are innumerable marked routes, but these forests are industrial wood producers and are criss-crossed by loggers' trails. In the Finnish view, the true ski tourer does not depend on carefully planned trails but sets off with a *pulka*, dog and compass to move from one point to another, camping in the forest where necessary.

The terrain is rough but not particularly undulating. The common ski used by the Laps and the country folk is a heavy, long, wide ski with cable bindings known in Norway as a *landski*. The ultra-light racing or loipe ski would not survive well in these conditions.

In this kind of skiing, when long distances have to be covered, it is not unusual to use a dog or dogs to help to pull the light-weight *pulka* sledge. One man and a dog can manage about 75 kilos for a long distance in this way.

One particular centre is worth special mention and that is the Suommu lodge located exactly on the Arctic Circle. In fact, this hypothetical line passes through the middle of the lodge dining room. There is a skilift to the summit of Suommutunturi which gives about 300 metres of simple downhill running. For ski touring there are 500 miles of country stretching into the wilds of arctic Lapland. For a truly northern ski vacation complete with genuine (as opposed to electric) sauna, wild reindeer, good company and leg-wearying long distance touring mixed with a few shorter runs, this is an ideal place, even if it is a little hard to reach.

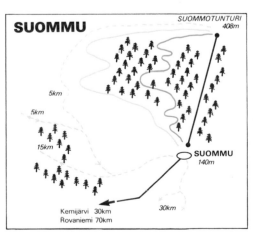

SCOTLAND
Aviemore/Glenshee/Glencoe
One way and another, Britain has contributed as much to modern, Alpine skiing as any other single nation, despite the fact that the country has neither a ski industry nor any major mountains. It is not surprising, however, that the efforts made over the last 70 years to establish the sport as a popular recreation in the United Kingdom should have had only limited success and a total of about 300,000 active skiers out of a population of 53 millions. Comparison with other countries, notably Germany, shows that the absence of an easily accessible, reliable and diverse skiable hinterland means that the sport remains a minority interest. Only Bavaria in Germany, which has its own mountains and access to Austria, has shown the type of growth comparable to that which the Alpine countries have experienced. The more distant parts of Germany, such as the Rhineland, continue to show statistics similar to those of Britain.

British winter snow cover is unreliable and in areas south of the Scottish border heavy falls are infrequent. In Scotland, where skiing has been practised for at least 1200 years and most actively for the past 40, snow cover is adequate but the heather growth requires a snow fall greatly in excess of that normally to be expected.

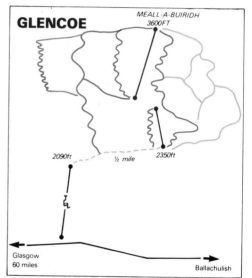

GLENSHEE

Glenshee on Deeside, not very far south of Aviemore, is essentially a club skiing area with limited facilities and limited runs. It is used largely by the clubs and the universities of Dundee and St Andrews and their enthusiastic student members. The atmosphere is friendly and entertaining rather than commercial, and for a novice, providing the weather is good, this is a very pleasant place to learn to ski.

GLENCOE

Glencoe, 60 miles (96 kilometres) north of Glasgow, is probably unique as the only resort in the world which can be hired, by an individual, a club or any other group, by the day or even for a week.

The area can also provide the most difficult and most entertaining skiing in Scotland, and the rewards for the walk from the first chairlift to the bottom of the skiing area are more than adequate.

Despite popular belief fine weather is not an unknown quantity in Aviemore, nor is the skiing constricted or excessively crowded.

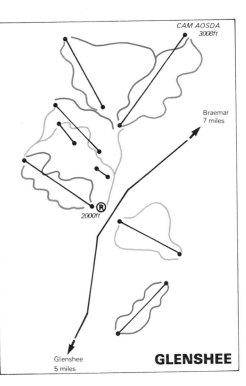

GLENSHEE

AVIEMORE

Of the three centres only Aviemore, in the Cairngorms, has become an established resort. It is 40 miles (64 kilometres) south of Inverness with a direct train connection to the south. A modern sports and hotel centre has been created and the surrounding villages and townships have profited from the lift installations and have created for themselves a busy winter season.

Transport to the ski area on the Cairngorms is a problem for the bottom chairlift is eight miles from the closest hotel. Because of the very changeable and often inhospitable weather, it is frequently uncomfortable to have to remain on the mountain the whole day.

The skiing itself is reminiscent of that in some New England areas. It is relatively short, frequently icy, very windy and either extremely easy, or fairly difficult to very difficult.

Although the season lasts, officially, from December to April, the best time is late April and continuing well into June. This is due to the very thing which makes winter skiing here so uncomfortable, the wind, which transports quantities of snow into the corries where it lies hard and compact through much of the summer and provides a very good spring snow surface.

Fine weekends are often extremely crowded with as many as a dozen different ski schools working the slopes. It is best to ski on a weekday when, considering the limited height difference available, there is a great variety of runs to be found. The skiing came as a revelation to the international press in the winter of 1978 which saw Cairngorm's first international racing. The planned development of Corrie na Ciste, which will, it is hoped, unify the two skiing areas should add further point to Aviemore's claim to full ski resort status and bring many more visitors to the area.

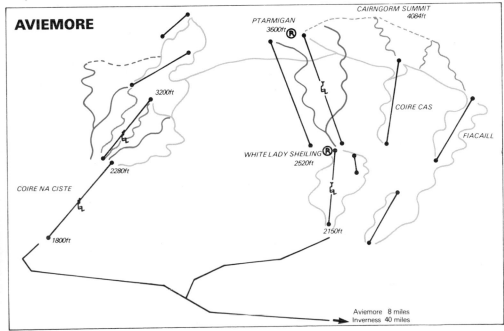

AVIEMORE

Eastern Europe and the USSR

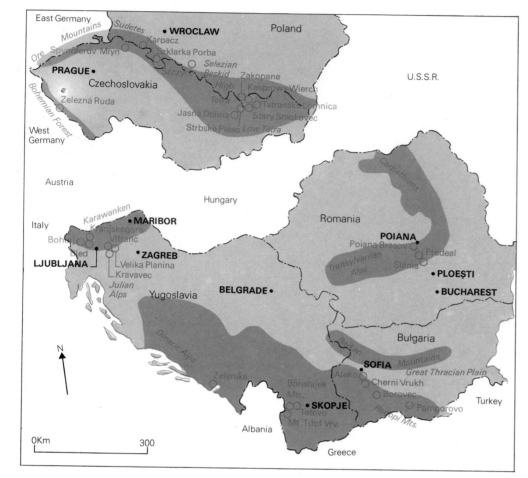

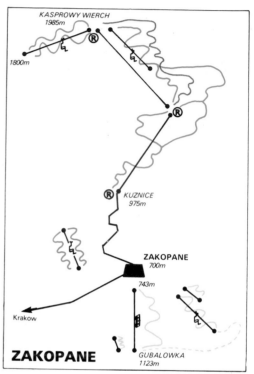

ZAKOPANE

The Tatras, the Carpathians, the Karawankens and the vast mountain ranges of the Caucasus, the Urals, the Altai and the northern outrunners of the great Himalayas could provide ski areas of unparalleled magnitude. For reasons of geography and ideology, the governments of the countries concerned have decided to promote Nordic rather than Alpine skiing, although there are resorts of great beauty, in the Tatras and elsewhere, that are publicized in the West, which offer both downhill and cross-country facilities.

CZECHOSLOVAKIA

Skiing is actively practised in ten mountain areas along three sides of the country. All are well mechanized and well provided with accommodation. In the south-west of the country adjoining Western Germany and Austria is the Bohemian forest, a wild, densely wooded area famed for its primeval state and concerned largely with Nordic skiing. The main centre is Zelezna Ruda. All the centres in this area are easily reached from

Karlovy Vary, 80 kilometres south of Pilsen.

The Krkonose, Olicke Hory and Jesenik (Giant, Eagle and Jesenice) mountains follow the northern frontier of the country. The main centre is Spindlerúv Mlýn, a very important Nordic centre and also the main training area for bob and luge experts. It was here that skiing was first introduced in 1892.

The Tatras, which range the eastern side of the country, are divided into the Malá Fatra (Small Fatra), the Velká Fatra (Great Fatra) and the Vysoké Tatry (the High Tatras). It is in the High Tatras that the most developed of all the Czechoslovak winter sports centres is to be found. This is Stary Smokovec with its two satellites, Strbské Pleso and Tatranská Lomnica. There is a great variety of downhill skiing around and from the summit of Lomicky (2632 metres) using a cable-car and a large number of other lifts. Unfortunately, there are few inter-linking runs.

The best skiing area in Czechoslovakia is in the Nizké Tatry, the Low Tatras, due south of the High Tatras. Based on Jasná Dolina, an assortment of 13 skilifts mechanize the Chopok mountain (2025 metres).

POLAND

Poland shares its ski mountains with Czechoslovakia, the summit ridge of the Tatras, a western continuation of the Carpathians, forming the frontier. Best known of all the Eastern European ski centres is Zakopane, a town devoted entirely to tourism. It was the site of the world's first F.I.S. World Championship to include a downhill race in 1929. The championship was held there on two further occasions, in 1939 and 1962. The main skiing is on the Kasprowy Wierch which is served by an ancient cable-car and two additional chairlifts leading to the summit. The skiing is moderate to difficult and the full run down to Kuznice is impressive. The additional skiing on the Gubalowka Hill and the nearby chairlift which starts at the front door of the luxury Kasprowy hotel is not very taxing. The area is a good starting point for a week-long high-Alpine hut-to-hut traverse of the Tatras and also for long cross-country treks through unspoilt farming.

Two other Polish ski centres deserve mention. Karpacz, based loosely on Wroclaw, has some simple chairlifted skiing and a link into the Szklarska Poręba area which is also mechanized. Together they provide about 1000 metres of downhill running. Szczyrk in the Silesian Beskid is of considerable importance as it is the main training centre for the Polish Ski Association and students. This organization has set up a very high standard of teaching and training, and through it the Polish ski industry now exports more ski bindings and boots made under licence than it imports, as well as producing locally-designed ski clothing.

ROMANIA

Although skiing was introduced into the Carpathians late in the nineteenth century, and the many foreign employees engaged in the oil industry at Ploesti prior to 1939 made the most of the facilities in the Sinaia area, little further activity has taken place. The installations at Sinaia itself have been allowed to decay and the once fashionable little town is a rather dismal place in the winter. Predeal, a small manufacturing town a few miles to the north of Sinaia is the traditional training ground for Romanian downhill skiers. The facilities here comprise a cable-car with a rise of some 400 metres and a chairlift with a further 300 metres. Most serious Predeal skiers commute to Sinaia where a two-stage cabin rises from the town at 800 metres to 1885 metres on the edge of the Bruceligor Plateau and a chairlift provides a further 500 metres of ascent. Provided there is good snow cover it is possible to ski from just below the summit of Virful cu Dor at 2029 metres into the town.

With a little imagination and effort a great deal could be made of Sinaia – certainly more than of the newly created centre of Poiana Brasov, some 13 kilometres above the old Hanseatic town of Brasov. Poiana Brasov is idyllically situated and is designed as both a summer and winter holiday resort. It lies exactly half-way to the Castle Bron, the legendary home of Count Dracul the Impaler who served as the model for Bram Stoker's Count Dracula. Intention and design seem to have been at variance here for the main uplift, a cable-car from the valley floor to the end station, the Cristianu Mare Hut, leaves the wretched novice and even moderate skier at the top of a vertiginous wall down which they must slither before reaching the three additional ski lifts which rise from the bowl below the hut. There is a further hill beyond the top cable-car station which one day should be mechanized. When that is completed Poiano Brasov, provided that something is done about the initial wall, will be a most welcoming winter-sports station.

The mountains in the Little Fatra rise out of the wide farming valleys like giants' teeth.

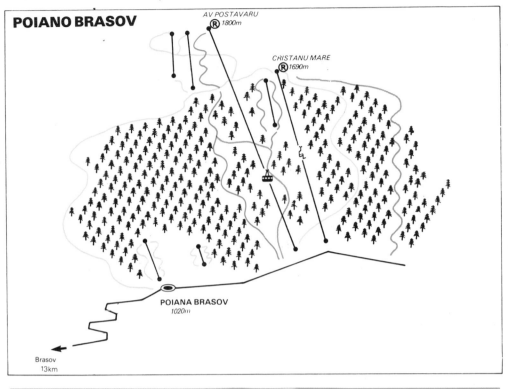

YUGOSLAVIA

Although better known as a summer mountain holiday area, Slovenia in northern Yugoslavia, has a long skiing history which dates back to the pioneer work of Matthias Zdarsky. With well-mechanized slopes in easy commuting distance of Zagreb, Ljubljana and Maribor and one of the largest ski factories, Elan, in the world, it is not surprising that skiing has an important place in the country's sport. Five resorts, all on the southern flanks of the Julian and Karawenken Alps, make up the formal list. Zelenika, 53 kilometres from Ljubljana, has two chairlifts and a T-bar which rise to a height of 500 metres. Velika Planina, a large, open, mountain plateau at about 1400 metres and reached by cable-car has wonderful cross-country skiing territory, based on the Simnovec group of huts and lodges, and it is only 20 kilometres from Ljubljana. Krvavec is the third day-skiing area in the Ljubljana area.

Kranjskagora, 20 miles from Bled, is the leading Yugoslav resort. It is comparatively well mechanized and based on a small village and hotel complex. The nearby summit of Vitranc is the start for a world cup downhill race through rough scrubby broken ground and the Planica giant jumping hill is five kilometres away. There are ambitious plans for a great extension of the skiing over the next few years to include the glacier slopes of the Razor.

There is unlimited and most attractive cross-country skiing around the lake of Bo-

hinj, based on any of the single, isolated hotels. The downhill skiing is in a great snowbowl based on the cable-car terminal Vogel. Although the actual height differences are limited, the area is very open and the variety is so great that the impression is of an extensive area. The return run from Vogel is a long, rough red route for which local guidance should be employed. Bled itself has little or no skiing and relies on nearby Ztrink which is reached by bus.

Maribor has its own mountain, the Mariborsko Pohorje, with a cable-car, four T-bars, and a chairlift serving a multitude of heavily forested trails.

For a number of years there has been talk of developing the Sar Planina, based on Tetovo in Macedonia. This could provide the best downhill routes in Yugoslavia with two mountains, the Borislajek and Titof Vrv, which are ideal for skiing.

Officially, there are 29 more ski centres in Yugoslavia. They provide basic downhill trails and moderate cross-country skiing.

BULGARIA

Bulgaria has three delightful, well-organized skiing centres, and the indigenous population seems to ski with enthusiasm which probably has a lot to do with the fact that they are now considered a major Alpine skiing nation of very good international standing.

Vitosha, near the suburbs of Sofia and reached by town bus, is a small range of hills on which the Aleko sports complex has been

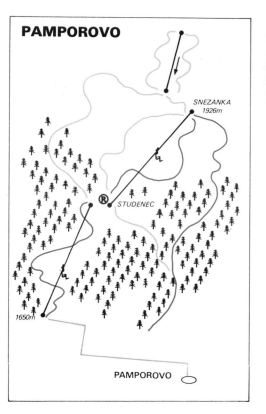

built. This comprises two large hotels and a number of lodges. There is a main chairlift to a summit at 2290 metres, which gives a drop of nearly 500 metres, in addition to several nursery lifts. A subsidiary centre reached from the valley by cable-car, Vodenicata, provides some skiing during winters with heavy snow and it is possible to ski from

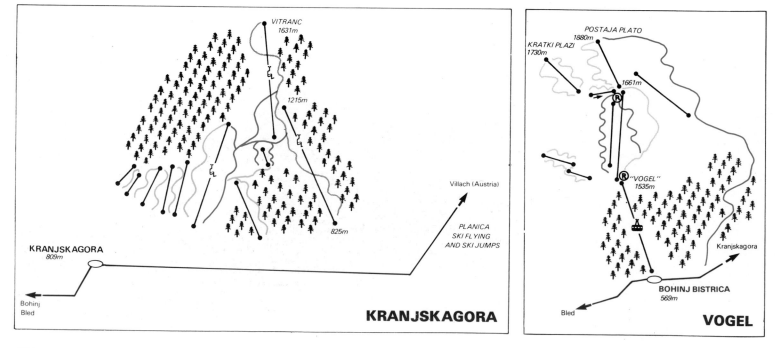

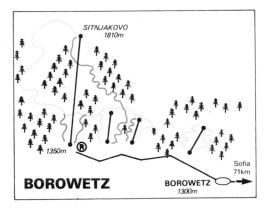

BOROWETZ

Cherni Vruh, the summit, to the valley.

Bulgaria's main ski areas are in the Rila and Rhodope mountains. Borovecs in the Rila mountains, 50 miles (80 kilometres) south of Sofia, is used as the main competition area and when the best skiing summit, the Jastrebec, is mechanized there will be a glorious 1000 metre run. For the moment the vacation skiing is restricted, but that is more than compensated for by the lovely forest setting of the resort and the great variety of Alpine and Nordic touring that is possible.

Pamporovo in the Rhodope Mountains, close to the Greek frontier, and lying above the Great Thracian Plain, is a loose scatter of hotels and lodges, hidden in the forest, and has a two-stage chairlift to Snezanka summit at 1938 metres. The mid-station is where the nursery area is to be found and it is from here also that a great variety of cross-country trails start. By Alpine standards, the skiing is restricted, but the atmosphere is so relaxed and friendly and the potential for any adventurous skier so great that both areas deserve to be much better known.

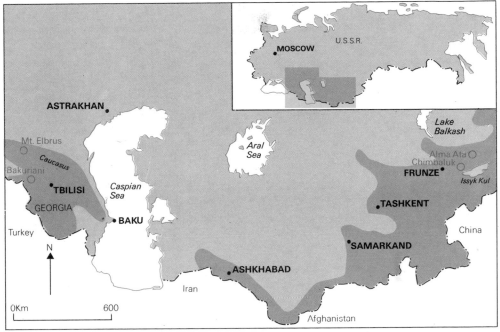

USSR

Considering the size of the Soviet Union, the unimaginable vastness of the mountain regions and the enthusiasm with which almost any sport is practised, it is surprising that it is only possible to show one Alpine ski resort – Bakuriani in the Caucasus, 150 kilometres south-west of Tblisi. This ski complex consists of two 2-stage chairlifts and a couple of nursery tows. French consultants have sketched out a massive development for the area which, if ever completed, envisages no fewer than 31 lifts which will mechanize the chain of

Jahorina in Bosnia, Yugoslavia has been the venue for a number of international downhill races.

mountains extending behind Bakuriani and rising to an average height of 2800 metres.

A well-developed chain of mountain huts and refuges covers the whole of the Northern Caucasus range and are the bases for extensive high-altitude ski mountaineering and summer mountaineering expeditions, which include Elbrus, at 5633 metres.

One further high-altitude centre is known about and that is Chimbaluk, not very far from Alma Ata in the Altai mountains of Khzakstan. It is believed that this is the main, all-year training centre for Alpine skiing. It is also in this region that prehistoric skis, dating from about 2500 BC, have been found.

Nordic disciplines are practised throughout Russia and there is active, competitive cross-country skiing both in the Moscow and Leningrad regions.

BAKURIANI

The Mediterranean

GREECE

Strange as it may seem to those for whom Greece is an automatic reminder of summer vacations and archaeological visits, skiing in Greece has been actively practised for very many years. The Hellenic Federation of Mountaineering and Skiing has been responsible for the development and operation of Mount Vermion, Mount Kissavos, Mount Pieria, Mount Menalon, Mount Pagaion, Mount Dirfy, Mount Vitsi, Mount Tymfristos, Mount Vrondon, Mount Falakron and Mount Pindos. The majority of these areas have a mountain refuge and a small rope tow or brief chairlift. However, three are the equal of many small Alpine resorts and can supply a full ski package. The accommodation is often some way from the slopes and visitors are limited in their choice.

The most important resort is Parnassus, 32 kilometres from Delphi on a good, snow-free road. The mechanization comprises a chairlift from Fterolaka at 1600 metres to the main ski area at Kontokredo where two Pomas provide access to slopes where novices and moderate skiers can have lessons. A long chairlift to Arnovryssi at 2050 metres opens up a truly surprising variety of runs from a very good, black, steep trail to a pleasant moderate red. Winter 1979 will see the opening of the new ski area Kellaria, which will be reached by gondola from the Arakhova road. Two or three chair and Poma lifts will mechanize a very large snowbowl to 2250 metres and also link with the Kontokredo installations at Arnovryssi.

Some hotel accommodation is available, but it is not the tourist season for Delphi and there is no transport available to the ski area. It is more lively to stay in the small village of Arakhova which most skiers like. Itea on the Gulf of Corinth is a pleasant excursion and it has restaurants with excellent seafood.

The vista from Parnassus leaves an indelible memory of blue skies, ranges of snow-capped mountains and plunging views to an unbelievably luminous sea.

The Killini range of mountains, in the northern Peleponese, is the site for a new centre at Trikala.

The skiing on Pilion, above Volos, is more limited than on Parnassus. The mechanization consists of two chairlifts and a small nursery lift providing 350 metres of downhill running through clearings cut in the dense birch, alder and Mediterranean pine scrub. Accommodation is available at the Alpine Club hut or 16 kilometres lower down at one of the hotels in the holiday centre of Portaria, above the busy town of Volos.

Vermion, in central Macedonia, is the oldest of the Greek ski centres, and one which has done most for the development of the sport in Greece. Based on the tiny hamlet of Seli, it has a two-stage chairlift and a Poma which provide very much more skiing than a first impression of the barren, rolling hills would suggest. Two more lifts planned for the near future will more than double the ski area. Seli has one small hotel, and there are two club lodges at Phterolakos. Additional accommodation can be found in Veria, 30 kilometres away, and many skiers commute to Thessaloniki, 75 kilometres to the east.

For ski mountaineers, Olympus, 2917 metres high, is an obvious target. The Hellenic Mountaineering Club maintains a chain of huts on both faces of the mountain and can also provide qualified ski mountaineering guides. The late winter season is well worth the journey and it is very unlikely that the mountain will ever be mechanized.

PARNASSUS

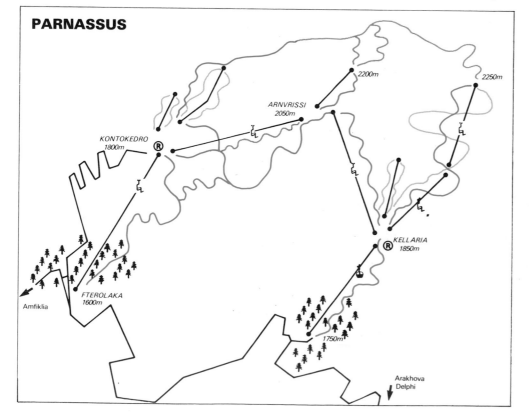

LEBANON

Skiing in Lebanon, until the current outbreak of hostilities, had reached an international standard and provided an intriguing alternative to Alpine skiing.

There was a list of eight centres, most of which were little more than a rope tow and a nursery slope, but the resort known as The Cedars, some 80 miles (126 kilometres) inland from Beirut, was a fully mechanized ski centre with magnificent, open, go-anywhere slopes with a potential vertical drop, after a short climb, of about 600 metres. The season is long, lasting well into April.

There is very considerable Alpine and Nordic touring potential in the Lebanon which has hardly been touched upon but it would require expedition equipment as the huts are very few and mostly unsuitable for winter occupation.

The full list of ski centres in the Lebanon is: Syr Mghabbine, Laklout, Sannine, Baidar Kneisseh, Barouk and Mount Hermon. A new resort was in the course of construction at Faraya-Mzur.

TURKEY

Although a number of ski mountaineering expeditions have climbed Mount Ararat and although the skiing potential is considerable, access to this region is almost impossible as it is close to the Soviet border and is classed as a military area.

A resort has been built at Bursa, which is due south of Istanbul across the Sea of Marmora. The season is short, from January to March, and the limited skiing takes place between 1370 and 2500 metres. A combination of train, ferry and bus from Istanbul is needed to reach the ski fields.

CYPRUS

There is a centre with limited facilities in the Troodos Mountains, which was created by a private club and was formerly supported by the British Armed Forces ski clubs. However, since the division of Cyprus, this centre has become little used as it lies very near the Green Line separating Turkish and Cypriot spheres of influence.

Skiing in the Troodos Mountains was a club activity and was patronized particularly by British army skiing enthusiasts.

Japan

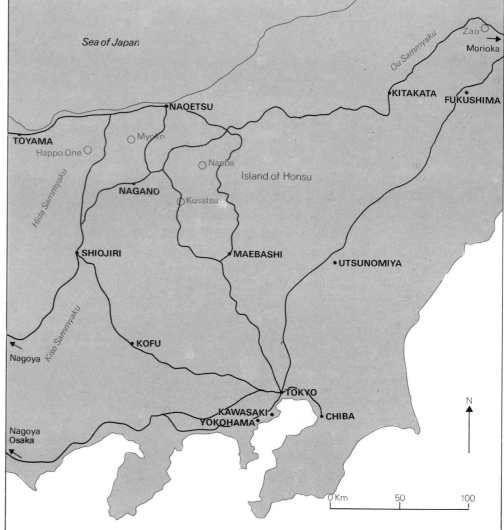

Skis were first seen in Japan in 1911 when they were introduced by Theodor von Lerch, an Austrian General and pupil of Matthias Zdarsky. Von Lerch wrote about his skiing experiences in his autobiography covering the period 1910–1912 during which time he was posted to Japan. His first ski attempts were made in the Niigata Prefecture. It is very doubtful whether he would believe the evidence of his eyes today were he able to witness between five and ten million Japanese skiers attempting to find snow space in anything from 280 to 400 ski centres.

The numbers are inevitably approximate for the definition of a 'skier' and a 'ski centre' are essentially vague. Competent authorities estimate that about ten million 'person-ski-events' take place every winter and that of those 'events' or attempts at skiing about half are very transitory. According to the Red Guide to Japanese Skiing Areas of 1978 there are 280 serious ski centres, that is to say places where there are more than two lifts and which are open all winter for skiing activities. The guide also categorizes the following main areas involved in serious skiing: Hokaido, Thohoku, Jhoetsu, Shinetsu, Chyuouo Ohito, Hokuriku Takayama, and Kansai Chyugoku.

Although there are 28 mountains over 3000 metres, 507 over 2000 metres and 661 over 1600 metres, the skiing is, with very few exceptions, on dormant or extinct volcanos below 2000 metres, over ground that is heavily vegetated, though not, in the Alpine sense, forested and there is not more than 600 metres

vertical height available. The lift base can be as low as a few hundred metres above sea level and the snow cover is often scant and the surface more often than not icy. The weather is extremely variable and frequently excessively unpleasant with much wind, a high humidity and low temperatures. Powder snow is rare and spring snow of very short duration. The scenery is frequently very beautiful, often dramatic and centres are in rural settings. Access is very easy, virtually all centres are directly reachable by rail with only a short inclusive bus journey. Road access is good with well-graded roads leading off from the main highways and very ample parking space is provided.

With the exception of a few major centres, accommodation is simple, often

primitive and for a Westerner probably unacceptable being in the form of communal dormitories with none of the amenities which the Western skier has come to accept as normal.

By Alpine standards the frequently meagre ski slopes are grossly over-lifted. With virtually no exception, all lifts are chairs, with an occasional gondola or cable-car in the major resorts. The reason for this is logical for a chairlift permits skiing over the ground occupied by the cables and pylons of the chair – a fact that is of considerable importance where ski-room is at a premium. The lifts are mostly short – again to reduce and disperse crowds and to cater for the relatively low standard of performance among the casual visitors. The Japanese novice is nothing if not adventurous and it is common to find a virtual beginner casually proceeding up the nearest lift, irrespective of its length or difficulty, and launching himself down the fall-line with total trust in fate and Isaac Newton, relying on natural cloth to snow friction and the presence of obstructing skis and bodies to terminate any untoward fall. Crowds are the norm. I recall on one crowded Sunday afternoon in Switzerland commenting to a Japanese colleague with whom I was skiing on the impossibly crowded trail, to which he replied 'like a week-day at home'.

Resorts and centres in Japan are called either after the local mountain ('Yama', 'San' or 'Dake'), the local village (frequently with the suffix 'Onsen' meaning 'shot springs') or by a fanciful pseudo-Alpine name.

The trails are labelled 'Easy', 'Moderate' and 'Difficult' and are further subdivided by using a combination of any two of these designations, one below the other, separated by a dot, so that you can find a trail starting 'moderately easy', becoming 'easy to moderate' and finishing 'moderately difficult'.

A ski area has the generic name 'gelende', a single Kanji character which is the close phonetic equivalent of the German term 'gelände'.

Equipment, clothing and technical expertise is extremely good in Japan and shows an inventiveness which should be the envy of the Western trade. After a lengthy period of importing European skis and bindings followed by an equally long period manufacturing under licence, there is now a major Japanese ski industry whose products are beginning to find their very competitive way into the Western market. However, for any Westerner going skiing in Japan, it would be only prudent to take boots and clothes for Japanese sizes are two to

three numbers smaller than those customarily worn in Europe or North America. Skis, on the other hand, should present no difficulty as the compact ski is well established in standard lengths and the bindings are capable of being adjusted to the feet of Western skiers.

It is, unfortunately, not possible to follow the general principle adopted throughout this atlas of showing the exact heights and summits of lifts. No Japanese publication lists these facts and all lifts are shown only in terms of length. As a general rule it can be taken that the average vertical skiable height will never exceed 600 metres, the average mid-mountain lift will not be over 200 metres long and the base lodge will usually be well below the 1000 metre level. The timber line can be taken to run at around 1500 metres, though scrubby growth making free skiing virtually impossible extends to above the 2000 metre level.

The Japanese call these weird snow-crusted trees Chouoh. The resort of Zao in Yamagata is famous for them.

JAPANESE SYMBOLS	
初級 *EASY*	スキー場
上級 *DIFFICULT*	*"GELENDE"—from German GELÄNDE used to designate any ski area or centre and, by custom, has come to mean ski area.*
中級 *MODERATE*	

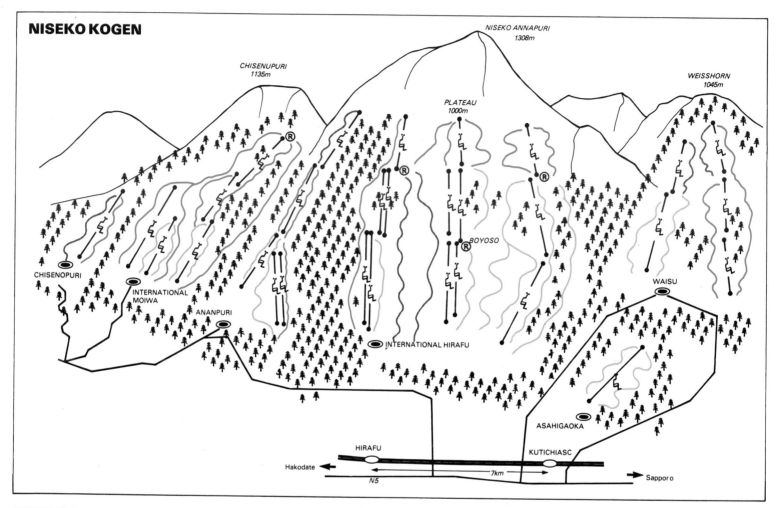

NISEKO KOGEN

CHISENUPURI
1135m

NISEKO ANNAPURI
1308m

WEISSHORN
1045m

PLATEAU
1000m

CHISENOPURI

INTERNATIONAL
MOIWA

ANANPURI

BOYOSO

INTERNATIONAL HIRAFU

WAISU

ASAHIGAOKA

HIRAFU

KUTICHIASC

Hakodate

7km

Sapporo

N5

NISEKO KOGEN *Hokaido*

Although most people associate skiing in Japan with Sapporo and the Winter Olympics, Sapporo itself has no permanent ski centre and the entire Olympic Alpine structure had to be removed and the National Park in which it took place restored to its natural state.

Niseko Kogen is a more representative centre for the island of Hokaido. Very exposed, suffering a violent and unpredictable weather pattern, it is generally not rated as being reliable for skiing until February. Unlike most of the other Japanese ski areas, the upper levels are treeless and the so-called 1000 metre Plateau is rated as being extremely dangerous in bad weather.

The centre consists of six separate accommodation areas of which International Hirafu is the one chosen by Western skiers.

The unlifted north slopes of Niseko Annupuri are one of the few areas where powder snow can be found and can be skied for more than an hour or so.

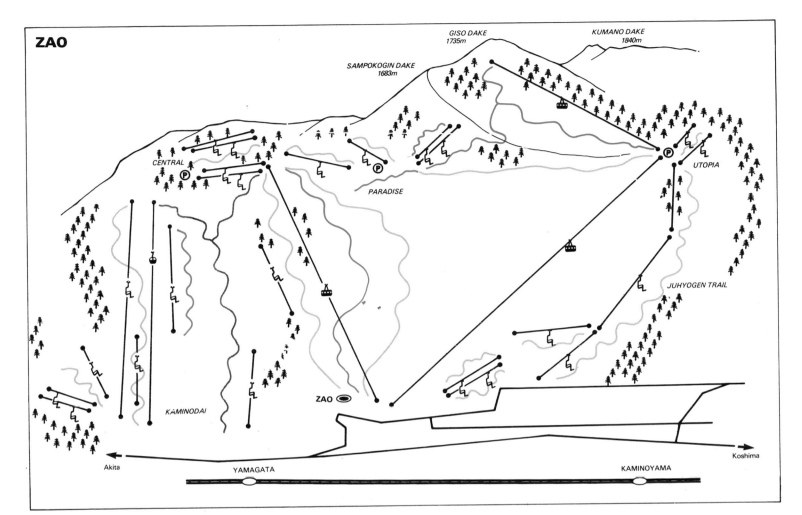

ZAO

GISO DAKE
1735m

KUMANO DAKE
1840m

SAMPOKOGIN DAKE
1683m

CENTRAL

UTOPIA

PARADISE

JUHYOGEN TRAIL

KAMINODAI

ZAO

Akita

YAMAGATA

KAMINOYAMA

Koshima

ZAO *Tohoku*

Zao is one of the larger and more modern of the Japanese ski resorts with three cable-cars and a gondola and three interconnected areas. However it does suffer from extremely violent and unreliable weather and extremely low temperatures. There is a local saying that when there is cloud on Giso Dake, go home.

However the adverse weather does have its compensations for the central ski area where, at the summit area, there is a whole lift system through a small forest of low stunted pines. In winter, these pines become completely mummified by hoar frost and blown snow so that they stand like a pigmy forest of weird snow shapes through which the trails wind. They are known as *Chouoh* and are a prominent feature of Japanese mountain art.

The main parking lot has room for 3000 automobiles and the hotel village is 11 kilometres from the railway station.

Into on Hokaido is surprisingly treeless and the skiing is open in attractive alpine scenery.

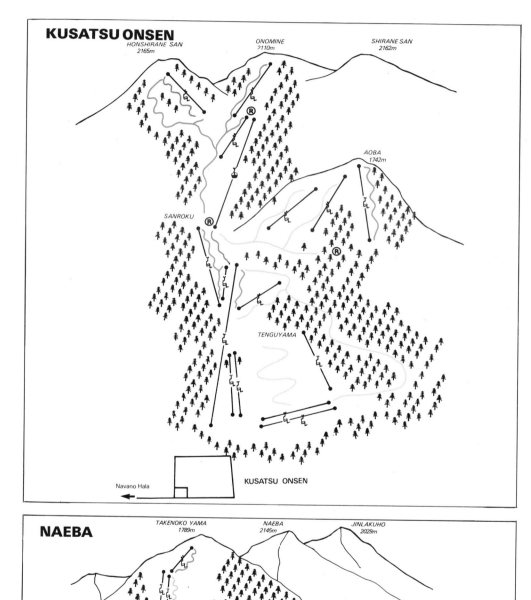

KUSATSU ONSEN

HONSHIRANE SAN
2165m

ONOMINE
2110m

SHIRANE SAN
2162m

AOBA
1742m

SANROKU

TENGUYAMA

KUSATSU ONSEN

Navano Hala

NAEBA

TAKENOKO YAMA
1789m

NAEBA
2145m

JINLAKUHO
2029m

Sangoku
Toge

A17

NAEBA

Echigo
Yusawaeki

KUSATSU ONSEN *Jhoetsu*

Rated as a very fine, old-fashioned summer and winter resort with very attractive hot springs, this small, popular centre deserves a very special place in the world's list of ski resorts.

Whether the Women's Liberation Movement and similar organizations approve or not is a philosophical problem, but this resort is, as far as I know, the only one in the world where ski classes are strictly divided by sex and the majority of the classes are for women only. The classes are also divided not only by standards of proficiency but by each individual's body structure or shape. It is a

novel, eminently sensible development and one which would appeal to nations other than Japan.

The skiing is close to the main residential area and the vertical distance appears to be above average. This centre also boasts the longest (and some say the slowest) chairlift in the country. It is one-and-a-quarter kilometres long over a very exposed hill-side. Since the area is famous for its wine, called Shirane, no doubt compensation can be found at Sanroku terminal for the cold journey on an open chair.

A typical day in the life of a Japanese skier.

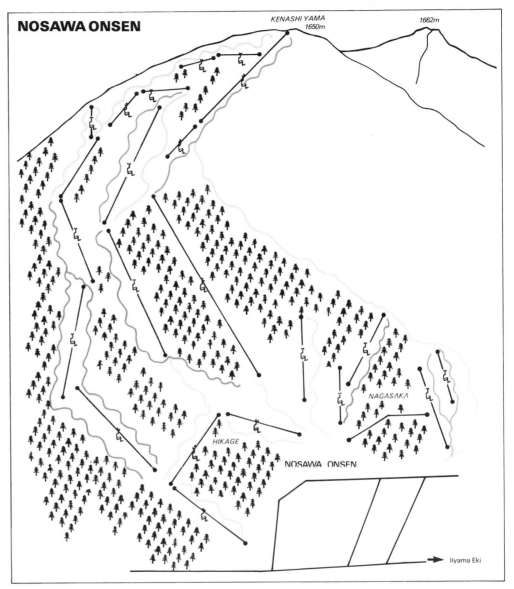

NOSAWA ONSEN *Shinetsu*

This is a small, very simple ski centre based on a genuine rural village. Accommodation is mostly in local inns, where only beds are provided, or in rooms let by the local farmers. The area is famous for its hot springs and the normal après ski activity here is soaking in one of the many communal hot spring baths.

The skiing is simple, shallow and, for beginners, the two areas Hikage and Nagasaka are larger and give more freedom than the customary clearings through trees and brush, which can present difficulties.

The area is also known for the cultivation of Nosawana, a form of cabbage-like vegetable known as *Nosawa Greens* which is a popular dish throughout Japan.

NAEBA *Jhoetsu*

Naeba is probably the most popular ski centre in Japan. The Naeba Prince Hotel is world famous, the visitors are very fashion conscious and the wealthy young people can find all they want in an ambience very similar to that in any other international resort. The 'village' is close to the ski area, the lifts are interconnected by a wealth of trails and the skiing is sufficiently difficult to provide the trail hounds with good ground to demonstrate their most exotic ski techniques.

The area is also of interest to the clubs and organizations which can hire a race-course – downhill, Giant Slalom or Slalom – or all three – complete with flags, marshalls, starting and finishing gates and electronic timing.

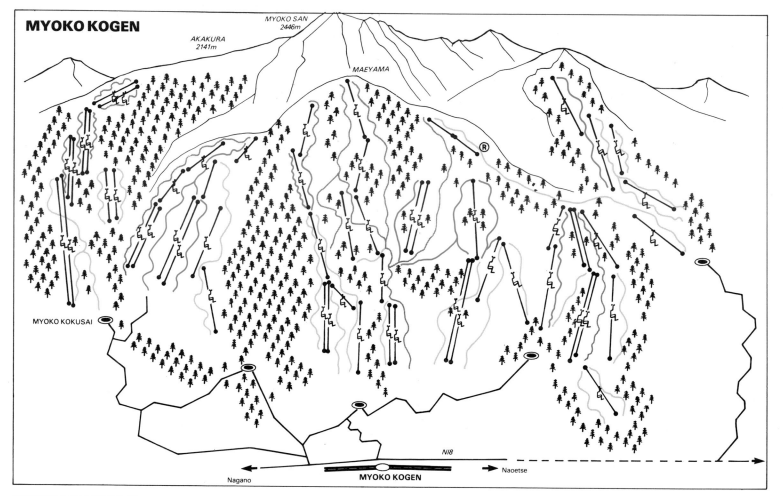

MYOKO KOGEN

AKAKURA
2141m

MYOKO SAN
2446m

MAEYAMA

®

MYOKO KOKUSAI

N18

Nagano ← → Naoetse

MYOKO KOGEN

MYOKO KOGEN *Shinetsu*

Myoko Kogen, a complex of five distinct
areas, is considered the most international (or
Western) of all the Japanese ski areas. The
scenery is magnificent and the view from the
summit of Maeyama dramatic. The skiing is
extensive and, with the exception of Kyoko
Kokusai, lift-linked. The season is long and
generally considered to be reliable, opening in
December and lasting until the middle or the
end of April. The clearings in the pine and
birch scrub are wider than is customary and
while the expert has a number of full-length
runs from summit to base, the novice has
wide and ample nursery fields, all close to the
residential area.

The distance from the nearest railway
station is considerable but here, as in all other
ski centres, there is ample and efficient public
transport to the ski areas. Special weekend ski
trains are customary.

*Not all Japanese mountains are volcanos and the
Japanese Alps rival anything European scenery
can offer.*

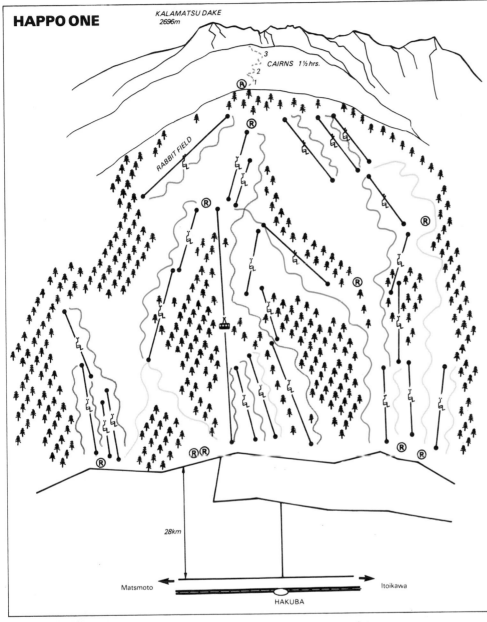

HAPPO ONE

KALAMATSU DAKE
2696m

3
CAIRNS 1½hrs.
2
1

RABBIT FIELD

28km

Matsmoto ← HAKUBA → Itoikawa

HAPPO ONE *Chyuo Ohito*

Happo One Ski Gelende, an important centre with some long and difficult skiing, is based on a small village with a number of tiny hotels and local inns. There are a mass of snack bars and it is popular with the younger generation.

The total vertical ski height can be extended by climbing on foot from the summit lifts towards Kalamatsu Dake, following a line of cairns set at 30 minute intervals which should give a further 450 metres of height.

The general standard of trail grooming is not high and this centre boasts a difficult run, which is known as the 'Rabbit Field' on account of the many and large moguls. According to a Japanese acquaintance, these moguls make you bounce just like a rabbit hopping. It is not a recommended method of tackling any mogul field, even very tame mole hills. The area is also particularly noted for some very special carp dishes. Speaking purely personally I find that the time I take picking unlikely fugitive bones from this highly prized delicacy reduces the gastronomic pleasures of this fish despite its wonderful flavour.

The Japanese Alps in winter can be as impressive as a Himalayan landscape and it is not surprising that the Japanese are such outstanding mountaineers. The contrast with the average ski mountain is quite startling and ski mountaineering in this area is rare.

Australia

There is no specific Australian ski style and it is impossible to identify any skiing as being characteristic. The influence has been mainly Austrian and American.

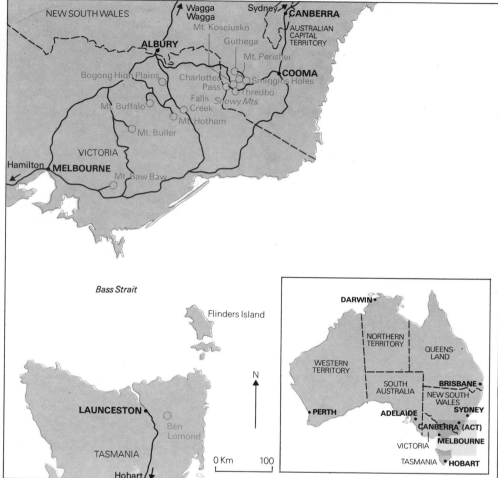

Skiing in Australia has continued since the founding of the Kiandra Snowshoe Club in 1861. It is a minority sport practised in a limited region, the Snowy Mountains and, to an even lesser extent, in Tasmania. The Australian Ski Federation lists 39 centres where organized skiing takes place, but of these only 11 can be classed as public or commercial ski centres and the remainder are club-operated huts or lodges.

Australian skiing grew up through local and regional clubs. They built dormitories in their huts, saved up and ran raffles to buy and build themselves the simplest of rope tows and provided the enthusiasm and perseverance that eventually led to the formation of the few commercial centres. Even these centres are still largely club dominated with most of the accommodation provided by and reserved for members. In many ways Australian skiing is an

object lesson to other ski nations.

The season begins, regardless of weather or snow cover, on the Queen's Birthday in June and finishes at the end of September, usually coincidentally with the Melbourne Show. The Snowy Mountains are a straggly range of very ancient geological formations that form a gentle arc about 400 kilometres long, from Canberra in the east to Melbourne in the west, never more than a 150 kilometres from the sea and whose highest point is Mount Kosciusko at 2230 metres. The resorts are spread equally between Victoria and New South Wales. Access from the New South Wales side is by air to Cooma and from there by automobile or from Melbourne by automobile. Many skiers drive directly from Sydney or Canberra for a long weekend in the more easterly resorts. The conditions resemble those of Scotland or New England; the weather can be very inclement, characterized by

high winds. The snow cover is often meagre but as the ground is rock-free this is not a great problem. Powder snow is a rarity and spring snow a very transient pleasure. In all resorts considerable emphasis is placed on cross-country touring and there are a number of long and extremely exciting routes which can resemble mini-expeditions as huts are scarce and distant. Skiing standards are moderate to high with enthusiasm and hardiness substituting devotion to style.

It must come as a surprise to realize that there has been an unbroken history of skiing in the Snowy Mountains which is longer than that of the Alps and, to be pendantic, longer than that in Oslo. Kiandra has a lot to be proud of.

Kiandra mining settlement finally vanished a year or two ago. Fortunately a contemporary kept a complete photographic record of the activities of the Kiandra snowshoe club.

THE ALPINE CLUB

THREDBO *New South Wales*

Thredbo is to Australian skiing what St Moritz, Gstaad, Davos, Val d'Isère and Aspen is to the rest of the world. Almost equidistant from Sydney (319 miles, 513 kilometres) and Melbourne (329 miles, 526 kilometres) and reachable over snow-free roads and only 56 miles (90 kilometres) from the nearest airport, Cooma, it is well placed for a busy winter season. It came into being through the efforts of Tony Sponar, a Snowy Mountains Authority hydrographer. The Authority was running a road through the valley and, with Karel and Sasha Nekvapil, fellow Czechs who were ski-teaching in nearby Charlotte's Pass, Sponar started to plan a resort. The original village was designed by Eric Nichols and in 1957 the nucleus of the resort was built. In 1961 the major expansion took place under the auspices of the Land Lease Corporation acting through the Kosciusko Thredbo Pty. Ltd.

The history is worth recording for what now stands in the valley is an object lesson to all mountain developers. Taking all that was best of the North American style of development and the attractiveness of an Alpine village, Thredbo became a real village with its own very special ambience – and that, today, is quite an achievement.

The skiing is interesting, moderately difficult and extensive. The loosely grouped mountain gum trees provide just enough shelter from adverse weather but not enough to prevent some delightful birdnesting skiing through dense shrubs in deep powder snow. The view from the gondola summit is awe-inspiring and a journey by snow-cat to the summit of Ramshead over a wild, desolate landscape is one of the highlights of a skiing visit to Thredbo.

RAMSHEAD 2178

THE BASIN 1966

KRACKENBACK TERMINAL 1990

TOP STATION 1850

KAREELA STATION 1806

MUNDI STATION 1539

T10 STATION 1501

MERRITT'S SPUR

1829

1667

CREEK STATION

THREDBO 1370

MLYNN 78

FALLS CREEK *Victoria*

This is a pleasant, very well-organized, small ski centre, 236 miles (380 kilometres) from Melbourne and accessible by either rail or road. One chairlift and eight ski-tows mechanize a good variety of moderate-to-expert slopes. Skiing can start from the village centre and the capacity of the lifts is in excess of the dormitory capabilities of the village so that lift queues are the exception. Accommodation can be found in self-catering luxury apartments though, as in all Australian ski centres, ski club lodges predominate. The distance to Falls Creek does not preclude day visitors.

MOUNT BAW BAW *Victoria*

Mount Baw Baw has a reputation in Australian skiing circles as being a teenage playground. Relatively low (1570 metres) it is most attractively wooded with luxuriant mountain gums. It has a magnificent view over Western Gippsland and entertaining, moderately difficult runs. It deserves a better reputation.

Commercial accommodation is very limited though as Mount Baw Baw is being developed as a year-round activities centre this should improve in time.

MOUNT HOTHAM *Victoria*

For many years inaccessible except by backpacking, Mount Hotham enjoys the reputation of being the finest ski centre in Australia with the least development. A strange resort, with the tiny village on the mountain summit and the runs extending downwards, it also has the reputation of being the only Australian centre which can guarantee powder snow. The skiing is moderate to very difficult and it is an incomparable touring centre for the Bogong High Plains. Access is still problematical owing to frequent road blockages after blizzards, and the accommodation is very limited. Potentially it is the foremost Australian ski centre but it is likely to be many years before it even begins to be seriously developed.

MOUNT BULLER *Victoria*

Only 150 miles (241 kilometres) from Melbourne, Mount Buller is the most populous of all Australian ski resorts. It has 4500 beds, most of which are provided by large club complexes. It is however as a day-resort that Mount Buller flourishes and with 15 skilifts of one sort or another and a good expanse of easy and moderate slopes it is very popular

and most busy on weekends. It might be a better resort if there were not two rival lift companies and two rival ski schools. Australia should have learned from European mistakes of this sort.

MOUNT BUFFALO *Victoria*

A two-centre resort, Mount Buffalo is the oldest ski centre in Victoria. The area is a National Park and consequently there are no club lodges. The only available accommodation is in one of the two commercial lodges. One is run by the Victorian Government Railways and the other is a private enterprise. It is an old-fashioned resort with limited uplift – one chairlift and four draglifts mechanize the simple downhill trails. Mount Buffalo is however a major Nordic skiing centre. With the increasing interest in Nordic skiing a resort such as Buffalo could become increasingly interesting, even in a poor snow season.

BEN LOMOND AND MOUNT MAWSON *Tasmania*

Both these resorts are situated in Mount Field National Park and are relatively undeveloped and suffer from doubtful snow cover. They are mainly used for extensive ski touring and there is no public accommodation. The Northern Tasmanian Alpine Club operates a hut in the area provided with cooking facilities and utensils. To quote the official description: 'Skiing ... here ... provides an experience worth remembering for a life-time. (It) ... richly rewards the skier for the effort involved

in getting off the beaten track.'

Back-packing or rough living are part of the scene for any skier wishing to do more than try out the primitive skilifts.

CHARLOTTE'S PASS *New South Wales*

Charlotte's Pass is five miles beyond Perisher Valley but it cannot normally be reached by road in winter. It lies at the foot of Mount Kosciusko and has a single commercial hotel, The Chalet. Mechanization is by two Pomas and one T-bar and the principle activity is touring. It is a delightful, intimate and relaxed small centre.

GUTHEGA *New South Wales*

Lying in a valley roughly parallel to Perisher in the north, Guthega is not only one of the least developed of the Australian centres, it is also possibly the one which can offer the most diverse and difficult skiing in spectacular scenery. Mechanization consists of one draglift and one rope tow and one further lift is planned for Blue Cow Mountain and it should be possible to link Guthega with Perisher. This is specialist country and it is significant that the best skiers in Australia, both Alpine and Nordic, congregate there. Very comfortable commercial accommodation is available in the single lodge operated by the centre's owner and developer, Walter Spanring, and his wife Hannelore.

For anyone wanting to experience the real skiing spirit in Australia, a visit to Guthega is essential, though the approach is likely to keep all but the fittest away

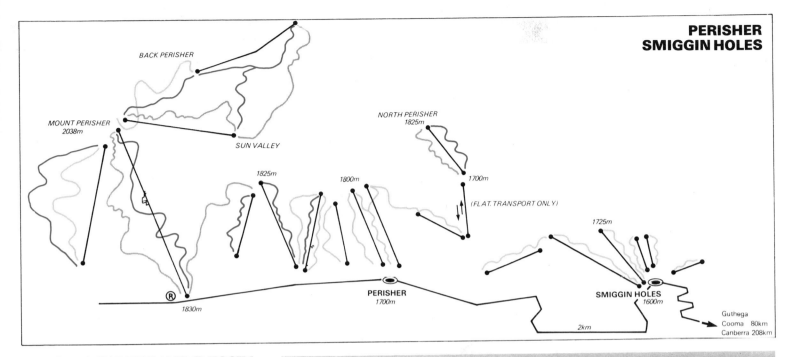

**PERISHER
SMIGGIN HOLES**

BACK PERISHER

MOUNT PERISHER
2038m

SUN VALLEY

NORTH PERISHER
1825m

1825m

1800m

1700m

(FLAT. TRANSPORT ONLY)

1725m

℞

1830m

PERISHER
1700m

SMIGGIN HOLES
1600m

2km

Guthega
Cooma 80km
Canberra 208km

PERISHER VALLEY AND SMIGGIN HOLES *New South Wales*

If ever a name fitted a location, it is Perisher. A long, virtually treeless valley, a funnel for every wind that blows, it presents an uninviting, straggly face with a long array of miscellaneous skilifts, one next to the other, rising a bare hundred or so metres to a scrubby ledge, scoured with erosion gullies and speckled with stunted mountain gums. It is also, with Mount Hotham, the highest of the Australian resorts and can boast the highest lifted summit – Mount Perisher. It is on this hill and on the slopes of Back Perisher and Sun Valley that the best skiing is to be found. The only problem is getting there for a zig-zag along the other lifts is not always possible, nor is it deemed practicable.

On the other hand, Smiggin Holes, the highest point to Perisher than can normally be reached in winter by automobile, does give some impression of cohesion with two sides of a concourse lined by shops, lodges and hotels. The skiing is elementary and most suitable for families with small children. It is loosely skilift-linked with Perisher though the return journey requires a little footwork. The name Smiggin Holes is an archaic Scottish term for *Licking Holes* and recalls the salt licks that were used by cattle grazed here in the 19th century. Cattle is no longer the main occupation of this recreational centre.

Though the accommodation in Perisher is scattered the resort is surprisingly popular and enterprising.

New Zealand

If you are looking for Alpine or North American resort development or even for club dominated, mechanized skiing, then New Zealand is the wrong country. The one exception is the Ruapehu Ski Fields of North Island. The truly magnificent skiing to be found, mainly on South Island, not only has to be worked for but comes into the category of serious ski mountaineering. Skins, ice axes, crampons and rope, a great deal of high mountain experience and the strength, equipment and expertise to deal safely with some quite atrocious weather are needed.

The accommodation is often simple, bordering on primitive, and access routes are difficult. The rewards are more than ample compensation for the effort – providing that groomed and patrolled trails are not the only kind of skiing in your repertoire.

The season is comparable to that in any Southern Hemisphere mountain region. It starts, rough speaking, in June and finishes in September, though for high expeditions in the Mount Cook and Tasman Glacier area late spring is probably more comfortable and practical than mid-winter.

SOUTH ISLAND

The Southern Alps of South Island are the great magnet for all serious New Zealand skiers. There are 17 recognized and established ski fields. Of these only seven are commercial and one, Tasman Glacier, is operated by the Mount Cook National Park. A further five commercial fields are being planned.

The principle difference between a club and commercial ski field in South Island, New Zealand is the fact that in the latter it is possible to book and pay for accommodation in the lodge or lodges. These can range from being relatively luxurious to simple, multi-bed dormitories. The trails are based on one or more relatively short rope tows and the resultant skiing is best described as training and instruction. The main activity is ski mountaineering and, in many cases, air-lifted glacier skiing. Access in virtually all cases is difficult and over partially unmetalled roads with little modern snow-clearing equipment. Many visitors prefer to fly in on short-landing light aircraft and those who cannot afford such luxury drive in as far as possible and finish their journey on foot.

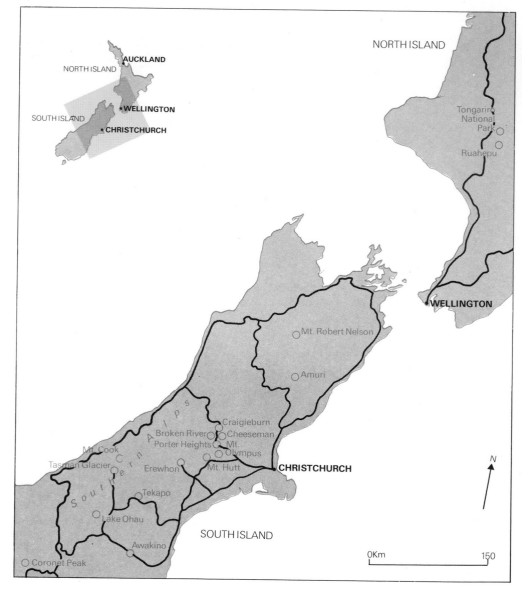

MOUNT HUTT *South Island*

Mount Hutt, in Canterbury, is the most advanced and ambitious of the South Island commercial fields. It has relatively high skiing above the 2000 metre mark and the four T-bar lifts provide a maximum height difference of just on 700 metres. Unique to South Island, there is a snow-grooming machine and regular race training takes place during a very long season. Access is good but the accommodation is outside the ski area.

CORONET PEAK *South Island*

Coronet Peak, operated by Mount Cook Airlines, is possibly the most popular commercial ski field and the one most visited by overseas skiers. It is only 19 miles (30 kilo-metres) from Queenstown with a good access road. There are two chairlifts and two Poma draglifts. The maximum drop is in the region of 350 metres.

TASMAN GLACIER *South Island*

Tasman Glacier, Mount Cook offers either pure ski mountaineering or air-lifted high-Alpine skiing, which is based on the luxury lodges, the Hermitage and Tasman, or at one of the nearby hotels or youth hostels. It can only be reached by light aircraft to one of four airstrips of which Tasman Saddle, 2393 metres, is the highest. There is a maximum run of 21 kilometres if snow conditions permit though the drop is, by Alpine standards, slight – about 600 metres.

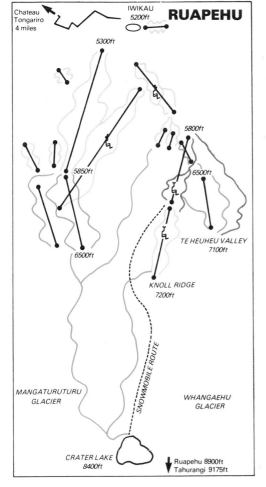

RUAPEHU

IWIKAU
5200ft

Chateau
Tongariro
4 miles

5300ft

5800ft

5850ft

6500ft

6500ft

TE HEUHEU VALLEY
7100ft

KNOLL RIDGE
7200ft

MANGATURUTURU
GLACIER

WHANGAEHU
GLACIER

SNOWMOBILE ROUTE

CRATER LAKE
8400ft

↓ Ruapehu 8900ft
↓ Tahurangi 9175ft

RUAPEHU SKI FIELDS *North Island*
Roughly equidistant from Auckland and
Wellington in the Tongariro National Park
and bordering the Hauhungatahi Wilderness
Area, Ruapehu is New Zealand's only fully
developed commercial ski area. Based on
Iwikau village but including Chateau Tongariro as the dormitory area, the skifields
extend about a mile-and-a-half southwards
towards Tahurangi Peak with a maximum
mechanized drop of 2000 feet (610 metres).
The skiing is open, moderately steep but can
be excessively difficult early in the season
because of ice and marble crust. No fewer
than 55 club huts and lodges occupy the
village area, and this gives some idea of the
preponderance of club over commercial
activity. Many of the smaller lifts are club-
owned and operated. There is a high degree of
mechanization with 15 chair and draglifts.

*The skiing ambience of Ruapehu ski fields is
unique and, except in Chile, the only place a
smoking volcano is going figure in every picture.*

South America

trails are moderate to extremely difficult and the maximum drop is 750 metres – which at those heights and starting from 3500 metres is further than many people expect it to be. The season lasts from June until mid-October.

Portillo is however not the only ski resort in Chile. There are nine others and, while they may not be as well known, most are preferred to Portillo by the Chileans. Farelones is an hour's drive from Santiago and its satellite resort La Parva is considered by Chileans as the best downhill resort in their country, even though it may be crowded at weekends. Almost as close are Lagumillas (2285 metres), Chillan (1800 metres), Villaricas (1200 metres) which was recently damaged by a volcanic eruption, and La Picada (950 metres).

The favourite ski touring area (both Alpine and Nordic) is Llaima (1500 metres) where the skiing is around and below a mildly active volcano. For those who like exotic skiing ambience Llaima can produce trails slaloming between dense monkey-puzzle trees.

Antillanco, which is reached by road from Osorno, is the least accessible and the latest of the Chilean resorts to be developed. The most southerly organized skiing in the world is at Punt Arenas in Patagonia. There is at present only a single rope tow there.

ARGENTINA

There are four established skiing centres in Argentina, but only two of these have achieved international recognition. San Carlo de Bariloche is in the Nahuel Huapi National Park, only 19 kilometres from the Chilean border. It is a sizable village created as a holiday centre in the style of an Austrian village. Skiing is on the slopes of Cerro Catedral and is mechanized by a cable-car, four chairlifts and five draglifts. Although the resort itself is low (about 1000 metres) the skiing reaches up to 2400 metres and though the lower slopes are heavily forested, the upper slopes are good open skiing country. The standard varies from moderate to easy.

A neighbour to Bariloche is the newly developed centre of San Martin de los Andes where the skiing takes place on the slopes of the Cerro Chapelco. Mechanization is two chairlifts, a Poma and three nursery T-bars.

In addition to these two resorts, skiing has been developed at Porterillo (Mendoza) and Los Vallecitos.

The skiers on the right are above Bariloche in Argentina, with the Andes in the background.

CHILE

Portillo, 150 kilometres by road north of Santiago, has become something of a by-word in North American skiing circles, for not only is it the target for all the year-round ski fanatics, it also hosts a Flying Kilometre world-record week. The World Alpine Championships were held there in 1966. The resort is at 2890 metres which can cause some people some acclimitization problems. There is a wide variety of lifts – chairlifts, T-bars, Pomas and an assortment of rope tows hauling as many as six skiers at a time. The

Asia

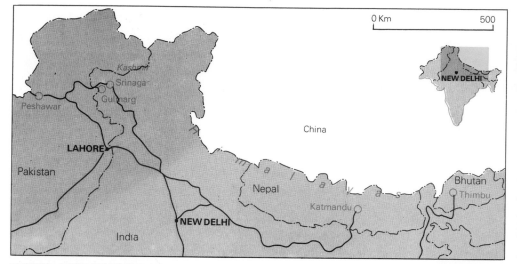

INDIA AND PAKISTAN

Skis have been used both for pleasure and transport in the northern, mountainous borders of the Indian sub-continent, from Peshawar in Pakistan, to Bhutan and in the foothills of the Himalayas. Distance and problems of access have limited the sport to occasional forays by Himalayan expeditions or home-sick British and European officials.

For a number of years there has been talk of establishing a winter and summer holiday centre in Peshawar, but this has never proceeded beyond the planning stages.

One single resort has, however, been established and has enjoyed some success. Gulmarg is 28 miles (45 kilometres) by road from Srinagar in the Kashmir. Known as the *Meadow of Roses*, it is about 2600 metres above sea level and lies just below the Firozpur Pass and Mount Aphara. Nanga Parbat is the dramatic backdrop to this tiny ski resort and the notoriously rainy climate of Kashmir assures an ample snow cover. The season runs from December to mid-April.

A chairlift provides about 180 metres of downhill running and there is a nursery rope tow and a further two T-bars serving steeper slopes. Two more lifts are being planned and it is possible to use a jeep for transport to the top of the pass for a more rewarding run back to Gulmarg. There is a ski school operating under Austrian direction and employing about 20 Austrian and Indian instructors. The principal foreign visitors come from Hong Kong from where there is a regular tour operator package available. Accommodation is in a three-star hotel. Recent information suggests, however, that this pioneer resort is gradually decaying and the installations are in a poor state of repair.

IRAN

Although Damavand, at 5604 metres, is the customary goal for visiting mountaineers, Iran has three mechanized, downhill ski centres, all within 65 kilometres of the capital, Teheran. Of these, Shemshak is the most popular, with Lashgarak and Abe-Ali close runners up. As might be expected, weekends are very crowded, though few people go to ski, but during the week the slopes are almost deserted. The operating times of lifts are haphazard and it is also possible for the entire area to be closed if a member of the Shah's household has decided to go skiing.

For some time there has been talk of developing a super-resort in the Karaj Valley under Austrian supervision. The plans foresaw a large international centre.

No serious skier can visit Iran without being fascinated by the sight of Damavand (right).

It has become quite common to take skis on an Everest expedition and their use has saved many a long hour's downhill trudge. It is however one mountain that will never see either skilift or trails.

TAIWAN

Taiwan, formerly called Formosa, is a large island 50 miles (80 kilometres) off the southeast coast of mainland China. A wild and largely inaccessible range of mountains, the Miitaku, has 62 summits in excess of 3000 metres. It is on one of these mountains, the Hohuanshan, 3460 metres, that there is some limited skiing in January and February.

The ski area is approached from the new east-west highway by a side road which leads to the Sung Hsueh hostel. This is a simple but comfortable establishment at 3275 metres. Its name means pines and snow. There is a skilift which gives a few hundred feet of downhill skiing. There is considerable potential in these mountains, and their foothills to the east of Taipei have always been a location for holiday homes, but problems of access and similar considerations have resulted in a lack of customers.

Africa

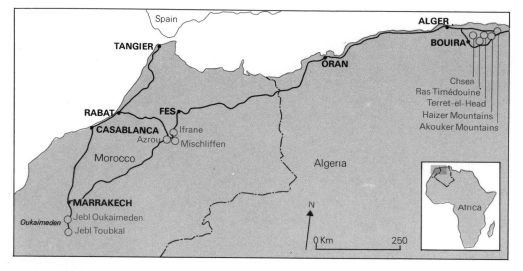

ALGERIA

There is some limited skiing in Algeria but the sport has not received the interest that it has in neighbouring Morocco. The main area is Chséa in the Djur Djura mountains, 135 kilometres south-east of Alger. The centre is at 1860 metres and with the aid of skins an ascent of Dju Djura, at 2508 metres, is feasible. There is some skiing at Terret-el-Head, on Ras Timedouine (1950 metres).

Tizi'n Ticha Pass in the High Atlas is the inhospitable country bordering the skiing areas.

MOROCCO

The High Atlas run in a semi-circle south of Marakesh to the Atlantic. There are more than a dozen peaks over 4000 metres and in the centre of this mountain range is the major African ski centre, Oukaimeden, 2650 metres high and 47 precipitous kilometres from Marrakesh. At the bottom of a great snow-bowl, it is a tiny hamlet of two hotels, several lodges and hostels and a small army camp.

Oukaimeden was founded by the French Alpine Club in 1939 and is now administered by the Royal Moroccan Federation of Winter Sports. There are six lifts – a chairlift and five draglifts of various lengths. The chairlift rises straight up the bowl to the summit, at 3225 metres, of Jbel Oukaimeden, which is at the foot of the highest of the High Atlas mountains, the 4165 metre Jbel Toubkal.

The terrain is completely treeless and is roughly divided into three very wide, shallow gullies which run into the bowl from the long southerly ridge that limits the skiing area. There are no trails as such and the skiing is free, ungroomed and varies from difficult to moderate. The 600 metre drop cannot be extended but the actual length of the run can be, by judicious traverse-zig-zagging using one or two of the intermediate lifts. Oukaimeden is a convenient starting point for the major ski mountaineering expeditions that use the loose network of huts and shelters available to the mountaineer.

In addition to Oukaimeden, there are three further ski areas, Ifrane and Mischiffen in the Middle Atlas and Azron-Bordz in the Northern Atlas. Of these Mischiffen is the most interesting though the interest is purely Nordic. The main skiing is on Jbel Hebri, an extinct volcano, 2035 metres high. You can meet chamois and ibex in the Alps, a singularly ugly beast, the wombat, in the Snowy Mountains, but on Jbel Hebri watch out for packs of Barbary apes.

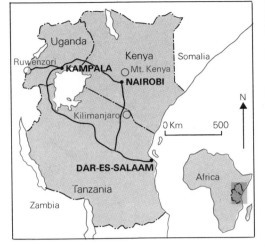

EAST AFRICA

Access problems, and very slight potential has limited skiing in Kenya, Uganda and Tanzania to expeditions of curious explorers using skis on Kilimanjaro (5963 metres) and Ruwenzori (5119 metres). Mount Kenya, 5202 metres, is generally considered to be quite unsuitable. In all three cases, the very long and arduous approach through tropical jungle and mountain forest makes skis an unnecessary burden for an already difficult undertaking.

SOUTH AFRICA

South Africa is one of the more unlikely places to find organized skiing. An increasing number of skiers living in the Republic are making use of the long Christmas vacation period, which is mid-summer in the Southern Hemisphere, and the cheap charter flights to the Alps. Lack of finance, doubts about the popularity of skiing and a deep-rooted disbelief in such a sport in an area more attuned to summer activities have left the considerable skiing potential undeveloped.

Cape Town Ski Club and the Ski Club of South Africa have the lease on some ground near Ceres, a summer resort 77 miles (123 kilometres) to the north of Cape Town on the slopes of the Matroosberg (2250 metres), where they operate a ski lodge and a rope tow.

There has been considerable planning activity surrounding the creation of a summer and winter season, multi-sport and recreation centre based on Witsies Hoek, a small township close to Golden Gate National Park on the borders of Lesotho. This dramatic location, on the northern slopes of the Drakensberg Mountains and below the 3220 metre Cathedral Peak and 3300 metre Mont aux Source, would give skiing access to this part

This face of Mount Kenya is the least skiable side though as a mountain it is not very snowy.

of a large range of mountains. The area is already busily skied by mountaineers during a good, four-month snow season. A further area is also being considered, on the eastern borders of Lesotho, where a jeep track climbs up from Underberg over the Sanie Pass and into the high mountain plateau below Thabana Ntlenyama, at a height of about 3000 metres. This resort would be in Lesotho and consequently visitors could enjoy the non-apartheid pleasures which make this country so attractive to South African holiday-makers and other visitors.

Unfortunately skiing and the pleasures of snow – known to most South Africans only as a distant view of white-capped mountains – are not fully appreciated by the authorities. On one famous occasion, when the mountains were particularly inviting, a party of skiers was subjected to a forced evacuation by helicopter. The South African Air Force had thought they were in dire distress because of the heavy snow falls.

The World Ski Atlas

Acknowledgements

Full-colour maps by Harry Clow,
Mike Lynn and Geoff Nicholson
Two-colour maps by Helen Downton
Location maps by Arka Graphics
Illustrations: Page 6/7 David Worth;
10/11 Paul Buckle; 12/13 Harry Clow;
18/19 Paul Buckle; 20/21 Mike Saunders;
22–27 QED.

Photographs by *(reading from left to right across the page and from top to bottom)*:

Endpapers Paulo Koch: 1 Paulo Koch;
2 Paulo Koch; 4/5 Picturepoint; 8 Jon
Wyand, Mansell Collection, Mary Evans
Picture Library, René Dazy, courtesy
Swiss National Tourist Office;
9 Swiss National Tourist Office,
B. Duthrie, Mary Evans Picture Library,
J. Allan Cash; 12 Swiss National Tourist
Office; 14 J. Allan Cash, Picturepoint,
Swiss National Tourist Office, Zefa;
15 Paulo Koch, K. Farrant, Zefa,
Bill Holden; 16 French National Tourist
Office; 17 Pictor International, Zefa,
French National Tourist Office,
K. Farrant; 22 M. Heller, Robin Day;
23 Robin Day; 24 M. Heller; 25 S.E.F.;
26 Paulo Koch; 27 Paulo Koch;
28 Picturepoint; 30 EISL; 32 Paulo Koch;
34 Pictor International; 40 F.K. MacNeill;
41 courtesy Big Sky; 44 FPG; 45 courtesy
Breckenridge; 46 FPG; 50 courtesy
Ernie Blake; 51 courtesy Gore Mountain;
52 courtesy Hunter Mountain;
61 courtesy Alberta Government;
62 Robert Harding, Peter Wingle,
Canadian Mountain Holidays;
63 Gill Durance, Canadian Mountain
Holidays; 65 Edi Klopfenstein,
Canadian Mountain Holidays;
69 Swiss National Tourist Office;
70 Swiss National Tourist Office;
71 Swiss National Tourist Office,
J. Allan Cash; 73 Swiss National Tourist
Office, J. Allan Cash; 74 J. Allan Cash;
75 Swiss National Tourist Office;
77 Swiss National Tourist Office;
80 Swiss National Tourist Office; 81 Zefa;
85 Swiss National Tourist Office;
87 S.E.F.; 91 Picturepoint, Zefa; 93 Zefa;
96 Swiss National Tourist Office;
97 Swiss National Tourist Office; 101 Zefa;
114 Kaernten; 114/5 J. Allan Cash;
126 Zefa; 127 J. Allan Cash; 131 Zefa;
133 J. Allan Cash; 148 courtesy French
National Tourist Office; 149 courtesy
French National Tourist Office;
153 Barnaby's Picture Library;
160 courtesy French National Tourist
Office; 164 courtesy French National
Tourist Office; 166 J. Allan Cash;
167 courtesy French National Tourist
Office; 169 J. Allan Cash, courtesy French
National Tourist Office; 170 J. Allan Cash;
171 Barnaby's Picture Library; 178 Zefa;
179 Bill Holden; 180 Bill Holden;

182 Photographer's Library;
184 Photographer's Library;
185 Picturepoint; 187 J. Allan Cash;
189 J. Allan Cash; 192 J. Allan Cash;
194 J. Allan Cash; 201 Photographer's
Library; 203 J. Allan Cash; 204 Ente
Nazionale Italiano Per Il Turismo;
205 Zefa; 208 J. Allan Cash; 209 J. Allan
Cash; 210 Ente Nazionale Italiano Per Il
Turismo; 211 Mark Heller;
213 Mark Heller; 216/217 Mark Heller;
218 Robert Harding; 219 Mark Heller;
220 courtesy Scottish Tourist Board;
221 courtesy Scottish Tourist Board;
223 Zefa; 225 Tanjugfoto, Belgrade;
226 J. Allan Cash; 227 Barnaby's Picture
Library; 229 Japan National Tourist
Office; 230 Japan National Tourist Office;
231 Japan National Tourist Office;
232 Japan National Tourist Office;
234 Barnaby's Picture Library;
235 Japan National Tourist Office;
Barnaby's Picture Library;
236 Picturepoint; 237 National Library
of Australia; 240 J. Allan Cash;
241 Pictor International; 242 courtesy
New Zealand High Commission;
246 Pictor International;
247 Robert Harding; 248 J. Allan Cash;
249 Barnaby's Picture Library.

Index

Figures in italics refer to maps